D0086859

Rewriting the Women of Camelot

**Recent Titles in Contributions to the
Study of Science Fiction and Fantasy**

Rewriting the Women of Camelot

Arthurian Popular Fiction and Feminism

Ann F. Howey

Contributions to the Study of Science Fiction and Fantasy, Number 93
C. W. Sullivan, III, Series Adviser

GREENWOOD PRESS
Westport, Connecticut • London

Library of Congress Cataloging-in-Publication Data

Howey, Ann F., 1967–
   Rewriting the women of Camelot : Arthurian popular fiction and feminism / by Ann F. Howey.
       p.   cm.—(Contributions to the study of science fiction and fantasy, ISSN 0193–6875 ; no. 93)
   Includes bibliographical references and index.
   ISBN 0–313–31604–X (alk. paper)
   1. Arthurian romances—Adaptations—History and criticism.   2. English fiction—20th century—History and criticism.   3. Fantasy fiction—Women authors—History and criticism.   4. American fiction—20th century—History and criticism.   5. Women and literature—History—20th century.   6. Historical fiction—Women authors—History and criticism.   7. Feminist fiction—History and criticism.   8. Women in literature.   9. Middle Ages in literature.   I. Title.   II. Series.
   PR888.A76H69   2001
   823'.91099287—dc21   00–042226

British Library Cataloguing in Publication Data is available.

Copyright © 2001 by Ann F. Howey

All rights reserved. No portion of this book may be reproduced, by any process or technique, without the express written consent of the publisher.

Library of Congress Catalog Card Number: 00–042226
ISBN: 0–313–31604–X
ISSN: 0193–6875

First published in 2001

Greenwood Press, 88 Post Road West, Westport, CT 06881
An imprint of Greenwood Publishing Group, Inc.
www.greenwood.com

Printed in the United States of America

The paper used in this book complies with the Permanent Paper Standard issued by the National Information Standards Organization (Z39.48–1984).

10 9 8 7 6 5 4 3 2 1

Copyright Acknowledgments

The author and publisher gratefully acknowledge permission for use of the following material:

Excerpts from Marion Zimmer Bradley, *Mists of Avalon* (1984). Courtesy of Russell Galen Agency.

Excerpts from Fay Sampson, *Black Smith's Telling* (1990), *Herself* (1992), *Wise Woman's Telling* (1989). Courtesy of Headline Book Publishers.

Excerpts from Fay Simpson, *Daughter of Tintagel*. Courtesy of Fay Simpson.

Excerpts from Gillian Bradshaw, *In Winter's Shadow* (1983), *Hawk of May* (1992). Courtesy of Dorian Literary Agency.

Excerpts totaling 418 words from *The Last Enchantment* by Mary Stewart. Copyright © 1979 by Mary Stewart. Reprinted by permission of HarperCollins Publishers, Inc. William Morrow.

Excerpts totaling 318 words from *The Wicked Day* by Mary Stewart. Copyright © 1983 by Mary Stewart. Reprinted by permission of HarperCollins Publishers, Inc. William Morrow.

Excerpts from *The Last Enchantment* and *The Wicked Day* by Mary Stewart. Reproduced by permission of Hodder and Stoughton Limited.

An earlier version of chapter 7 appeared as "Queens, Ladies, and Saints: Arthurian Women in Contemporary Short Fiction," *Arthuriana* 9.1 (Spring 1999). Courtesy of *Arthuriana*.

For Mom and Dad

Contents

Preface

This book examines the intersection of popular fiction and feminism, using popular rewritings of the Arthurian legend as sample texts. In this examination, the book combines my love of popular fiction, my enchantment with the Arthurian legends, and my belief in feminism. This book, however, is also the product of a combination of my commitment and energy with the financial and emotional support of others.

For financial support at early stages of this project, I would like to acknowledge the University of Alberta for the Sarah Nettie Christie Ph.D. Scholarship and a Province of Alberta Graduate Fellowship, as well as various teaching appointments with the Department of English. I would also like to acknowledge the staff of the Department of English, who have always been willing to help (usually with last minute-problems): thank you to Kim Brown, Kris Calhoun, Theresa Daniels, Mary Marshall Durrell, Marina Menze, and Gayle Spencer.

There are a number of scholars who have influenced and inspired me. I wish to thank Charlotte Spivack of the University of Massachusetts and Marisa Bortolussi of the University of Alberta for commenting on this work at an earlier stage; their enthusiastic and critical engagement was invaluable. I would also like to thank Muriel Whitaker, Douglas Barbour, and Jo-Ann Wallace (all of the University of Alberta) for their interest, encouragement, and challenging questions; they have helped me think about all aspects of my work in new ways. I particularly want to thank Stephen Reimer of the University of Alberta for supporting what I do and for challenging me to do better. I am very glad to have had the opportunity to work with all of these scholars, and I know my project has benefited from them; whatever mistakes remain are mine alone.

I am also grateful for the support of my colleagues. I would like to thank, in particular, David Annandale, Carolyn Guertin, Maureen King, Steven Scott, Karys Van de Pitte, and Sheryl Vint for always being willing to discuss popular culture.

I also thank Karys and Mary Beth Wolicky for proofreading. I wish to thank Jane Magrath for her encouragement and helpful criticisms, and Lisa LaFramboise for her confidence in my work and her willingness to read last-minute drafts; most of all, I am glad for the friendship of these two intelligent and sympathetic colleagues.

Finally, to Doug, Diana, Nancy, George, Susan, Kevin, Jason, Sam and Donovan—thank you for always being there for me. And to Hugh and Mabel Howey—thank you for everything, especially your love and encouragement.

Introduction

What we use we must remake. . . . The myths we imagine we are living
(old westerns, true romances) shape our choices.
Marge Piercy, *To Be of Use*, 72

In our culture, myths circulate, at least in part, through popular fiction. Stories
repeated through the years in oral tales and literary works are now rewritten once
again and marketed to audiences increasingly interested in the past. The Arthurian
legend is just one example of a group of old stories that have been reworked in
contemporary popular fiction.[1]

But the stories told by popular fiction are not simply about particular events
or characters. The masses of colourfully jacketed novels represent in their pages
millions of details of our society, reinscribing certain behaviours or social
relationships as normal, challenging other behaviours, other relationships. Our
debates over values, beliefs, and the institutions that embody them occur in various
political, educational, religious, and cultural contexts; they also occur between
these bright, dramatic covers. This book studies the way Arthurian popular fiction,
in particular, explores, reflects, and contributes to contemporary North American
and British engagement with feminism as a social and political movement.

Several factors make Arthurian novels and short stories particularly suitable
for a study of popular fiction and feminism. They well represent popular fiction
because of the popularity of the legend itself and because of the increase in the
amount of Arthurian fiction published in recent years. Furthermore, more women
writers now than ever produce Arthurian fiction. In addition, the legendary
settings for these novels provide the quality of "estrangement" that can allow a
critical perspective, and thus in some cases a feminist perspective, on our own
culture. Finally, Arthurian rewritings, because they each tell the same basic story,
allow comparisons between the approaches the writers choose to take to that story;
such comparisons highlight the feminist ideas influencing narrative strategies, plot,

and characterization.

The Arthurian legend pervades Western culture. Norris Lacy suggests that "the popular notion of Arthur appears to be limited, not surprisingly, to a few motifs and names"; nevertheless, the legend has survived centuries to be "profoundly embedded in modern culture at every level" (364). It is beyond the scope of this discussion to itemize all the possible examples of Arthuriana in Western culture; some examples of the many areas in which the legend appears, besides that of literature, will suffice. Hollywood movies such as *Excalibur* (1981) or *First Knight* (1995) tell substantial portions of the Arthurian story for a wide audience; other movies, such as *Monty Python and the Holy Grail* (1974), become cult classics satirizing it; yet others, such as *The Fisher King* (1991) or *The Mighty* (1998), use only certain elements from the legend. "The Sword of Kahless," an episode of the television series *Star Trek: Deep Space Nine*, involves the search for a lost sword of a Klingon mythic hero; this is just one example of Arthurian echoes to be found in contemporary television. Commercial ventures also use the legend. "Avalon" and "Camelot" appear in names for cars, housing, building contractors, publishing ventures, and other shops,[2] and the Round Table helps General Foods sell its Berry Black flavoured Jell-O. One can add to Lacy's list of "comics and cartoons, festivals, objects and memorabilia" (363) role-playing games and music (from New Age to rock) without exhausting the supply of Arthuriana around us. The legend possesses great cultural currency.

The popularity of Arthurian fiction can be gauged by the increasing amount of it published. Maureen Fries, in "Trends in the Modern Arthurian Novel," calls the prevalence of Arthurian prose fiction "the most surprising development in the last hundred years" of the legend's history (207). Raymond H. Thompson, in his 1985 study *The Return from Avalon*, also notes this increase in Arthurian prose (especially novels), and he goes on to give a statistical image of this growth: "Whereas the first half of this century produced less than fifty novels of Arthurian provenance, the last thirty years have yielded more than twice that number" (3). Bibliographies record twenty-three Arthurian novels published from 1950 to 1959; from 1960 to 1969, there were thirty-three; from 1970 to 1979, there were seventy-one. This adds up to 127 in total for the thirty-year period.[3] The statistics for Arthurian fiction between 1980 and 1996 are even more impressive. For the years 1980–89, bibliographies list 120 examples of long prose fiction and a further 39 short stories. From 1990 to 1996, the number of short stories more than doubled (to 83); the number of novels stood at 97, about 80 percent of the total of the previous decade.[4]

Women writers have participated in this burgeoning market. Marion Wynne-Davies observes that "in twentieth-century Arthurian literature . . . women begin to use the mythology for their own purposes, whether feminist or not" (4); many women writers have become influential in the tradition as it now develops. Moreover, the number of women writers (or collaborators) of Arthurian novels has been steadily increasing; surveying bibliographies, one finds nine examples in the 1950s, thirteen in the 1960s, then thirty-one and forty-eight in the 1970s and 1980s, respectively. Since 1990, thirty-eight Arthurian novels have been published by women, 79 percent of the total of the previous decade.[5] Women are also well represented as writers of Arthurian short fiction. Bibliographies show no short stories written by women from 1950 to 1979. During the 1980s, a third of all short stories (twelve of thirty-nine) were written by women; in the 1990s, 47 percent (thirty-nine of eighty-three) were.[6]

The setting of the story in a legendary past may be partly responsible for the popularity of Arthurian fiction among readers and writers. Arthur's validity as a historical figure inspires continuous speculation among scholars and enthusiasts, though "most . . . continue to believe in a post-Roman war leader who led the British to a temporary victory over the Germanic invaders during the late fifth and early sixth centuries" (Thompson 33). Theories about who this leader was, how he lived, where he fought, and whether or not he won are available in every form from academic treatises to coffee table books[7] to, of course, popular novels. David Lowenthal, in *The Past Is a Foreign Country*, analyses the nostalgia expressed by our Western society for the past.[8] This nostalgic attitude is just the latest shift in approaches to history; our culture has moved from seeing history "as a fount of useful exemplars" (xvi), to preserving items from the past, to being obsessed with pastness. The past, Lowenthal says, is "[n]ow a foreign country with a booming tourist trade" (xvii), and fiction is one of the vehicles people take to get there: "Fictional returns to previous times attract massive audiences" (xix). The Arthurian past has an advantage because of "the very uncertainty about what really happened . . . since it allows [writers] greater freedom in shaping the various details to fit their own literary purposes" (Thompson 33). Although writers must accommodate, to some extent, audience expectations derived from the Arthurian literary tradition, a wide range of treatments of that tradition is possible.

Besides explaining some of the popularity of Arthurian fiction for writers, the legendary setting helps make familiar (and hence invisible) social structures unfamiliar, and thus proves useful to novelists who wish their rewriting of Arthur's world to comment on our own culture. Analysts of science fiction, such as Carl Malmgren, identify "estrangement" as a key device in the cognitive effects of that genre: "SF presents the reader with . . . an estranged world, the nature of which necessarily comments upon the basic narrative world. The estrangement which a reader experiences while concretizing and assimilating an SF world compels him or her to bring that world into relation with the basic narrative world, establishing models of correspondence between the two worlds. . . . [I]n establishing systems of correspondence, the reader comes to know or understand his or her own world better" (27).[9]

Anne Cranny-Francis explores the importance of estrangement in feminist science fiction (SF) and fantasy, where "the (contemporary) reader is positioned to examine critically her / his own society from a different, other world perspective" (77–78). From this perspective readers may understand "the constructedness of their own society, the inflection of discourses which constitutes the contemporary hegemonic bloc" (78). The worlds of Arthurian historical fantasies are both similar to our reality since they occur (supposedly) in our past, and dissimilar to it since events can happen in that world (such as magic) that cannot happen in ours. The peculiar advantage of historical fantasies is that they can suggest a past time when sex roles, for example, were different from those of today. Marion Zimmer Bradley, in particular, chooses to set her Arthurian novel at the (imaginary) historical moment when such roles changed to limit women's power.

Arthurian novels offer an analytical advantage to a study of popular fiction and feminism as well. Each novel, series, or short story rewrites elements of the same basic story, and therefore, like a rewriting of a fairy tale, each offers "two narratives—the revised version of the traditional narrative and its discursive referent, the traditional narrative" (Cranny-Francis 89). Consequently, changes in plot, characterization, and ways of telling the story become obvious as each new version is read against, or in comparison to, all previous versions. Feminist ideas may influence such changes; the decision to have the queen tell her own story, for example, may be part of a desire to explore the woman's role in the legend, or to make a woman the subject of her own story, instead of an object of desire in someone else's. The metafictional aspect of all Arthurian rewritings, therefore, makes it easier to perceive the feminist ideas influencing choices made by particular ones.

The Arthurian novels that will be discussed in the following chapters are by four women writers: Mary Stewart's *The Crystal Cave* (1970), *The Hollow Hills* (1973), *The Last Enchantment* (1979), *The Wicked Day* (1983), and *The Prince and the Pilgrim* (1995); Gillian Bradshaw's *Hawk of May* (1980), *Kingdom of Summer* (1981), and *In Winter's Shadow* (1982); Marion Zimmer Bradley's *The Mists of Avalon* (1982); and Fay Sampson's *Daughter of Tintagel* series, which consists of *Wise Woman's Telling* (1989), *White Nun's Telling* (1989), *Black Smith's Telling* (1990), *Taliesin's Telling* (1991), and *Herself* (1992). All of these authors create substantial rewritings of the legend; Bradley is the only author who tells the tale in just one book, but it is a very long novel, almost nine hundred pages in its trade paperback form. All of these authors begin their tales near or before the beginning of Arthur's reign and finish them at its end; thus they treat the entire legend, not just a small part of it.

Since the earliest of these novels appeared in 1970, the latest in 1995, this sample of rewritings spans two decades. Although feminism has been a political force throughout this time (it is generally accepted that "second-wave feminism" began to develop through the 1960s and has been a political and social force since 1970 [Tuttle 222]), the nature of that political and social force has changed, as have society's responses to it. Thus the later novels are products of a culture where feminism is more generally recognized, and where different varieties of feminism offer different (sometimes incompatible) explanations of the sources and degree of women's oppression, and consequently different solutions to the problem of women's oppression.[10] Examining these novels, therefore, will indicate not only the ways that popular fiction engages with feminism but also the changes in that engagement over time.

The novels will also present a range in the degree to which they are influenced by feminist ideas. Stewart's novels tend to show awareness of feminist issues through the representation of some of the female characters of the legend. Bradshaw chooses Gwynhwyfar as one of her narrators; her rewriting also raises interesting questions about the use of binaries in structuring narrative. Bradley focalizes[11] her narrative through several women; her rewriting is the one most often identified by commentators as feminist. Sampson's series also uses multiple narrators; her final novel also explicitly questions the tradition and its conventions and is thus one that most proclaims feminism as an influence. The theoretical basis of these strategies will be discussed in Chapter 1; later chapters will explore the way these strategies work in these books.

Novels, however, are not the only forms of popular fiction. The short story genre is a growing area for Arthurian fiction, and there, too, one can find many examples of women writers and of stories engaging with feminist ideas. Thus I have devoted one chapter to examining six stories in some detail: Jane Yolen's "The Sword and the Stone" (1985), Phyllis Ann Karr's "The Truth about the Lady of the Lake" (1990) and "Galahad's Lady" (1996), Mercedes Lackey's "The Cup and the Cauldron" (1992), Heather Rose Jones's "The Treasures of Britain" (1996), and Diana Paxson's "Lady of Avalon" (1996). Like the novels, the stories vary in the way they recreate legendary characters and events. Yolen's story rewrites the queen's traditional characteristics; the stories of Karr, Lackey, Jones, and Paxson have female protagonists, or in Lackey's story, two female protagonists. Because of their length, short stories cannot recount the entire history of Camelot. These authors focus on specific episodes and characters, some traditional to the legend and some the authors' inventions, but all take place in Arthurian worlds. The depictions of such worlds, furthermore, challenge assumptions about how the Arthurian world (or our own) should work.

This study differs from previous scholarship in its approach and emphasis. Many studies of popular fiction, that of Anne Cranny-Francis, for example, tend to survey the field rather than intensively analysing specific examples; such analysis is usually confined to articles. The same is true of studies of Arthurian fiction: Thompson's *Return from Avalon*, for example, surveys and categorizes examples of Arthurian novels from throughout the twentieth century. Barbara Ann Gordon-Wise's book on Guenevere represents another trend, in which the focus is on one character, and consideration of contemporary works follows discussion of the entire tradition. My selection of these texts as examples of the intersection of popular fiction and feminism also differs in emphasis from other studies; Charlotte Spivack's *Merlin's Daughters*, for example, focusses on ten authors including Bradley, Bradshaw, and Stewart, but she discusses these in terms of the fantasy tradition. My approach also emphasizes the feminist cultural work of these texts; studies such as the one by Cranny-Francis, as mentioned earlier, valorize more heavily transformed texts or conclude by dismissing positive contributions to feminism made by these texts as outweighed by their conservatism. Although I acknowledge certain limitations of the strategies employed in the novels I study (see the Conclusion in particular), I reassert the value of such novels for our society's continuing engagement with feminist ideas.

Before the detailed study of these primary texts can begin, however, the definition of several concepts is required and the legend's history must be summarized. Chapter 1, therefore, establishes the parameters of this study through discussions of theoretical issues surrounding popular fiction, feminism, and readership; Chapter 2 discusses the cultural work and legacy of two important medieval Arthurian source texts. These discussions provide the framework for the later chapters: Chapters 3 and 4 examine two common Arthurian character types for women, queens and sorceresses; Chapter 5 investigates the use of female protagonists and communities of women; Chapter 6 discusses narrative techniques; and Chapter 7 considers the techniques of short fiction.

NOTES

1. I use the phrase "the Arthurian legend" to refer to the huge, ever-changing mass of stories (oral, written, traditional, modern) that centre on the figure of King Arthur and the members of his court.

2. Edmonton, Alberta, for example, has a travel agency called Camelot Travel and Tours. Toyota has named one of its cars Avalon. A publisher, Avon, has a line of children's books called Camelot, which according to a 1981 advertisement, was the "fastest growing line of children's paperbacks" (Avon Camelot Books 42). Using the legend as a source for names of commercial ventures is not new: Rocque's plan of London, England (1744–46), shows a tavern at New Tunbridge Wells called Merlin's Cave (Barker and Jackson 61).

3. The bibliographies from which I compiled these and the other statistics in this section are "The Arthurian Legends in Contemporary English Literature, 1945–1981" by Stephen R. Reimer (1981), and "The Arthurian Legends in Contemporary English Literature, 1981–1996" by Ann F. Howey and Stephen R. Reimer (1997). These bibliographies also provide updates on materials published before 1950; see also "The Arthurian Legends: Modern Retellings of the Old Stories" by Clark S. Northup and John J. Parry (1944), and "The Arthurian Legends: Supplement to Northup and Parry's Annotated Bibliography" by Paul A. Brown and John J. Parry (1950).

4. The statistics for the novels suggest that the 1990s will at least have kept pace with the 1980s, though there will not likely have been the kind of dramatic increase in numbers of Arthurian novels that occurred in the 1980s and 1970s compared to preceding decades.

5. The bibliographies surveyed for the statistics in this paragraph are mentioned in the earlier note. As with the category of Arthurian novels in general, those written by women seem to be keeping pace with the totals of the 1980s.

6. Three of these were collaborations between women and men.

7. Geoffrey Ashe's works continue to be popular and to influence writers about the "facts" of Arthur's time; Marion Zimmer Bradley, for example, thanks Geoffrey Ashe in the Acknowledgements to *The Mists of Avalon*. The variety of treatments of the history of the legend and its figures is as wide as the interpretations of it in literature. For example, C. Scott Littleton and Linda A. Malcor's *From Scythia to Camelot* gives Sarmatian origins for Arthur. One of the many Arthurian coffee-table books is David Day's *The Search for King Arthur*, which has a foreword written by Terry Jones (one of the writers of *Monty Python and the Holy Grail*). Day's book combines beautiful reproductions of Pre-Raphaelite paintings with discussion of and excerpts from the literary tradition, as well as some historical data. Other titles, such as *King Arthur: The True Story* by Graham Phillips and Martin Keatman, try to persuade readers that the final solution to the mystery has been found, but the debate continues.

8. Lowenthal mentions the film *Excalibur* (1981) as one indication of the nostalgia our culture expresses for real or imagined pasts.

9. The theory of "estrangement" as a device is similar to the Russian formalist notion of defamiliarization: "A novel point of view, as [Victor] Shklovsky points out, can make a reader perceive by making the familiar seem strange" (Lemon and Reis 5). Shklovsky argues that "[t]he purpose of art is to impart the sensation of things as they are perceived and not as they are known . . . to make objects 'unfamiliar'" (12). Malmgren recognizes these similarities but argues that SF takes the process further since it is "not simply an estranged object but an estranged world" (27) that is presented.

10. See Jennifer Wicke's discussion of celebrity feminism and Judith Grant's overview of feminist theory.

11. Gérard Gennette, in *Narrative Discourse*, argues that the term "point of view" causes "confusion between the question *who is the character whose point of view orients the narrative perspective?* and the very different question *who is the narrator?*" (186, emphasis in original). Genette introduced the term "focalization" to clarify the difference between the perspective through which events are experienced and the narrator who encodes the events. There ensued much debate about the meaning and usefulness of the term among narratologists such as Seymour Chatman ("Characters and Narrators: Filter, Center, Slant and Interest-Focus"), William Nelles ("Getting Focalization into Focus"), and Mieke Bal (*On Storytelling*, especially chapters 4 and 6), among others. Although "focalization" has suffered from some of the same vagueness of usage as point of view, it has become accepted in narratology. As I use the term, "focalization" refers to the perspective used in the recording and interpreting of events; "narration" refers to the voice that speaks of the events.

Chapter 1

Definitions and Other Theoretical Issues

POPULAR FICTION

The term "popular fiction" needs to be defined because the adjective "popular" appears in our culture in various contexts, and, as Jean Radford points out, it has therefore "accumulated a number of contradictory senses of both a positive and negative kind" (3). On the one hand, "popular" is used positively to describe culture produced and circulated by the working class. On the other hand, it is used pejoratively to describe products created by a capitalist industry.[1] Neither of these meanings adequately defines "popular" for my purposes; the first excludes the mass-market fiction to which my sample texts belong, and the second abhors such fiction as "imposed mass culture produced and distributed by commercial apparatuses over which 'the people' . . . have no control and which offer them no creative, productive involvement" (Bennett 16). Furthermore, as John Fiske argues, such definitions are based on "two romantic fantasies" (*Reading* 4): the first idealizes "a folk art in which all members of the tribe participate equally in producing and circulating their culture" (4–5); the second, in scorning "mass" culture, idealizes "the penniless artist, dedicated only to the purity and aesthetic transcendence of . . . art" (4). These fantasies create models in which cultural production is separable from economics; as a result, they do not describe our society (Fiske, *Reading* 5). These definitions are also inadequate because they rely on a vague notion of who the people are,[2] and, in the second case, because they make moral judgements on the people's tastes. As Stuart Hall observes, "The notion of the people as . . . purely passive, . . . is a deeply unsocialist perspective" (232); denigrating popular-defined-as-mass culture dismisses the fact that people make choices in entertainment.

Another possible definition uses what Stuart Hall labels "the most commonsense meaning: the things which are said to be 'popular' because masses of people listen to them, buy them, read them, consume them and seem to enjoy them to the full" (231). This "'market' or commercial definition" (Hall 231) contains its own contradictions, however. We all have a general idea of the type of fiction to qualify as "popular" under this definition, but how do individual books fit into it? How many copies sold of particular novels indicate that "masses of people . . . [have] read them" (Hall 231)? And does this mean that a book does not belong in the category of popular fiction when it first arrives in bookstores, only fitting into that category later after a certain number of copies have been sold? Obviously audience reaction alone does not adequately define popular fiction for my study; rather I shall consider how the cultural institutions market their products, and how the institutions themselves are situated within our culture. As Peter Humm, Paul Stigant, and Peter Widdowson argue, "One characteristic of 'popular' fiction must be that *its* relationship to the market, *its* place in the socio-economic relations of production is different from that of 'non-popular' fiction" (8, emphasis in original).

Pierre Bourdieu's discussions of literature in "The Field of Cultural Production, or: The Economic World Reversed" and in "The Production of Belief: Contribution to an Economy of Symbolic Goods" help clarify what is "different" about the production of popular fiction. In the first article, Bourdieu theorizes a field of class relations; at the dominant end of this field lies "the field of power" (37), which Randal Johnson interprets as consisting of "the ruling classes" (14). Within this smaller field, in "a *dominated position* (at the negative pole)" (Bourdieu, "Field" 38, emphasis in original), lies what Bourdieu calls "the literary or artistic field" (29) or "the field of cultural production" (29). Despite its location in the field of power, the field of cultural production exists in "relative autonomy with respect to it, especially as regards its economic and political principles of hierarchization" (37–38). This means that economic capital does not necessarily determine success within the literary sub-field.

Bourdieu bases his analysis of the cultural field, therefore, on the belief that "the interests and resources at stake in fields are not always material" (Johnson 7). Agents within the field of cultural production may instead compete for other kinds of capital, which may be represented as fame, honour, or cultural consecration. Furthermore, possession of economic capital may prohibit consecration in this field; because of its autonomy in the field of power, the field of cultural production can invert "all ordinary economies: that of business (it excludes the pursuit of profit and does not guarantee any sort of correspondence between investments and monetary gains), that of power (it condemns honours and temporal greatness), and even that of institutionalized cultural authority" (Bourdieu 39). As with Fiske's image of the penniless artist (*Reading* 4), this is art produced for an audience of other, like-minded producers.

Not all art or literature is produced for such a small, exclusive audience, however, and this is where popular fiction appears in Bourdieu's schema. In "The Production of Belief," Bourdieu identifies an opposition in the field of cultural production "between small-scale and large-scale ('commercial') production" (82). The sub-field of small-scale production depends substantially "on symbolic capital and . . . is marked positively" (Johnson 16) in the literary or artistic field; it tends to direct its products toward a smaller audience whose members have more education and higher social position, and who thereby possess greater "cultural competence" (Johnson 24). In contrast, the sub-field of large-scale production depends much more on economic capital and "the broadest possible audience" (Johnson 16). However, these two categories are not static; the field of cultural production is always a site of struggle as the two sub-fields continually compete to determine the criteria of value.

This division of the literary and artistic field into two sub-fields provides the possibility of a different definition of "popular" based on the characteristics of the field of large-scale production. These include "the primacy of marketing, audience, sales and success measured quantitatively"; "immediate, temporary success of bestsellers"; and "production which secures success and the corresponding profits by adjusting to a pre-existing demand" (Bourdieu, "Production" 82). Bourdieu's analysis thus suggests that the type of publisher and that publisher's position in the cultural field define what is "popular" fiction.

In "The Production of Belief," Bourdieu examines two publishing houses to find the differences between a "commercial" firm and a "cultural firm" (97). He states, "A firm is that much closer to the 'commercial' pole (and, conversely, that much further from the 'cultural' pole), the more directly and completely the products it offers correspond to a pre-existent demand, i.e. to pre-existent interests in pre-established forms" (97). Such "pre-established forms" include genre or category fiction, whose formats are well known and expected by their audiences; in the publishing industry, as David G. Hartwell explains, "[a] category is a response to a specific audience demand" (222). Large-scale firms use "marketing circuits and presentational devices (eye-catching dustjackets, advertising, public relations etc.)" (Bourdieu, "Production" 97) to ensure that consumers recognize books belonging to their preferred categories; this helps to guarantee sales and a return on the publisher's investment (Bourdieu, "Production" 97). Bourdieu also analyses companies' numbers of employees, of new titles published, and of bestsellers produced, as well as the size of the sales department and the investment in advertising (99). Commercial firms have much higher numbers in all of these categories; as well, their need for "safe investment" often leads to the publication of "famous names" (99).

Consequently, popular fiction, as I will be using the term, indicates works produced in this sub-field of large-scale production, promoted by large publishing firms, and marketed with the intent to reach a wide audience. This definition comes close to the culture-industry definition quoted earlier, but it lacks the pejorative implications of the idea of "imposed mass culture" (Bennett 16) for two reasons. First, Bourdieu focusses on economic relations rather than questions of literary value as he traces power and influence between institutions with different cultural roles. Second, although large publishing companies may try to "impose" their cultural offerings, Bourdieu's analysis reveals that their attempts to do so are not necessarily successful. For example, authors with many previous bestsellers may lose their following as other authors become recognized; the field is always a site of struggle, and audience reaction affects those struggles, either through the actual sales of individual books, or through audience members' becoming producers of popular fiction themselves.[3] Fiske, when discussing all consumer goods, emphasizes the effect of people's reactions to products: "The cultural industries, by which I mean all industries, have to produce a repertoire of products from which the people choose. And choose they do; . . . despite all the pressures, it is the people who finally choose which commodities they will use in their culture" (*Reading* 5). Emphasizing the production of a work within specific cultural institutions also avoids a strictly sales-oriented notion of "popular": a novel, paradoxically, can still be popular fiction even if its sales are limited, though it is not economically successful popular fiction.

All of the texts I have chosen for this study fit into this definition of popular fiction. The novels have been published by firms in the field of large-scale production; the short stories have appeared originally, or have been reprinted, in anthologies directed at a target market by similar large-scale producers. In many cases, the scope of these publishing firms means that the books in question can be distributed in a wide variety of countries; Arthurian popular fiction is thus part of an international network of myth making.[4]

FEMINISM

"Feminism," like "popular," has acquired differing meanings. Judith Grant, in *Fundamental Feminism: Contesting the Core Concepts of Feminist Theory*, presents the current situation in feminist theory with this statement: "The orthodoxy goes like this: There is no one feminist theory. Rather, feminist theory is multicentered and undefinable" (1). Grant cites liberal, radical, psychoanalytic, Freudian, Marxist, socialist, cultural, and postmodernist (1–3) as some of the types of feminism. Each of these derives from different perspectives on the causes of women's subordination and on the best ways to correct them. I will present the definition of feminism that I find most useful and give some reasons for its usefulness.

In trying to define feminism, I have found Rita Felski's arguments particularly persuasive. Felski adopts "Alison Jaggar's formulation, which defines as feminist all those forms of theory and practice that seek, no matter on what grounds or by what means, to end the subordination of women" (Felski 13).[5] Both Felski and Jaggar recognize that this is an inclusive definition, and that is why I shall also adopt it; it allows consideration of a variety of approaches to analysing women's place in contemporary society. This inclusiveness is important when discussing the intersection of popular fiction and feminism. Popular fiction, as I have defined it, is produced by large-scale publishers and marketed to a large audience in the hope of appealing to large numbers of readers; feminist discourses informing these texts must also be those perceived to be relevant to a wide range of people.

A definition of feminism that has more criteria (and is thus less inclusive) tends to exclude much popular fiction, for many writers of popular fiction challenge generic formulas in some ways, by using a female protagonist, for example, only to reinscribe other conventions, such as narrative unity. As a result, some critics believe "that mass-produced art forms . . . are ideologically conservative in the sense that they restore at least temporarily the claims of presently existing institutions" (Radway 221).[6] Anne Cranny-Francis, in *Feminist Fiction: Feminist Uses of Generic Fiction*, admits that writers can express "oppositional views" while using conventional narrative forms, but she wonders whether such views are effective, given "the conservatism that colours the text as a whole" (1).   Criticism of texts that, to some extent, work within the system originates in a belief that the only meaningful resistance to ideology is radical resistance. Texts that are less than radical, that maintain some conventions while challenging others, are believed "to strengthen the system and to delay any radical change in it" (Fiske, *Reading* 11). To people who believe this, popular fiction is a safety valve, useful for containing radical ideas.

However, I would argue that expressions of "oppositional views" play a vital role in our society. Writers and readers use them to imagine alternative social relations in a context that is non-threatening because of the generic or narrative conventions that remain familiar. Such alternative visions highlight certain assumptions made by our society, about gender for example, or about the "natural" way of storytelling. For some writers and readers, the tension within popular fiction between old conventions and new ideas may mirror inner struggles to reevaluate personal beliefs in the wake of such radical ideas as feminism. Thus, popular fiction, like popular culture generally, can cause "political gains in the specificity of everyday life" (Fiske, *Reading* 11). Fiske suggests that such gains "are progressive rather than radical" (*Reading* 11), but that does not diminish their importance. Gains in individuals' power at the "micro level" work against the system from within. Because I believe in the potential progressive effects of popular fiction, I, like Felski, define feminist literature as "all those texts that reveal a critical awareness of women's subordinate position and of gender as a problematic category, however this is expressed" (Felski 14). In order to analyse popular fiction, I will examine three possible strategies for presenting feminist "oppositional views" in otherwise conventional popular fiction.

The first two strategies used in the novels that I discuss require focus on characterization, so I will elaborate here my reasons for including both of them. The first strategy, discussed in the chapters "Images of Royal Women" and "Images of Magical Women," involves the representation of female characters in ways that challenge social and literary stereotypes of women and their roles in society.[7] The second strategy, discussed in the chapter "Women as Protagonists," makes female characters the centre of the story being told, often by using these protagonists as narrators to present the narrative from a woman's point of view. Not all feminists agree on the political efficacy of changing representations of women and portraying them as protagonists; much French feminist theory, to give one example, chooses language as a site for analysing political resistance in texts. However, the historical context of these novels demands consideration of characterization. Even though all the novels I study are "contemporary," those published in the 1970s and early 1980s are products of a somewhat different historical period,[8] one characterized by liberal feminist analysis of representations of women. Furthermore, examination of characterization and women's experience as represented in popular fiction is crucial if we are to understand the way such texts engage in political debates.

The novels that I examine were published between 1970 and 1996, and eight of fourteen appeared by 1983. This period witnessed the emergence of the Women's Liberation Movement, or what Felski calls "the recent cultural phenomenon of women's explicit self-identification as an oppressed group" (1). In its beginnings in the mid-1960s and throughout the 1970s, North American and British feminism primarily investigated the ways women were portrayed by and treated in society and attempted to recover or promote the telling of women's stories.[9] For example, feminists linked cultural stereotypes of women's abilities and proper work to the predominance of women in lower-paying jobs and, by emphasizing personal experience, were able to address publicly the problem of wife battering. This process of growing feminist awareness resulted in the establishment of several organizations during this period.[10] In the United States, the National Organization for Women, "the largest, most visible and most broadly-based feminist organization" (Tuttle 218), appeared in 1966 and campaigned in the attempt to pass the Equal Rights Amendment in the late 1970s and early 1980s. In Britain, the first National Women's Liberation Conference was held in 1970 (Tuttle 221); Britain's first shelter for battered women was established a year later (Tuttle 31). *MS*, an American magazine, was begun in 1972 "as a way of spreading word of the Women's Liberation Movement to non-political women" (Tuttle 210), a project it continues to pursue today. Other feminist publishing enterprises appeared on both sides of the Atlantic during the 1970s: The Feminist Press in the United States in 1970 was created to recover "the lost heritage of women's words, lives and history" (Tuttle 109); The Women's Press in Toronto appeared in 1970 as well (Tuttle 363); in Britain a publisher of the same name appeared in 1977 in connection with the Women's Liberation Movement (Tuttle 363); Virago, a British feminist publishing imprint, was founded in 1975 (Tuttle 335). On the academic front, many institutions established women's studies programs during the 1970s and 1980s (Felski 13). Also during this time, the following works of feminist literary criticism appeared: Kate Millett's *Sexual Politics* (1970), Susan Koppelman Cornillon's *Images of Women in Fiction* (1972), Ellen Moers's *Literary Women* (1976), and Elaine Showalter's *A Literature of Their Own* (1977). All these texts show their authors' concerns with representations of women in fiction and society, and with recovery of women's experiences by retrieval of women's literature from the past. Consequently, critical evaluation of the characterization of women (in society or in fiction) and celebration of women's points of view make up part of the social context surrounding the production of these popular novels, so I examine the way these texts become involved in the debates over women's place in society as they were framed at the time.[11]

Furthermore, the fact that these are works of popular fiction means that they need to be accessible to a wide market. Feminist strategies that do not deconstruct all generic and narrative conventions are most likely to be found in popular fiction, because of this need for accessibility; challenging stereotypical representations of female characters and presenting a woman as a protagonist of her own story can leave many other conventions intact. Feminist texts that radically subvert language and narrative are likely to be published as something other than popular fiction.

Subverting linguistic, narrative, and generic conventions does allow exploration of the relationships among power, knowledge, language, and ideology; however, it also raises questions of political efficacy. Stressing language as gendered leads, in various French feminist theorists for example, to a search for a feminine language, but as Felski argues, these explorations can reinforce traditional stereotypes of women: "Feminine writing is 'that which cannot be defined,' in other words the same old equation of the feminine with the negative, mysterious, unknown" (43). Furthermore, subversion of language is only metaphorically feminine, since "linguistic playfulness and nonlinear syntax are in no sense unique or specific to women but are indicative of a more general cultural shift away from analytical and discursive modes and a blurring of the distinction between literature and theory which marks a range of contemporary critical and metacritical discourses" (Felski 37–38). In addition, as Toril Moi observes, focus on language often ignores the "material factors" of women's lives, "the actual inequities, deprivations and violations that women, as social beings . . . must constantly suffer" (123). Thus, such texts leave the question of contemporary social action aside. By rejecting "the social and political realm as repressive and 'phallocentric'" (Felski 40), writers criticize aspects of existing institutions and the hegemony of our society, but they also "reaffirm . . . women's traditionally marginalized role" in those institutions (Felski 40).

French feminist writers, however, are not the only ones to subvert linguistic, narrative, and generic conventions. Anne Cranny-Francis discusses the subversive strategies of feminist writers who transform "generic texts." She remarks that "this [transformation] can be costly. The readership may find a heavily transformed text unreadable, no longer recognisable as a member of the generic family from which it developed" (19). Ultimately, this may mean "a loss of readership" (20). Cranny-Francis's own definition of what feminist fiction should be valorizes texts that are "heavily transformed" (19); other kinds of texts, ones in which male and female roles are simply reversed, for example, are problematic because they do "not challenge the nature of the role itself" (84). However, she also acknowledges that some compromise between feminist transformation and generic conventions may result in larger audiences. In her discussion of Anne McCaffrey's novels,[12] for example, Cranny-Francis suggests that the main character "becomes effectively an honorary man" (70) in that "the victory is for a girl who makes herself look and act as nearly as possible like a boy" (71). Cranny-Francis concludes that the novels "challeng[e] the reader's acceptance of conservative ideological discourses, rather than completely deconstructing them" (71). She goes on to ponder the value of that challenge: "Unlike the other texts discussed, . . . McCaffrey's novels are best-sellers and it is useful to consider whether her less radical political stance, which is obviously a factor in her success, her texts being less problematic for (conservative) readers, is a useful compromise given the size of the audience she therefore reaches" (71). As I have argued previously in defining feminist literature,

I believe that progressive (rather than radical) texts *are* useful. More importantly, these less radical texts make up more of the popular fiction published, and more of the fiction read by most people. We need to be aware of the uses such texts make of feminism.

So far I have argued that subversion of language, genre, or narrative should not be taken as the ultimate factor in determining whether a text is feminist. But why should representations of character matter? Susan Koppelman Cornillon suggests that readers turn "to literature, and especially fiction, for answers, for models, for clues to the universal questions of who we are or might become" (ix), and that if certain stereotypes predominate we are in effect "alienated from ourselves" (ix). This suggests that "we learn from lives" (Howe 255); literature, therefore, is not just drawn from life experiences: it influences life experience. This view, however, can make troubling assumptions about literature's *reflecting* life. As Toril Moi argues, assuming literature reflects life leads to a problematic theoretical position in which "writing is seen as a more or less faithful *reproduction* of an external reality to which we all have equal and unbiased access" (45, emphasis in original). Emphasizing "authenticity and truthful reproduction" (Moi 47) ignores "the basic facts of textual creativity" (Moi 45): writers select only certain details to give the impression of a "real" world populated by "real" characters. Moreover, form and convention affect this selection process.

Thus, literature cannot reflect life in any simple way. Yet many people, some writers among them,[13] strongly believe that there is a correspondence between art and life, and that fiction can therefore influence "the ways in which women learn to be women" (Howe 254). This does not mean that readers simply mimic fictional characters, or even that they believe such mimicking would be possible or desirable. Nevertheless, literature provides "symbolic fictions by means of which they [readers] make sense of experience" (Felski 7). John Fiske uses the term "production of relevance" to describe the process whereby people "make popular sense out of popular social experience" (*Understanding* 133). Fiske emphasizes that this process is not a simple identification of text with material experience, but a production of "relevances through which the two can be made to interact and inform each other" (*Understanding* 133). Fictional characters allow readers positions to occupy in imagination, and occupying those positions may lead such readers to question the differences between (or disturbing similarities of) fictional and real social relations.

Fiction with female protagonists gives readers both interesting positions to occupy in imagination and potentially new perspectives on society. Some radical feminists argue that such perspectives are the basis for social change. For example, Catherine MacKinnon argues that "to know the politics of woman's situation is to know women's personal lives"; this leads her to claim, "Feminism, on this level, is the theory of women's point of view" (120), because women's experiences are important in both defining oppressive social structures and imagining solutions to them.[14] Felski also argues that "a literature which articulates female experience is a legitimate cultural need of an oppositional movement," such as feminism, "which has sought to give cultural prominence to the depiction of women's experiences and interests" (7). If reinterpretation of the world happens in stories of women's lives, it can happen whether the women are real or fictional. In fact, fictional characters offer advantages to a writer, for fictional women, unlike real ones, do not have to be subject to the gendered structures of our society.[15]

Consequently, the chapters "Images of Royal Women," "Images of Magical Women," and "Women as Protagonists" examine the way the novels challenge traditional stereotypes. Such challenges may be evident in the way female characters are not presented as simply evil (or passive, or nagging, or angelic) only because they are women; instead, the narratives give reasons for actions and show a complex of motivations.[16] Some of the novels also create new roles or perspectives for the female protagonists. These chapters, therefore, analyse the ways in which the novels exhibit an awareness of feminist issues regarding representations of women, the ways in which they try to present complex women, and the ways in which the use of a woman as the protagonist of the narrative changes the Arthurian story.

The third strategy, discussed in the chapter "Narrative Techniques," explores the relationship between structure and feminist ideas. First, I examine the use of binary oppositions as a structuring device of the conflicts in Bradshaw's and Sampson's series. Since fantasy tends to depend on a fundamental opposition between good and evil for its structure, and since feminist theorists often suggest that structures based on binary oppositions reinforce cultural values around the opposition "male" and "female," the use of binaries would seem to be a context in which feminism and popular fiction are at odds. My discussion, therefore, analyses the extent to which certain writers question such binary structures even as they employ them. Second, I examine the use of multiple perspectives in Bradley's and Sampson's rewritings. Using several perspectives from which to tell the story can promote feminist ideas; the conflicts and similarities between these perspectives prevent any one of them from becoming authoritative, while emphasizing the biases that shape every narrative. My discussion speculates on the effects of such a strategy on the usual expectations created by popular fiction.

In the chapter "Rewriting Arthurian Women in Short Fiction," I examine the way short fiction uses the three strategies I have defined: the representation of traditional female characters, the use of such characters as protagonists, and the employment and questioning of narrative structures. The chosen stories employ these strategies to undermine traditional symbols of power, to redefine the heroic, and to problematize binary oppositions. Length does affect the use of these strategies: it is more difficult to fit multiple narrators into a short piece than into a long novel, for example; Lackey's story is the only one to focalize the narrative through more than one character, and she uses just the two female protagonists. Short stories, however, have techniques available to them that might be difficult to sustain in a novel: Karr's "The Truth about the Lady of the Lake," for example, relies more obviously on intertextuality than any of the novels, for Arthurian characters are never named; as a result we are positioned to view our traditions from the perspective of outsiders. Highlighting the variety of approaches to the legend and to feminism contained in this sampling of stories is one of the main purposes of this chapter.

In discussing these strategies I do not claim that the writers necessarily define themselves as feminists.[17] Instead, I will use these Arthurian popular fictions by women authors to examine the ways in which feminist ideas have become part of a popular culture that writers explore and sometimes question in their fictions. I will therefore study the role of popular fiction in circulating, exploring, and promoting these ideas. In addition, I will analyse the effects of feminism upon the conventions of popular fiction.

THEORIZING THE READER

If popular fiction circulates feminist ideas, among whom does this circulation take place? Literary critics have become increasingly sensitive to theorizing the reader when discussing the effects of literary works. The difficulty is to allow for the multiple numbers of readers, each with differing responses to any given text at any moment in time, while at the same time being able to make useful generalizations about the way literature works in the world.

One of the ways to theorize readers and reading is to recognize that reading, although undertaken by individuals, is also a social practice. Mary Louise Pratt points out that "literary works are public speech acts (in the sense that they are institutional, and have no personalized addressee)" ("Ideology" 8). They are institutional because, unless a friend hands you an unpublished manuscript, books are made available to us through the publishing and book-selling industry. This industry does not market products to an individual consumer, but to similarly disposed groups of readers. David G. Hartwell, in discussing the editing of science-fiction novels, describes the categories that the industry uses to ensure readers find the type of books they like: "A category is a kind of publication separated out from 'general fiction' to reach a specialized audience" (222). When individuals read, therefore, they each have idiosyncratic responses, but they also "are playing generalized social roles" (Pratt, "Ideology" 8). In fact, they need to play these roles, or, as Peter Rabinowitz phrases it, to become part of "a particular social / interpretive community" (22), in order to understand what they read.[18] Consequently, reading is not just the knowledge of the printed characters on the page, but also an "unspoken, culturally-shared knowledge of the rules, conventions, and expectations that are in play" in a literary work (Pratt, *Toward a Speech-Act Theory* 86). Because of these rules, we know what to privilege in a text, and how to relate elements; in addition, the rules delimit the types of plots, characters, and reading strategies required.

Readers use various means to decipher the interpretive community most suitable for any given text; one of the most important is genre. Frederic Jameson calls genres "essentially contracts between a writer and his readers . . . based on tacit agreements" ("Magical Narratives" 135); Janice Radway calls them "a set of rules for the production of meaning, operable both through writing and reading" (10). A book's genre, therefore, provides clues to the reader as to the unspoken assumptions that she or he will need to make in order to understand the story.[19]

Pratt argues that

> the reader who picks up a work of literature of a given genre already has a predefined idea of "what the nature of the communication situation is." Although the fictional discourse in a work of literature may in theory take any form at all, readers have certain expectations about what form it will take, and *they can be expected to decode the work according to those assumptions unless they are overtly invited or required to do otherwise.* (*Toward a Speech-Act Theory* 204, emphasis in original)

My study of popular fiction's engagement with feminism examines the way that engagement disrupts the conventions and expectations of the most likely reading communities for these works.

Because the novels I study are Arthurian rewritings, they cross generic lines, bringing different reading communities into play. First, there are the reading communities shaped by the genres of the works: historical fiction and fantasy.[20] For members of these groups, explicit comment on the status and roles of women may challenge the expectations of the genres; the play with narrative techniques will also be noticeable. Second, these novels can be expected to be read by Arthurian enthusiasts; for this group, familiar with at least one or two other versions of the legend, the changes to plot and characterization will be the most noticeable.

This book, therefore, focusses on the textual conventions rather than reader response, and I recognize that this focus, as John Fiske says, "artificially freezes that circulation [of meanings] at a particular (if convenient) point and overemphasizes the role of the text within it" (*Understanding* 124). Nevertheless, although analysis of the role of the text is not the only analysis that needs to be done, it is important. As Fiske admits, "not . . . all texts are equally political (even potentially), . . . [nor are] all politicized meanings . . . equally available in any one of them" (*Understanding* 168); those (potentially) politicized meanings can be analysed through "the discourses that comprise" the text (*Understanding* 168). In these rewritings, the discourses involved include the conventions of popular fiction, the continuing social / cultural formulation and articulation of feminisms, and the Arthurian literary tradition.

NOTES

1. Tony Bennett, in "The Politics of 'the Popular' and Popular Culture," The English Studies Group, in "Recent Developments in English Studies at the Centre," and Stuart Hall, in "Notes on Deconstructing 'the Popular,'" among others, discuss these two general poles of meaning that commonly appear in Marxist criticism.

2. Because of such vagueness, definitions of the popular often only make sense "*in relation* to what it is being opposed to in a historically given instance" (Radford 3, emphasis in original). Throughout his article Tony Bennett also analyses the way vague definitions of "popular" depend on often equally vague notions of "the people."

3. This happens most frequently in the romance genre, but also in the genres of science fiction and fantasy, in which readers may write for large publishing firms or for their own "fanzines."

4. For specifics about the publishing network supporting these texts, consult Appendix A.

5. See Jaggar's discussion, "Feminism as Political Philosophy," in *Feminist Politics and Human Nature* (3–13).

6. Janice Radway, in her study of romance reading, repeats this charge, which she says her "study does not challenge absolutely" (221).

7. These chapter titles echo the title of Susan Koppelman Cornillon's collection of essays, *Images of Women in Fiction: Feminist Perspectives* (1972).

8. One of the changes that have occurred during this period is the emergence of what Jennifer Wicke calls "celebrity feminism." Wicke defines this "zone" as "the public sphere where feminism is negotiated" (757), a sphere that exists in, and because of, the growing media presence in our society. Wicke suggests that if "academic feminism has an opposite, it is . . . the celebrity pronouncements made by and about women with high visibility in the various media" (753). As a result, the public profile of feminists and feminism has been continually increasing over the last three decades, so that feminism "is now in most active cultural play" in this "celebrity zone" (757). As I will discuss in my Conclusion, popular fiction's engagement with feminism intersects with other cultural engagements with feminism, such as those Wicke documents in her article.

9. Judith Grant, reviewing the development of feminist theory, indicates that in the early stages of that development feminists "grappled with . . . the stereotypes of women" (21) and "define[d] 'oppression' subjectively. Oppression included anything that women *experienced* as oppressive" (30, emphasis in original). The importance of experience to feminism led to the slogan "The personal is political" (33).

10. My examples of these institutions and organizations are drawn from North America and Britain, where the authors I study reside.

11. It should also be remembered that liberal feminism is not just a stage that is over; its ideas still exist today.

12. Cranny-Francis chooses *Dragonsinger* as her focus. In this novel, Mennolly, despite being a girl, becomes the apprentice to the Masterharper. McCaffrey thus makes a woman the protagonist of the novel and emphasizes the problems this character encounters because she fills an unconventional role for a woman in her society.

13. Marion Zimmer Bradley, in an article entitled "Responsibilities and Temptations of Women Science Fiction Writers," says that one of the responsibilities is "to tell a good story" (37); another "is to provide role models of women in society" (37).

14. As Judith Grant phrases this philosophy, "One solution to male domination is reinterpretation of the world from 'women's point of view'" (76).

15. This happens most often in science fiction and fantasy. Because of estrangement, as Anne Cranny-Francis observes, "science fiction (and fantasy) can present women in new roles, liberated from the sexism endemic to their society even in its most emancipated state" (42).

16. This is, of course, harder to demand of minor characters, since they are almost by definition those whose characters are only briefly sketched. This leads then to the importance of portraying women as protagonists.

17. The definition of feminism I gave earlier is, as previously mentioned, quite inclusive, but many definitions are not. One of the problems that feminism faces, Donna LaFramboise argues, is that "the mainstream of the movement refuses to distance itself from extremist elements; . . . in fact, it embraces them" (19). Women unwilling to align themselves

with the (often vocal) extremes of the movement may reject the description of "feminist" entirely.

18.   This approach explains failed readings or alternate readings: the reader has assumed the wrong, or a different, social / interpretive community and interpreted the conventions of the text accordingly.

19.   This applies to broad generic categories such as poetry, short fiction, novels, essays, and drama, but also to more specific sub-categories: science fiction, mysteries, historical fiction, and so on.

20.   Arthurian popular fiction most often appears in these categories, but the placement often depends on what the particular author has published previously. Thus, *The Mists of Avalon* usually appears in science fiction / fantasy sections because of Marion Zimmer Bradley's popular fantasy series, the Darkover novels; occasionally it appears in general or historical fiction. My preference would be a category called historical fantasy; it would include virtually all rewritings of the Arthurian legend, the Robin Hood story, or other works that reconstruct a historical or mythical time.

Chapter 2

The Medieval Legacy

The history of the legend in English literature provides a rich tradition for contemporary writers to work within or to work against. In particular, various aspects of the conditions of the production of the medieval versions of the legend, and the reception of those versions now, make this story amenable to feminist reinterpretation. I will briefly discuss two medieval texts in terms of their cultural use of the legend, in order to provide a context for contemporary uses of it; I will also summarize the legacy of events and characters, particularly female characters, that these medieval texts have bequeathed to today's rewritings.[1]

THE CULTURAL WORK OF MEDIEVAL TEXTS

As in contemporary society, in medieval times versions of the Arthurian legend circulated among many people and performed important cultural work.[2] Geoffrey of Monmouth's *Historia Regum Brittanniae* and Sir Thomas Malory's *Le Morte D'Arthur*,[3] both important texts in the development of the legend in English and the sources that have the greatest influence on the Arthurian rewritings I study in this book, construct Arthurian tales that speak to current issues of nationalism in their respective cultures.

Geoffrey of Monmouth's *Historia Regum Brittanniae* (c. 1139) chronicles the exploits of the British race from the time of their settlement on the island of Britain. In a work of twelve books that records events from the Trojan War to the reign of Athelstan (c. 738), Geoffrey spends five books depicting the time during which Arthur's family, and then Arthur himself, came to power.[4] Some of the information Geoffrey presents was already known; the chronicle *Historia Britonum* (c. 826) of Nennius, for example, includes Vortigern's story (29–31) and lists Arthur's battles (35); it is also possible that parts of the Welsh tradition pre-date Geoffrey. Lucy Allen Paton concludes "that before the beginning of the twelfth century to the name of the historic Arthur, the successful British leader, there had already become attached much legendary and even mythological material" (xiv) that Geoffrey could use. However, Geoffrey also added characters and events of his own making, shaped the story significantly by making Arthur a national hero with international importance, and, by writing in Latin, established the currency of the British hero's story for a continental audience. As a result, Geoffrey "gave a dignified place in literature" to the Arthurian legend (Paton xxiv). The fact that there are two hundred Latin manuscripts of the *Historia* extant (Hammer 3) indicates the immense demand for Geoffrey's version.

The Arthur that Geoffrey makes famous in the *Historia* is the conqueror of Europe. Although Saxon armies had beleaguered British leaders since Vortigern's reign, Arthur defeats the Saxons so decisively that there is peace for twelve years after (164); they only regain their influence when Mordred enlists them in his rebellion against Arthur (197). As R. William Leckie, Jr., notes, Geoffrey thus diminishes the Saxon conquest of the island and inflates the importance of the Britons. The date 449, when Hengist and Horsa arrived in Britain, traditionally marked the beginning of Saxon control (Leckie 3). In contrast, Geoffrey gives the Britons more influence in shaping a longer period of history. First, the Saxons are welcomed by treacherous usurpers (Vortigern, then Mordred); they do not overcome unified British resistance. Second, Arthur defeats the Saxons decisively; Geoffrey portrays Badon "not [as] the final memorable triumph of a declining people" (Leckie 63), but as one triumph among many, since Arthur goes on to conquer Hibernia (Ireland), Iceland, Gothland, and the Orkneys (*Historia* 164). Furthermore, Geoffrey then has Arthur fight the Roman empire; he conquers most of Western Europe but has to turn back from taking Rome itself "when message was brought him" of Mordred's treachery (196).[5] Geoffrey, therefore, gives Arthur and the Britons international significance.

Although some of his own contemporaries questioned the veracity of his account,[6] Geoffrey made Arthur a compelling figure for future generations. He is a king, practically an emperor; he saves his beleaguered people from foreign conquest and makes them, in their turn, the conquerors.[7] As a result, Geoffrey provides reasons for national pride since the British once held an empire comparable to Rome's. He also acts as a source for the "new" Norman kings to legitimate their conquest; because of the later exile of many of Arthur's people to Brittany and northern France, the Normans could claim Arthur as an ancestor. Moreover, since the dukes of Normandy were now also kings of England, he gives a precedent for Britain and her leaders' ruling over France. Geoffrey was used for these purposes as late as the reign of Henry VIII, who attempted to use Geoffrey in the negotiations of his divorce (MacDougall 16–17).[8]

Sir Thomas Malory's version, first published by William Caxton in 1485, appeared when the legend was still being used for political purposes; Henry VII claimed descent from Arthur and Cadwallader, then "christened his eldest son Arthur" (Merriman 35) in 1486. George D. Painter suggests that such uses of the legend would have increased demand for Malory's version of it, remarking that after the christening "Caxton must surely have done a roaring trade with his *Morte d'Arthur"* (167). James Douglas Merriman also speculates on the appeal of Malory's work and the nature of its audience: "The relatively large number of chivalric narratives published in expensive folios—such as all the Tudor editions of Malory—indicates that the audience for these works was still extensive in aristocratic or moneyed circles during the first three-quarters of the sixteenth century" (33). The demand for romances in general declined thereafter, and the questioning of the historical veracity of Arthurian stories helped diminish the legend's appeal; nevertheless, in the century and a half after Caxton's there were "six separate editions of Malory" (Merriman 21).

Written during the Wars of the Roses, *Le Morte D'Arthur* participates in the glorification of the English nation, but it criticizes that nation as well. *Le Morte D'Arthur*, like Geoffrey's *Historia*, establishes Arthur's reign as part of England's glorious past. As Elizabeth T. Pochoda argues, frequent references to events taking place in past days, as well as the combination of elements from the chronicle genre with those from the romance genre, suggest that "Malory had a definite sense of an historical *past* of which Arthurian society is a part" (59, emphasis in original). Also, certain changes made to the story, whether designed for political purposes or for reconciliation of conflicting sources, aggrandize Arthur's achievements. The Roman War, for example, culminates in Arthur's being crowned emperor (1:192); in Geoffrey's account Arthur had to turn back from the crowning because of Mordred's usurpation of the kingdom. Arthur's realm, in Malory, thus equals the Roman empire. This ending to the Roman War episode parallels the fifteenth-century vision of England as "the incarnation of that immortal justice which had previously been the province of Rome" (Pochoda 53).

Having established the glory of Arthur's realm, Malory uses differences from its virtues, or similarities to its faults, to chastise his own time. A narrative comment comparing love in the writer's time to love in Arthur's, for example, describes the fickleness of the new age in contrast to the virtues of the old: "Right so fareth love nowadays, soon hot soon cold: this is no stability. But the old love was not so; . . . then was love, truth, and faithfulness" (2:426). Mordred's usurpation, however, provides an example of political faithlessness that the writer sees in his own society: "For he that was the most king and knight of the world, and most loved the fellowship of noble knights, and by him they were all upholden, now might not these Englishmen hold them content with him. Lo thus was the old custom and usage of this land; and also men say that we of this land have not yet lost ne forgotten that custom and usage" (2:507). By such comparisons, Malory criticizes the "great default of us Englishmen, for there may nothing please us no term" (2:507). *Le Morte D'Arthur*, therefore, can be interpreted as a comment on the political upheavals of the time.[9]

Caxton's preface suggests another type of cultural work of *Le Morte D'Arthur*. He asserts that he has published the text "to the intent that noble men may see and learn the noble acts of chivalry, the gentle and virtuous deeds that some knights used in those days, by which they came to honour" (1:5). In Caxton's view, *Le Morte D'Arthur* acts as a reminder of the values that the nobility should follow. That this was Caxton's intention in publishing the text is reinforced, as J. R.

Goodman argues, by the other texts that Caxton was printing at the time; Malory's work is one of a series that "returns again and again to his [Caxton's] unifying themes—the three Christian Worthies, the need for a reformation of English knighthood, and the attractions of a crusade against the Turks" (266). Consequently, Malory's text, like Geoffrey's, illustrates the way that medieval authors shaped the Arthurian legend to engage with the political debates of their day. This reshaping of the legend occurs in the twentieth century as well; as Marion Zimmer Bradley points out, "every new society rewrites the Matter of Britain in its own way, to explain the legend to their own time" (Godwin, "Road" 9).

THE ARTHURIAN LEGACY OF MEDIEVAL TEXTS

Perhaps the first thing to be said about contemporary use of medieval Arthuriana is that it tends to be selective rather than slavish. Writers who retell Malory, for example, often write for children and in the process of simplification choose certain characters and incidents to work with rather than others. Authors who rewrite the legend for older audiences also select their material, choosing characters, incidents, and themes from disparate sources. They weave these borrowed strands with many of their own imagining, creating a new pattern, with new themes and emphases. Even John Steinbeck, as Raymond Thompson notes, exemplifies this process: though he begins *The Acts of King Arthur and His Noble Knights* determined to add nothing to Malory, Steinbeck "in the second half of his book . . . departs increasingly from Malory, 'opening it out'" (Thompson 11). Thus, medieval Arthurian works provide inspiration for quite new and different versions of the legend.

Contemporary writers have a large number of medieval versions now available, often in translation from medieval English or French, from which to find such inspiration. Although now, as in Victorian times, Sir Thomas Malory's *Le Morte D'Arthur* "continues to exercise by far the greatest influence upon modern authors" (Thompson 12), that influence is challenged by English chronicles, such as Geoffrey of Monmouth's *Historia Regum Brittanniae*; French romances, such as those of Chrétien de Troyes; and Welsh depictions of Arthur such as those in the *Mabinogion*. These works often provide contradictory information about characters and events that the contemporary author selects from or reconciles. Although the treatment of medieval sources varies with each rewriting, certain characters and events commonly appear in today's Arthurian fiction, often drawn from the versions of Geoffrey of Monmouth and Sir Thomas Malory.

For today's writers, Geoffrey of Monmouth supplies everything from names to ways of interpreting events. Some writers, for example, choose to make Bedevere Arthur's chief knight; Geoffrey names Arthur's butler Bedevere (170). But Geoffrey's chief contributions are the character and role of Merlin, the theme of war with the Saxons, and the names and roles of Arthur's family, particularly that of his nephew.

Mary Stewart comments that the *Historia* gave her the inspiration for her Arthurian novels, since Merlin "usually just appears as an old man in King Arthur stories" (Robertson 18). Geoffrey, then, is an important source for events before Arthur's conception, and for Merlin's characterization. In the *Historia*, Merlin possesses supernatural origins and attributes. Merlin's mother testifies that his father was some sort of supernatural force who "haunted" her and caused her to conceive (114). Merlin also exhibits magical abilities: he is able to prophesy the future to Vortigern when other magicians cannot (Book VI chap. xix, and Book VII); he later builds the Giant's Dance (138–41) and interprets the stars at the king's death to predict Uther's and Arthur's reigns (143–44). Geoffrey also makes Merlin Uther's advisor in the matter of Igerne, and it is through the magician's "leechcrafts" (149) that a disguised Uther impregnates Igerne with Arthur. Geoffrey thus uses Merlin to increase Arthur's stature and importance. First, Merlin's ability to prophesy makes him seem to be "possessed of some spirit of God" (115); the fact that he twice prophesies Arthur's coming (117, 144) thus suggests that Arthur is a hero divinely ordained to "succour" (117) his people. Second, the help Merlin gives Uther means that Arthur, as a hero should, has a mysterious and even magical beginning.[10] Though Geoffrey does not make Merlin involved in any later events (in taking the baby Arthur away to be fostered, for example), he gives the character an important role and thus makes him available for further duties in later versions.

Geoffrey also supplies a history of warfare between Britons and Saxons.[11] In the *Historia*, Vortigern welcomes Hengist and Horsus as allies against the Picts (104); however, these allies soon take control of the kingdom. Every king thereafter has to battle the Saxons to secure his reign until Arthur's decisive victory at Badon. The idea of a hero able to defend his country and culture, and, in effect, to rescue civilization, attracts today's writers, many of whom explore the implications of one culture's battle for survival against another. Issues of power and conflicts between cultures are thus important themes in many rewritings, and Geoffrey's version supplies a basis for those themes. Moreover, for writers attempting historical depictions of Arthur's time, Geoffrey provides a historically plausible enemy; Saxons likely would have been Arthur's opponents.

Most notable of Geoffrey's contributions, however, is the villainy of Mordred. Earlier chronicles simply list "[t]he battle of Camlann, in which Arthur and Medraut fell" (Nennius 45); Geoffrey cements the tradition that Mordred wanted the throne for himself. Geoffrey also involves the queen in this treason; Mordred "had linked him[self] in unhallowed union with Guenevere" (196). Although Geoffrey gives no details of the queen's motives or the degree of her complicity with Mordred, he suggests that she bears some guilt, for, when Arthur seems to be winning against his nephew, "she was forthwith smitten with despair, and fled from York unto Caerleon, where she purposed thenceforth to lead a chaste life amongst the nuns" (198). Some contemporary writers, such as Fay Sampson, keep Mordred as the queen's love interest, and therefore Arthur's rival personally and politically. Even some writers who include a Lancelot figure, Gillian Bradshaw or Mary Stewart for example, also incorporate Mordred's wish to marry the queen. Regardless, the precedent set by Geoffrey stands today: Mordred kills Arthur.

The Arthurian literary tradition was firmly established by the fifteenth century when Malory wrote *Le Morte D'Arthur*. Malory constructs his version from English alliterative and stanzaic poems, as well as from various French prose romances.[12] Thus, Malory is not the origin for Merlin's role as Arthur's advisor, the quest for the grail, Lancelot's status and love for the queen, or Mordred's parentage; nevertheless, it is Malory's version of these events that has made them accessible to English-speaking readers for the last five centuries.

The additions made to Merlin's role in *Le Morte D'Arthur*, as compared to the *Historia*, illustrate the way Merlin's character adds to Arthur's status (as it did in the *Historia*) but also the way he provides important information to other characters and to the reader. Merlin is involved in both hiding Arthur after his birth (1:14) and arranging the sword in the stone test that will prove Arthur's right to the throne (1:15).[13] Arthur thus grows up in secrecy and in ignorance of his parentage, and when he re-enters his society, he must prove his right to lead it; this cycle of exile, return, testing, and recognition has mythic aspects that add to Arthur's status as hero.[14] Merlin also informs the young king and the court (and thus the reader) of the background or hidden meanings to many events. Sometimes this information is political: he advises Arthur to ally with Ban and Bors, for example (1:24–25). Sometimes he makes accessible hidden knowledge of the past or the future: he reveals the name of Arthur's father (1:47), predicts that the eleven kings will be too busy fighting Saxons to bother Arthur (1:41), and foretells Arthur's downfall (1:48) and Lancelot's fame (1:118). Merlin also takes Arthur to find Excalibur (1:55) and informs him of the histories of such strange characters as Pellinor (1:55) and the damosel with the sword (1:66). Whereas Malory emphasizes Merlin's importance as Arthur's advisor, later writers, such as T. H. White, make him a teacher and mentor as well; his "shameful death" (1:48) through the wiles of a woman has fascinated writers as disparate as Alfred, Lord Tennyson, and Mary Stewart.

In telling the story of the grail quest, "a story chronicled for one of the truest and the holiest that is in this world" (2:372), Malory reduced the material in his sources by "sometimes omitting, sometimes telescoping" the marvels (Lawlor xv), and by "compressions of the passages featuring spiritual interpretations of dreams, visions, and historical events" (Plummer 109). Malory focusses on the adventures of Galahad, Percival, Bors, and Lancelot and gives the narrative the cyclical structure of challenge-adventure-return found in chivalric quests. Many writers of contemporary popular fiction reduce the grail story further. They focus on specific events, like the two appearances of the grail,[15] and skim over the episodic adventures between them. Alternatively, they focus on a specific character, so that the grail quest becomes another event that shapes or explains the psychological portrait being created.[16] The grail primarily provides an opportunity for authors to explore issues of religion and spirituality, but this can be done earnestly or ironically, with the confidence and earnestness of religious belief or with scepticism and mockery.

By Malory's time, the legend included Lancelot as Arthur's chief knight and Guenevere's lover, and Mordred as Arthur's son by his sister. Raymond Thompson remarks that even writers determined to create historically plausible portraits of Arthur's time cannot ignore "two motifs that are later accretions to the legend: the love between Lancelot and Guenevere, and the incestuous birth of Mordred" (34). Much of the power of the story comes from the conflicts caused by this love; much of its tragedy comes from the relationship between Mordred and the man he betrays.

In Malory's text, the conflicts caused by the love affair are both internal and external. Lancelot cannot reconcile his love with his duties to God and his king. He admits: "All my great deeds of arms that I have done, I did for the most part for the queen's sake, and for her sake would I do battle were it right or wrong" (2:272). The first part of his admission contradicts the knight's duty to work for God; the latter clearly violates the knight's oath, which requires "that no man take no battles in a wrongful quarrel" (1:116). Thus, Malory's portrait of Lancelot suggests, as Marion Zimmer Bradley notes, "a man tormented by conscience" (Godwin, "Road" 7), and this characterization is often emphasized in contemporary rewritings. Furthermore, the external conflicts caused by the love affair drive much of the plot of the latter part of *Le Morte D'Arthur*. Quarrels between Guenevere and Lancelot cause the latter to go mad (2:202) or send him away when he is needed to protect the queen, as in the episode of the poisoned apple (Book XVIII, chap. 1–7). The revelation of their love and Lancelot's killing of Gareth put Arthur and Lancelot at odds, and the resultant seige by Arthur of Lancelot in France provides the opportunity, which in earlier versions had been provided by the Roman War, for Mordred's usurpation. The importance of the love triangle can also be seen in the amount of Malory's story devoted to it; of the twenty-one books in Caxton's version, nine involve Lancelot's efforts to prove himself to the queen, to rescue her, to repent for his sin with her, or to fight Arthur because of her. Furthermore, four of those books are at the end of *Le Morte D'Arthur*; the love triangle thus provides climactic events to the story and is crucial to Malory's depiction of the end of Arthur's court. Contemporary writers usually follow Malory in emphasizing this love affair, though they tend to alter or expand upon the motives and feelings of each character and often more explicitly explore the sexuality of the characters.

Although the love between Lancelot and Guenevere weakens the realm, it is Mordred who mortally wounds Arthur (2:514). This is consistent with Geoffrey's account, but the relationship to Arthur differs. In Malory, when King Lot's wife arrives "to espy the court of King Arthur" (1:45), Arthur does not know that she is his half-sister, so he "desired to lie by her" (1:45). As a result, she conceives Mordred. Merlin explicates the significance of this act: Arthur will die in battle "for it is God's will your body to be punished for your foul deeds" (1:48), adultery and incest. Thus, Arthur's story becomes a tragedy; he is brought down in consequence of his own "innate failure" (Thompson 34).[17] Contemporary writers tend to explore this dimension of the story, in creating varying degrees of hostility between father and son or in apportioning blame between Arthur and his sister.[18]

Contemporary writers choose these elements from Geoffrey and Malory as opposed to others, all the tournaments in Malory's story of Tristram, for example. This indicates certain tendencies in Arthurian rewritings. First, authors seem to be attracted to episodes and characters that give the greatest scope for psychological expansion. For example, many contemporary writers create childhoods for important characters; this supplies a background to explain the characters' later actions or decisions. T. H. White, in *The Sword and the Stone*, began this practice, by recording Arthur's boyhood before he becomes king. Mary Stewart decided to "invent a life for Merlin" (Robertson 18); much of *The Crystal Cave* concerns his childhood, and the episode when he prophesies for Vortigern, his first appearance in Geoffrey, occurs more than halfway through Stewart's novel. Similarly, Marion Zimmer Bradley and Fay Sampson each give the child Morgan a role in events that happen before she is sent "to school in a nunnery" (Malory 1:12). Other authors, such as Persia Woolley, Sharan Newman, and Nancy McKenzie, explore possible childhoods for Guenevere. The early lives of the Orkney princes have been portrayed by White in *The Queen of Air and Darkness* and by Gillian Bradshaw in *Hawk of May*. In addition, contemporary writers explore possible feelings about, and reactions to, core events of the legend, such as Arthur's conception or Mordred's betrayal of Arthur. In part, such expansions on these events result from choice of genre; novels can explore the inner life of characters in ways medieval romances did not. I say "can explore" because, as Thompson notes, some contemporary novels, like some medieval romances, are "preoccupied with adventure for its own sake" (45). However, writers who want their Arthurian characters "to be credible as ordinary people" (Thompson 35) try to give motivation to characters' actions.

Second, contemporary writers tend to explore issues of power, and this influences their choice of narrative elements. These explorations may be about personal power—the ability (or inability) of an individual to determine his or her own fate. They may concern interpersonal relationships—the power one person wields over another as a result of personality, circumstance, or social structures. They may also concern power within a state or between states—how it is gained, how it is used, and its effects on history and on the individual.[19] Feminist ideas can influence such explorations by emphasizing the role of gender in social structures of power, or by criticizing as destructive the obsession with "power for the sake of power" (Spivack 12) that manifests itself in heroic stories in the warrior's code.[20]

Besides the suitability of the legend for examining issues of power, several other aspects make it amenable to feminist reinterpretation, if by that one includes, as I have argued earlier, a focus on women's stories, women's perspectives. On the one hand, courtly love literature (which includes many medieval Arthurian romances) attributes to women certain power over men, and the genre was influenced as it developed by several powerful women of the twelfth century. Eleanor of Aquitaine and her daughter, for example, patronised and perhaps commissioned[21] courtly romances; Marie de France wrote *lais* in the courtly love tradition. In comparison to chansons de geste or the chronicle tradition, courtly love literature makes women essential to the exploits of the men and gives ladies power over their knights. In Malory for example, a rebuke from Guenevere makes Lancelot into a madman (2:202). Contemporary writers interested in portraying strong women or exploring issues of gender and power are, in some ways, participating in a tradition when they choose the Arthurian legend to do so.

On the other hand, the women in medieval versions still tend to be adjuncts to the men, as shown in Maureen Fries's discussion of the roles of female characters in Arthurian romances, "Female Heroes, Heroines and Counter-Heroes." For example, many damosels come to court to request help of Arthur's knights and often ride with them as guides; these female heroes facilitate the male heroes' adventures. Guenevere inspires Lancelot's deeds; throughout Book VI, Lancelot overcomes knights and requires them to "go unto the court of King Arthur and there . . . yield . . . unto Queen Guenever [*sic*]" (1:215). The focus remains on Lancelot as subject of the story; it is the way *he* acts because of his love for her that shapes it. The legend, therefore, provides contemporary writers with many interesting women whose stories have not been told to use as protagonists, or whose characters can be elaborated on through the addition of past experiences. Furthermore, the medieval characterizations of these women often contain contradictory elements, depending on the roles they play in relation to the story's heroes.

Geoffrey's *Historia* supplies three female characters: Igerne, Anna, and Guenevere; Arthur's mother, sister, and wife, respectively. Another work by Geoffrey, *Vita Merlini*, mentions Morgan as the leader of nine sisters in Avalon who greet the wounded Arthur. Malory's version also contains Igraine as Arthur's mother and Guenevere as Arthur's wife; however, Arthur here has three half-sisters, named Elaine, Margawse, and Morgan. *Le Morte D'Arthur* also contains other courtly ladies, like the two Elaines who each fall in love with Lancelot, and numerous feys, like the Lady of the Lake and Nimue.

Several contemporary writers have chosen such minor characters, particularly the ones with magical powers, as the focal characters for Arthurian rewritings because of the possibilities for explication of motives. Nimue, for example, as she appears in *Le Morte D'Arthur*, possesses somewhat contradictory traits. When she entraps Merlin, she would seem to be at odds with Arthur's court; Tennyson focusses on this aspect of the character in creating his Vivien. However, Malory's Nimue then proceeds to protect Arthur and his knights from the wiles of other women: she rescues Pelleas from his destructive obsession with the cruel Ettard (1:157); she saves Arthur from Morgan's machinations during the battle with Accolon (1:130–33) and in the episode of the poisoned mantle (1:142). She is therefore helpful to Arthur,[22] yet autonomous from the court because of her magic. Contemporary writers use Nimue to explore the issue of women and power, though some follow Tennyson's lead to focus on the destructive possibilities of such power.

The most powerful and ever-present of the legend's sorceresses, Morgan, does not appear in Geoffrey's *Historia*. In his later work, *Vita Merlini* (c. 1150), however, she receives the wounded Arthur after Camlann (103). This Morgan is a beneficent and beautiful healer who combines the qualities of a shape changer (101) with those of a scientist (her knowledge of plants and of astrology). *Le Morte D'Arthur*, in contrast, presents Morgan almost always as Arthur's enemy. Arthur gives her the sword and scabbard for safe-keeping (1:77), but she arranges with "crafts and enchantments" (1:129) for a battle between Arthur and Accolon in which the former carries a false sword and Accolon carries Excalibur (1:130–35).

She steals the scabbard and drowns it so that it will not benefit Arthur (1:140). She sends gifts designed to kill or cause confusion at court: a poisoned mantle (1:142), a horn that tests the faithfulness of the wives who drink from it (1:163–64), and a shield depicting the love of Lancelot and Guenevere (1:463–64). At various times she also tries to trap Lancelot (1:198, 1:422–23) or Tristram (1:428–29). As in *Vita Merlini*, she has the ability to heal, but more harm usually follows her healing; thus, she cures Alisander but then drugs him to keep him with her in her castle (2:73–74). Despite all of these machinations against Arthur, she is one of the women at the end who collected the wounded king (2:519), who "wept and shrieked" for grief (2:517). Many contemporary writers find this sorceress figure fascinating, in part because of the contradictions in the Arthurian tradition from Geoffrey to Malory: she is both healing goddess and destructive witch. The metamorphosis of Morgan into "Arthur's worst enemy and nemesis" suggests, as Marion Zimmer Bradley argues, "a religious or cultural bias" that contemporary writers can question by revisioning the character ("Search" 107). Morgan also appeals to contemporary writers because of the current revaluing of witches in Neo-paganism, and in our culture more generally, as emblems of powerful women.

Perhaps the most famous female character of the legend is Guenevere, Arthur's wife. In the *Historia*'s chronicle, she is a minor character whose birth and beauty are mentioned when Arthur weds her (164), but who receives little other mention until Mordred seizes the throne and marries her.[23] Her despair when Arthur returns and seems to be winning (198) suggests that she may have been Mordred's co-conspirator, rather than a victim of his plot, but Geoffrey does not make this clear.

As a queen and a courtly lover, Guenevere has much greater importance in *Le Morte D'Arthur*. Guenevere often appears in her role of queen of the court; she hosts tournaments (2:79–88) and dinners (2:376) and generally contributes to the court's stature with her beauty and fame. She also plays the role of courtly lover by inspiring Lancelot's deeds of arms. This role also means that she inspires the plot of the work as a whole. First, she is often the mechanism by which Lancelot is sent from court on different adventures (for example, when they quarrel and she dismisses him). Second, she provides the framework for more examples of Lancelot's prowess; she is, at various times, kidnapped and accused of murder and treason and thus requires rescuing. Third, the revelation of their love sets in motion the feud that will take Arthur from England, allowing Mordred to usurp the throne.

There are thus contradictory attitudes surrounding Guenevere in the text. Although she often needs Lancelot to save her, she can also defend herself: when Mordred attempts to claim Guenevere as well as the throne, she tricks him and garrisons herself in the Tower of London (2:505–06). She inspires knightly action and is thus a model of the courtly lady; furthermore, her status as "a true lover" results in "a good end" (2:426). However, she, or love for her, prevents Lancelot from achieving the grail: the hermit explains that Lancelot will only acquire true worship if he promises to "never come in that queen's fellowship" (2:272). And as I mentioned earlier, Guenevere inspires action but is not the subject of it: they are all Lancelot's adventures. Guenevere thus provides contemporary writers with a female character whose importance to the legend's events is established, yet she can be used to elaborate her own story or psychological motivation in new ways, or she can supply a new perspective on the traditional events and characters of the legend. Guenevere also has been important to many subsequent writers (Tennyson and Morris as well as twentieth-century authors) because of cultural concern with sexuality and sexual freedom; for similar reasons she is important to contemporary feminist rewritings. Guenevere's story fits the slogan "The personal is political," for her love is both a personal expression of sexuality and an act of treason. The Arthurian legend as a whole and the queen's story in particular, therefore, allow exploration of the ways in which the personal impinges upon, or is bound up with, political acts.

NOTES

1. When discussing medieval texts, I spell character names consistently as Arthur, Guenevere, Igerne, Uther, Bedevere, Lancelot, Merlin, Mordred, Morgan, and Nimue. I have chosen this approach because spelling in general was not regularized until after the medieval texts were written and often varied within a work. However, when discussing contemporary works, I spell character names according to the usage of the author whom I am discussing at the time. Twentieth-century writers often choose particular spellings to complement their approach to the legend; spellings of Guenevere, for example, may depend on whether the queen is portrayed as Welsh or Roman. Because individual writers alter the legend's characters for their own purposes, I am including Appendix B to help my readers keep track of the various individuals to whom I refer. In some cases, authors only alter spellings of names; in other cases they dramatically change the relationships and roles assigned to their characters, by splitting one person into two, for example.

2. Because of their formation in a pre-industrial culture, medieval Arthurian chronicles and romances cannot be called "popular" in the sense that I defined earlier. Harriet E. Hudson reviews the difficulties of characterizing such works as popular but recognizes that there remains a "long standing identification of romance with popular literature" (31). In discussing the medieval works, I do not use the word "popular" to describe them, but I do demonstrate that they circulated widely for their time.

3. The spelling and even the title of Malory's text vary depending on the edition used; editions of Caxton's version of the text refer to it as a single entity, whereas Eugène Vinaver's editions of the Winchester manuscript refer to Malory's "works." Whereas Caxton treats the whole text as one work, dividing it into twenty-one books, each with various chapters, Vinaver's edition presents the text as eight separate, but related tales. Other textual variations include the shorter length of the Roman War episode in Caxton. Versions based on Caxton are still more readily available, so for my own quotations I use Janet Cowen's two-volume edition based on Caxton's Malory, and I therefore refer to the text as *Le Morte D'Arthur* since that is the title of her edition; the volume number is followed by the page number in the parenthetical citations.

4. Book VI concerns the kings Constantine (Arthur's grandfather), Constans (Arthur's uncle), and Vortigern; Book VIII, the reigns of Aurelius Amrosius and Uther Pendragon (Arthur's uncle and father, respectively); and Books IX, X, and part of XI, Arthur. Book VII contains the Prophecies of Merlin; near the beginning of these Merlin calls Arthur "the Boar of Cornwall [who] shall bring succour" to the people (117). Geoffrey had previously been "press[ed] . . . to make public an edition of his [Merlin's] prophecies" (116); they appeared separately circa 1135.

5. Malory has Arthur "crowned emperor by the Pope's hand" (1:192) because Arthur's downfall occurs much later in his account, after Lancelot's affair with Guenevere.

6. Leckie reviews several twelfth-century chronicles (73–101) and finds that many followed Geoffrey only when other sources gave no information. Therefore, Arthurian material was more often accepted than some of Geoffrey's other claims.

7. Evidence that this contributed to the legend's popularity can be seen in Layamon's use of the "Britonic hope" at the end of his *Brut,* where he says that "an Arthur should yet come to help the English" (264). The "English" who had defeated Arthur's people, the Welsh, had of course been defeated in turn by the Normans.

8. See Hugh A. MacDougall's *Racial Myth in English History: Trojans, Teutons, and Anglo-Saxons* for more examples of the way Geoffrey's *Historia* was used by British monarchs until the Renaissance. James Douglas Merriman, in *The Flower of Kings,* and Muriel Whitaker, in *The Legends of King Arthur in Art* (particularly pages 145–51), also examine Tudor uses of the legend.

9. See Pochoda's *Arthurian Propaganda* for a discussion of Malory's work as an engagement with fifteenth-century political theory.

10. Joseph Campbell observes that "the makers of legend have seldom rested content to regard the world's great heroes as mere human beings. . . . The whole hero-life is shown to have been a pageant of marvels" (319).

11. Malory, in contrast, has the newly crowned Arthur face other British kings in combat.

12. Malory's French sources were the Prose *Tristan,* the *Suite du Merlin,* and *The Vulgate Cycle.* Eugène Vinaver discusses these in his introduction (vii); there are numerous other studies of Malory's sources and the extent to which he followed them.

13. Merlin advises the archbishop as to the time and place for the nobles to meet to pray for guidance for their country, and it is while they are praying that the stone appears (1:15).

14. Joseph Campbell notes that "a prominent feature in all legend, folk tale and myth" is the "theme of the infant exile and return" of the hero (323). Arthur's fosterage with Ector fits this pattern, and the drawing of the sword marks the occasion "when, after the long period of obscurity, [the hero's] true character is revealed" (Campbell 329).

15. Marion Zimmer Bradley uses this technique, as do other writers who focus on female characters; since women are excluded from participating in the quest in the medieval and in many modern versions, they often only see the grail when it appears at court. Phyllis Ann Karr's "Galahad's Lady" is an exception to this tradition (see Chapter 7).

16. In Anne Eliot Crompton's *Percival's Angel,* for example, the grail quest enables Percival's growth in maturity and understanding, which the other protagonist of the story, Lili, has already acquired in the quest to reach Camelot safely.

17. Other medieval versions emphasized the tragic structure, often by including dreams of Fortune's Wheel. In *The Alliterative Morte Arthure,* for example, Arthur's rise and fall is tragic, but his fall results from his overweening pride and ambition; he starts his Roman expedition in order to redress wrongs but progressively becomes more ambitious and tyrannical. By rooting the tragedy in Mordred's conception, Malory makes Arthur unknowingly set the stage for his own downfall.

18. Malory does not specify whether Morgawse knew of their kinship, partly because such details of motivation are seldom explained, but several contemporary authors, including Stewart, Bradshaw, and Sampson, make the seduction of Arthur a deliberate, political act by his half-sister.

19. Marion Zimmer Bradley, in an interview with Parke Godwin, says, "To me, cultural shock, the clash of alien cultures, is the essence of literature and drama" ("Road" 6). Godwin, who has written his own version of the legend, agrees ("Road" 6).

20. Several of the short stories discussed in Chapter 7 undermine traditional symbols of power or question the sorts of power coded as indicators of heroism.

21. I refer here to the debate over the lines in Chrétien de Troyes's "Lancelot (The Knight of the Cart)," where he says that his "lady of Champagne" gave him the "subject matter and treatment" of the romance (185).

22. Sue Ellen Holbrook notes these traits in Nimue and argues that this Lady of the Lake "develops with acceptable logic: initially a damosel in distress, transitionally a sorcerer's apprentice, finally a benevolent sorceress" (175). Holbrook admits that the character "is not cut from whole cloth, and the seams are visible," but significantly Nimue remains "a consistently sympathetic figure" (175).

23. She is mentioned in the episodes of the crowning (170) and of the appointing of regents (178).

Chapter 3

Images of Royal Women

In practice, of course, novels can never be completely true to experience; however "realistic" their portrayal of events or characters, they cannot "reflect life accurately and inclusively in every detail" (Moi 45). Still, many readers expect novels to represent elements of the material world. For this reason, much feminist criticism of the early seventies examined the portrayal of female characters in literature, concerned with the ideas about women's "natural" attributes, abilities, and roles communicated by literature.

"Realistic" characters, by which I mean characters who go beyond stereotypes to have complex and believable motivations similar to those working in human beings, are one literary convention used to make a novel representational. In order to make characters "realistic," an author may seek to reveal the inner conflicts of characters. Such revelations help explain the motivations behind the actions in a novel, and they make it more difficult to assign a simple role (villain or helper) to a character. Moreover, as Raymond Thompson observes, they suggest struggles within characters "with feelings and doubts, with hopes and fears, and these encourage identification" (110). This identification on the part of the reader is not a recognition that the world of the novel (whether fantasy or historical fiction) reflects exactly the world in which the reader acts. Instead, "realistic" details, including plausible characters, allow the reader to recognize the ways in which the world portrayed by the novel is "analogous to reality" (Felski 80).

The fact that we, as readers, recognize the fictional world as analogous to our own enables us, first of all, to understand the story; the analogies provide points of reference. But because it is analogous, we also recognize ways in which it differs from or is similar to our own. Thus if the narrative persuades us that a situation or a system is unjust, we may realize that that injustice has parallels in our own world. Changes to traditional characters of the Arthurian legend that have been influenced by feminist ideas, therefore, help demonstrate that many stereotypes of or traditional roles for female characters, and by analogy actual women, are not inevitable or natural but are culturally constructed.

The Arthurian rewritings of Stewart, Bradshaw, Bradley, and Sampson are novels, and, as Ian Watt observes, "the novel is surely distinguished from other genres and from previous forms of fiction by the amount of attention it habitually accords . . . to the individualisation of its characters" (17–18).[1] Readers of novels expect, to some degree, "characters who are explicable in human terms, who are swayed by human emotions and who are psychologically plausible" (Dean 73). However, the types of changes made to traditional characters and the degree of complexity given in their representation still depend on the roles those characters play. In part this results from popular fiction's roots in medieval romance. As Northrop Frye demonstrates in *Anatomy of Criticism*, "the characterization of romance follows its general dialectic structure which means that subtlety and complexity are not much favored" (195). Consequently, roles shape characterization: "Characters tend to be either for or against the quest. If they assist it they are idealized as simply gallant or pure; if they obstruct it they are caricatured as simply villainous or cowardly" (Frye, *Anatomy* 195). Contemporary writers of popular fiction may meet this expectation in regard to the main protagonists of their novels while still using stereotyped characters to fill in the supporting cast and villains of the story. Even novels that engage with feminism illustrate this tendency, in that major female figures who are for the protagonist are made complex whereas villains remain stereotypes.

Arthur's queen is perhaps one of the most well-known characters of the legend, and she appears in almost every rewriting. Her characterization varies widely. In some versions she is selfish and shallow; in others she is hard-working and intelligent. In some her actions are blamed for the fall of the realm; in others her motives are validated even if the outcome remains tragic. The depth of her characterization often depends on her role: does she oppose the protagonist, as in Sampson's series; or does she support or act herself as the protagonist, as in Stewart's and Bradshaw's series; or is she a victim, as in Bradley's novel? This chapter examines Guenevere's character and those of a few other royal women in these four rewritings, focussing particularly on the way role affects characterization.

FAY SAMPSON

Sampson's is the most recently written series I consider. The five books give insight into many characters, but Morgan is always the main focus. *Herself* also alludes to Arthurian texts from throughout the legend's history, suggesting Sampson's awareness of the tradition and the way the tradition is currently evolving; she cites Mary Stewart's and Marion Zimmer Bradley's works, for example.

Nevertheless, Sampson's series vividly illustrates the influence of narrative role on characterization, particularly in the portrayal of Arthur's queen. Although Morgan is the central character, throughout the series Gwenhyvar is, intentionally or not, one of Morgan's opponents. Gwenhyvar's royal marriage destroys the possibility of Morgan's connection with Arthur, and her status as queen detracts from Morgan's influence. The main character of the series, then, resents Gwenhyvar, for the two often work against one another, and this narrative role affects Gwenhyvar's characterization.

Gwenhyvar, over the course of the series, is vilified. Unlike Morgan, Margawse, and Elaine, who become each aspect of the Goddess, Gwenhyvar remains always girlish, described as "light and shallow" (*Herself* 166), "light [and] lewd" (*Herself* 266). Morgan blames her for Camlann, though Gwenhyvar does not have the power of "spells and ritual. All the enchantment she needed lay in her own shy, sweetly-smiling self. Without high magic, she worked more harm than all the rest" (*Herself* 98). Gwenhyvar causes harm because of her capricious whims and her lack of maturity. She is "too shallow, vain and selfish" (*Herself* 281) to understand why Arthur must go away to fight; moreover, "she was bored" (*Herself* 281). As the final battle nears, her main concern is "what will happen to [her]" (*Taliesin* 255), rather than the fate of her people.

Although most of the negative portrayals of the queen come from Morgan, who admits she is jealous of her sister-in-law, there are no dissenting pictures of the queen given. Taliesin, for example, compares her to a camp-follower (*Taliesin* 147) because she does not have a land to govern when her husband goes off to war, unlike the other queens. Bryvyth the abbess rebukes Gwenhyvar for selfishness and declares, "That one was never strong enough to be the Pendragon's wife" (*Taliesin* 257). Gwenhyvar's narrative role as villain (and a minor villain at that) means that her characterization is one of the least complex in the series. We see little motivation for her actions, and what we are given does not encourage sympathy.

Sampson explicitly acknowledges the difficulty in creating a feminist version of the legend. Even if a writer does not "demonize" all the women (*Herself* 304), those cast in the role of villains often remain stereotypical characters. Despite her awareness of the problem, Sampson does not escape this "trap" (*Herself* 305) in her depiction of Gwenhyvar.

MARY STEWART

The first novels of Mary Stewart's series are the earliest of the rewritings to be considered. The five books are a historical reconstruction of the legend, set in Dark Age Britain. Stewart creates a predominantly masculine society, uses male narrators or focal characters, and emphasizes the importance of fathers and surrogate fathers to those characters. Nevertheless, the series engages with feminism explicitly through the characterization of several women. Issues of representation of women particularly arise in the emphasis placed on the strengths of four minor characters of royal birth—Niniane, Ygraine, Anna, and Alice—and in the changes made to the characters of Guenever / Guinevere.

Niniane's response to her father's questions about her lover illustrates her emotional and psychological strength, and the cost of resisting authority. Determined to protect Ambrosius, Niniane "was whipped till the women said she'd miscarry, but never a word" did she say about the father of her child (*Cave* 20); she knows her family would have Ambrosius killed if she named him. The king, her father, uses brute force and political power to intimidate people; he often "put himself in a passion" (*Cave* 20) to "frighten . . . men" (*Cave* 21). Yet Niniane maintains her silence on Merlin's paternity, refuses to marry, and continues to try to become a nun. Stewart's expansion of this character, in Geoffrey's *Historia* simply identified as Merlin's mother or as the "daughter of the King of Demetia" (113), emphasizes her strength and her resistance to male family members who wish to control her for their own political gain.[2]

Niniane's strength in resisting her father compares favourably with a masculine standard of strength: many men are frightened by her father's rages. Ygraine's strength of character tends also to be expressed in terms of a masculine standard. Merlin's praise for Ygraine focusses on the way she fulfills "manly" ideals: he admires the way that she is "direct as a man, and with the same high pride" (*Hills* 75). When she shows any inconstancy or hesitation, Merlin associates it with her female nature and calls it "her woman's weakness" (*Hills* 78). Thus just before Arthur's birth, he describes her fighting spirit as cloaked by "the milky calm that seems to come on women in pregnancy" (*Hills* 75), and her "mettle" and rationality are lessened by the fact that "she was a woman nearing her seventh month" (*Hills* 76). As a result, much of Ygraine's strength becomes a virtue borrowed or emulated from men; any weakness reveals her "female" nature. Nevertheless, Stewart's expansion of Ygraine's role in the story provides insight into the duchess of Cornwall's motivations during Uther's courtship of her, and her analysis of her own feelings and the situation reveals intelligence and a sense of honour.

Merlin admits that Ygraine "was cleverer than Uther, clear-headed, and . . . stronger too" (*Cave* 421), for although she is passionate about wanting Uther, she refuses "to lose her head" (*Cave* 418). She resists playing the role of a woman whose beauty devastates society; she declares that she is "no trashy Helen for men to fight over, die over, burn down kingdoms for" (*Cave* 419).[3] She asserts her right to be a person rather than the spoils of war, merely "a prize for some brawny victor" (*Cave* 419). Her attitude also shows that she understands the political consequences of her personal feelings.

Merlin also comments on the restrictions placed on women and the roles they play in the society depicted by the novels; such comments parallel those made by some contemporary feminists about our society. For example, in *The Crystal Cave* Merlin compares women's lot to that of slaves to explain Ygraine's ability to deceive: "Duchess or slut alike, they need not even study to deceive. I suppose it is the same with slaves, who live with fear" (*Cave* 426).[4] This passage suggests that even a strong, admirable woman like Ygraine is disadvantaged in her society because of her gender. Although such women may evade the restrictions of their society, or flout patriarchal authority, they need exceptional strength to do so.

The most recent addition to Stewart's series, *The Prince and the Pilgrim*, creates interesting portraits of two other royal women who are very minor characters in the Arthurian tradition. In this rewriting of Malory's story of Alexander le Orphelin and Alice la Beale Pilgrim,[5] Stewart expands the roles of

Anna (Alexander's mother) and Alice, and, like Niniane and Ygraine in Stewart's earlier novels, these women show exceptional strength of character in negotiating a patriarchal world that makes certain assumptions about them based on their gender.

Anna, wife of Baudouin and sister-in-law to King March of Cornwall, is a main character only in the first section of the novel, but her resourcefulness saves her son, who is a protagonist for much of the rest of the book. She first appears helping her husband prepare for an interview with March; in this scene (15–16), husband and wife appear to have an equal partnership. This sense of partnership grows after Baudouin's murder, for Anna and Baudouin together have prepared for this circumstance. Anna grieves at her husband's death, but she does not let emotion prevent her from acting. She identifies herself as "a princess and the mother of a prince" (20) who must tend to her duties even while she grieves. Because of her determination, she escapes March's castle. Her courage becomes even more evident when she faces the pursuers March has sent to kill her and her son. The description of Anna emphasizes stereotypical feminine qualities: her eyes are full of "fear" and also "appeal. Her hand looked small and fragile on the rein" (27). Sadok, the pursuer, thinks of her as "the fair . . . the chaste" (27). Yet the reader knows that the entire time that Anna looks fragile and vulnerable, "her right hand was steady on the hilt of Baudouin's sword" (27). Anna uses assumptions about the weakness of her gender to help persuade her pursuers to let her go, but she is always ready (and it would seem able) to use other, traditionally masculine means to defend herself and her son.

Stereotypical feminine traits are also used as a mask by Alice, a protagonist of the novel. She is introduced as a child interested in the insect world and wondering about the martial and sexual practices of the insects she observes. When she is called to her public duties, a transformation takes place. Dirty hands and feet are hidden by her dress; with "downcast eyes," she becomes "decorous," the "*Lady Alice*" (37, emphasis added). The novel emphasizes the complexity of her character, sometimes hidden, but never erased, by the traditional feminine roles her society expects her to fulfill.

Alice, like Anna, thinks and acts for herself. As her actions show when she is confronted by an assassin (155) or a murderous kinsman (274), Alice reacts courageously and effectively when she meets danger. Because of this, she is more active in events than many courtly lovers. She may inspire Alexander to greater prowess in combat (272), but she also offers more practical help, by giving him a dagger so that he is armed with the same weapons as his opponent and by dragging obstacles out of his way (274).

Despite her unorthodox early life and her active participation in political events, Alice does not violate the conventions of her society in terms of the life she lives when she grows up. As in Stewart's other novels, the female characters of *The Prince and the Pilgrim* live in a patriarchal world. From the beginning Alice has "two alternatives: she must marry some suitable man of her father's choosing, and bear his children, or she must take her vows and retire to a convent, a chaste and holy bride of Christ" (42). Her father, thinking that these alternatives are the only possible, natural ones, does not recognize that Alice could need "anything else to fill . . . her mind" (42). Although Alice marries a "suitable man," she is the one who chooses the groom. Her father informs Alexander: "She tells me that she is going to marry you. With your consent, of course?" (256). *The Prince and the Pilgrim*, therefore, portrays Alice as a strong female character who sometimes challenges, but often works within, the conventions of her society.

Stewart's series, particularly *The Last Enchantment* and *The Wicked Day*, also expands the roles of and offers some psychological depth to the character of Arthur's two queens, Guenever and Guinevere, although they remain supporting characters for the male protagonists. Stewart uses the Welsh tradition of multiple Gueneveres, but the two queens are described more fully than in Geoffrey's account; neither of them plays the role of courtly lover as in Malory.

Arthur's first wife, Guenever, has been groomed for her role as queen by Ygraine herself, and she demonstrates intelligence and political astuteness. Bedwyr describes her as "delightful. She's full of life . . . and she is clever. She plied me with questions about the wars, and they were not idle ones. She understands what he [Arthur] is doing" (*Enchantment* 200). Guenever and Arthur, therefore, share characteristics such as liveliness and interest in the country's future, and seem genuinely devoted to one another. When she dies while miscarrying his child, Arthur grieves over what "could have been a good marriage" (*Enchantment* 235). Although only a minor character, Guenever is represented as a person capable of loyalty, of affection, and of fulfillment of political responsibilities.

Stewart makes Arthur's second Guinevere share some of her predecessor's positive traits. She is also full of life and spirit; she possesses "a sort of outgoing gaiety, and a way of communicating joy" (*Enchantment* 265), and her ability to handle horses elicits admiring comments (*Enchantment* 268). Although Arthur declares that he loves her (*Enchantment* 295), her position as queen is not a secure one. In presenting this second Guinevere as an attractive, sympathetic character who is affected by her society's notions of proper womanhood, the novels confront the problem of gender discrimination.

The three most important men in the series, Merlin, Arthur, and Mordred, acknowledge the hardships of Guinevere's position as queen, and the difficulties created by society's expectations of a woman's "natural" roles. Merlin reflects that "to be Arthur's Queen was no mean burden, with all that it entailed of loneliness, and a life of banishment in an alien country" (*Enchantment* 305). Arthur's analysis of that burden recognizes it as the consequence of a society where women are the property of men, where "even royal ladies are bought and sold, and are bred to lead their lives far from their homes and their people, as the property of men unknown to them" (*Enchantment* 300). Furthermore, as a woman who is married to a powerful man, she is viewed as a tool to be used or an object to be possessed by "the flatterers, the power-hungry schemers, those envious of her rank or beauty, or—perhaps most dangerous of all—the young men ready to worship her" (*Enchantment* 305). Such attempts to use her for political advantage or to worship her beauty can threaten her physically; Melwas, for example, abducts the queen because of his "love" for her and would have raped her if Merlin had not found them (*Enchantment* 297). The only weapons society allows her are deception and fair speech: thus to defuse Melwas's anger and buy time for a rescue, Guinevere "smiled, and spoke him fair, and hid her fear. . . . She let him think that, with nightfall, he would have his pleasure, while all the time she hoped for rescue still" (*Enchantment* 300).[6] Meanwhile, her popularity with the people decreases because they expect her to bear Arthur's heir; because she "fails" in this mothering role by being barren, "there will always be those who start whispers, in the hope that [Arthur] will put her away" (*Enchantment* 301). These rumours make her position as queen insecure, and also threaten any personal emotional security she might have in Arthur's affection by reminding her of "the 'other Guinevere,' the pretty Queen who had conceived from the King's first bedding of her, and for whom he had grieved so bitterly" (*Enchantment* 305). Mordred, too, comes to realize that her position forces Guinevere to create a public image to hide harsher realities: "to him she had been the Queen, . . . a creature of gaiety and wealth and power and happiness. It was a shock to see her now, suddenly, as a lonely woman who lived with fear" (*Day* 335). By having these men comment on and understand Guinevere, Stewart influences the reader to sympathize with the queen, as well, and understand the motivations behind her actions.

Stewart also changes Guinevere's actions in terms of the love affair, making the feelings genuine but leaving the consequences of those feelings vague. Both Bedwyr and Guinevere suffer from their feelings for both are unwilling to betray Arthur and yet are unable to deny their love for one another. Although Arthur implies that she might have taken Bedwyr "to her bed" (*Enchantment* 354), Stewart's series, unlike many versions of the legend, never shows the queen and the best knight of the realm as sexual partners.[7] In the scene where the queen and Bedwyr are trapped in her bedroom, Mordred reports, "There was never any question of adultery. . . . The King had sent a letter to the Queen, which she wished to show Bedwyr. . . . I saw it there, in her chamber. And when we broke in, they were both fully clad—warmly wrapped, even—and her women were awake in the anteroom. One of them was in the bedchamber with Bedwyr and the Queen" (*Day* 294). The only report of the pair as lovers comes from Agravain, whose judgement on the subject is suspect because of his sexual jealousy and hatred of Bedwyr. Furthermore, Stewart follows Geoffrey's account and has Mordred's usurpation of the throne occur during Arthur's battle with Rome, rather than as a consequence of divisive effects of Guinevere's love affair. Neither does Guinevere encourage Mordred's love; she seems unaware of his feelings for her and assumes that he wants only "to bring her comfort and distraction" in her grief over Arthur's reported death (*Day* 354). As a result of these changes to her actions, Guinevere bears less blame in the deterioration of Arthur's realm, and her character illustrates some of the effects of women's position in patriarchal society.

Niniane, Ygraine, Anna, Guenever, and Guinevere are supporting characters in the drama that Stewart creates. Niniane, Ygraine, and Anna bear and protect the male children, Merlin, Arthur, and Alexander, who are the protagonists. Guenever and Guinevere support Merlin and Arthur's dream of the kingdom the men wish to create. Stewart gives these women complex motives, but they remain on the sidelines. Only Alice has the status of protagonist, and her role as an exceptional heroine will be considered in a later chapter.

GILLIAN BRADSHAW

In Bradshaw's series, Gwynhwyfar is both a minor character (*Hawk of May*, *Kingdom of Summer*) and a protagonist (*In Winter's Shadow*). In all three novels, she supports Arthur's vision of the kingdom and contributes very practically to its construction. Like Stewart, Bradshaw makes careful additions to the legend's traditional story so that the reader can understand and sympathize with Gwynhwyfar's character, particularly when she is charged with treason because of her affair with Bedwyr.

Gwynhwyfar is beautiful, and descriptions of her beauty emphasize warmth and light. Gwynhwyfar had "masses of deep red, wavy hair and smiling brown eyes. There was a warmth to her, and a grace that made her beautiful" (*Hawk* 288). Rhys compares her to "a candle flame, warm and shining" (*Kingdom* 107). But Gwynhwyfar's beauty is that of a mortal woman. She ages as the series progresses and occasionally reflects on the way life's stress has affected her appearance. In the epilogue to *In Winter's Shadow*, she describes herself: "The face I see is an old woman's, lined with use. Much use: many tears. . . . Lined with laughter, too" (317). Gwynhwyfar's beauty results from ordinary life and human sorrows; it is not a fairy-tale perfection.

Although Bradshaw informs us of Gwynhwyfar's beauty, it plays much less of a role in her life and gives her far less importance and power than her intelligence and education. Her father, a scholarly noble, educates her; she admits that she "shamelessly ran off . . . from the cooking and housekeeping" (*Shadow* 7) in order to study with him until eventually she "had read even more than her father" (*Hawk* 288). Ogyrfan recognizes her abilities and gives her the responsibility of making their "holding . . . a smoothly managed, effective base" for Arthur's men (*Shadow* 11). Her education gives her a bond with Arthur for she understands his "goal of preserving the empire . . . [and] the value of peace and impartial justice" that the empire could represent (*Shadow* 10).

Gwynhwyfar appreciates Arthur's philosophical vision; moreover, she becomes invaluable in the attempt to put it into practice. Bradshaw constantly reminds the reader of the hard work that the queen undertakes. Rhys lists some of her duties: "She determined how much wool we had and how much we needed to buy and how much each person could take; she saw to it that the cattle were slaughtered in the right numbers and that we had enough grain; she ordered major repairs, like thatching, and kept all the accounts" (*Kingdom* 107–8). In the typical day with which *In Winter's Shadow begins*, she must

buy grain to feed the fortress, . . . arrange a feast for the emissaries from the kings of Elmet and Powys, . . . allot some wool from the stores to the weavers of the fortress if all the Family were to have their winter cloaks in time. Soon, . . . [she] would have to find a new supply of iron for the smiths. . . . There would doubtless be some petitioners asking for a hearing. And there was the question of what [the] emissary must say to the king of Less Britain. (14)

After her expulsion from Camlann, Arthur confesses to her, "The fortress and the kingdom are almost ungovernable without you, because the affairs of the empire are in disorder and the servants and farmers sigh whenever you are mentioned" (*Shadow* 238). She later helps Sandde devise ways to raise supplies for the army (*Shadow* 276) and thus even in the final battle uses her administrative skills for Arthur's side.

Gwynhwyfar's talents extend beyond managing the fortress, for she is involved in all aspects of Arthur's campaign. "She was strong enough to help Gruffydd the surgeon with his work without flinching" (*Hawk* 288) and, for a while at least, able to keep the peace by persuading "many warriors into offering apologies" (*Shadow* 19) when conflicts arise in the Family. With Gwalchmai and Bedwyr, she joins Arthur in conferences on policy (*Shadow* 26–29). By often extolling Gwynhwyfar's abilities and responsibilities, Bradshaw emphasizes throughout the series the ways in which the queen is important to Arthur's dream; Gwynhwyfar is not just a figurehead, but gives Arthur practical assistance in running the kingdom.

Although Gwynhwyfar holds political power,[8] the society that Bradshaw depicts in her series is a patriarchal one. Women and men have particular roles, and for the most part women have charge of the domestic sphere and men take charge of war and law (*Shadow* 172). Exceptional women like Gwynhwyfar can find positions of power within that society, but those positions are tenuously held. Gwynhwyfar cannot command respect outside a controlled sphere. When she goes with Bedwyr to Less Britain, she finds that she is "useless and helpless" because Hywel and his warband see her only as a "stolen woman" (*Shadow* 195). She contrasts her treatment in the two courts: "I had been accustomed to responsibility and authority, and I had become a piece of Bedwyr's luggage, the trophy of a battle" (*Shadow* 195). Only a few people—Arthur, Bedwyr, Gwalchmai, Cei, Ogyrfan—realize that Gwynhwyfar is not a possession. The contrast between Gwynhwyfar's capabilities and the way she is perceived by people outside her court demonstrates both the irrationality and debilitating effects of gender prejudice in society.

MARION ZIMMER BRADLEY

Bradley's Gwenhwyfar is both antagonist and protagonist in *The Mists of Avalon*. She often opposes Morgaine, the central character, but she focalizes the narrative in several sections, so readers are given insight into her motives. Her upbringing and religion particularly contribute to the complexity of her character, a complexity that complicates the role she plays.

Gwenhwyfar's upbringing at the convent makes her more helpless than other women in Bradley's novel. When Gwenhwyfar is introduced, she is, significantly, lost, and must depend on Lancelet for rescue (who in turn follows Morgaine). When Bradley next depicts Gwenhwyfar, just before her betrothal to Arthur, some of the girl's fear and timidity is explained. Gwenhwyfar's agoraphobia results from poor eyesight. Her condition is not improved by the ridicule she receives from her father and stepmother. Although afraid of marrying, Gwenhwyfar feels that she would accept marriage for the chance to be in her own house, where "no one would dare to make fun of her" (252). However, when Arthur offers to allow her to "rule at [his] side" (273), she panics and refuses. She wants to be able to do things, to manage her life, but she is ultimately afraid to do so.

It becomes obvious that Gwenhwyfar has been trained to be a meek and mild creature. She speaks to Leodegranz "in her shyest little voice . . . [for] it displeased her father if she spoke out boldly" (254). Her moments of rebellion or boldness are smothered either by others in authority or by herself. For example, when she suggests that she should marry Lancelet, her father over-rules her; he feels she needs "a man to take care of [her], and better the King than the King's captain" (256). The logic of his argument and his assertion that it is for her own good silence her. Later, when leaving for her wedding, she becomes so angry that she thinks "she would smother with the rage . . . choking her" (268) because she feels she is "merely part of the furniture . . . not herself, . . . only some property" (268). Her reaction to this anger reveals the extent to which she has internalized and accepted her father's and the priests' view of women: she equates her anger with Eve's sinfulness, and her rebellion against her father's will as rebellion against the will of God. Her method of coping with this anger and guilt is to "will . . . herself into semiconciousness again" (268).

The Roman, Christian doctrine that Gwenhwyfar follows makes her more of a victim when she is raped. Morgaine reassures Gwenhwyfar that Arthur will not blame her for Meleagrant's actions because she was "trapped and beaten into submission" (527). Gwenhwyfar does not believe this for she has been taught "that no woman was ever ravished save she had tempted some man to it, as Eve led our first father Adam into sin" (527).[9] Thus Gwenhwyfar suffers physically with Meleagrant, but she also suffers spiritually because she believes "that she merited death for the sin of having lived to be ravaged" (527).

Bradley's portrayal of the unfairness of Gwenhwyfar's position is compromised, however, by the implicit comparison between Morgaine and Gwenhwyfar. Morgaine warns her not to go see Meleagrant without a proper contingent of Companions (507). Moreover, she delivers this warning, not by using some supernatural source that Gwenhwyfar does not possess, but by using common sense. According to Morgaine, "it needs no sorcery to know that a villain is a villain" (507). Gwenhwyfar's logic, that Meleagrant will not harm her because it would invalidate his kingship claim, loses persuasiveness for the reader since the possibility of "bedding with the Queen" to prove kingship has already been suggested by Kevin (473). Moreover, part of her decision is based upon pride and willfulness, for "whatever Morgaine said, Gwenhwyfar always felt compelled to do precisely other" (507), and Gwenhwyfar also wants to prove "that she . . . could . . . settle a matter of state when Arthur was absent" (507). Furthermore, the Church's example of "the Holy Virgin martyrs of Rome [who] had willingly died rather than lay down their chastity" (527) parallels Gwenhwyfar's own thoughts about how Morgaine "would have used that little dagger of hers" (516) to prevent being raped. Still, Gwenhwyfar's vulnerability is memorable, and the graphic details of the rape (514) also create sympathy for her character.

Although Bradley depicts Christianity as having negative effects on Gwenhwyfar, there are some positive traits in this religion, and Bradley's characterization of it, like her characterization of Gwenhwyfar, is rather complex. First, women do have some status and power in Christianity depending on the situation. The abbess of Igraine's convent, for example, does "not bow" to Gwenhwyfar, because "temporal power . . . [is] nothing" in the holy place that she supervises (361).[10] Second, most of the depictions of Christianity come from characters like Viviane or Morgaine, whose beliefs and ways of life are threatened by Christianity; they are biased. Gwenhwyfar's is the only view of Christianity that we get from a woman, and she represents an extreme view of the Church, one that does not represent all Christians. For example, when Gwenhwyfar confesses that she has thought barrenness would allow her to take lovers with impunity, the priest does not condemn her. Instead, he reassures her "that it was no more than reason that with her husband so long sick, her thoughts should turn to such things; she must not feel guilty" (333). Gwenhwyfar refuses to take this counsel; she always thinks that she is too wicked to be forgiven.

Christians in the novel do act prejudicially and unreasonably, but a desire for power usually lies behind their actions; they enforce their beliefs not for Christ but for their own interests. The priest who comes to Gwenhwyfar after her miscarriage does not hesitate to encourage her fears and feelings of guilt in order to gain greater power at Arthur's court. He reinforces the thought that "if there is fault, it must be [her] own" (391); consequently, since the only fault the queen can think of is Arthur's use of the Pendragon and not the cross as his symbol, the queen becomes more obsessed with making the court completely Christian. When Gwenhwyfar realizes that Arthur fathered Morgaine's child, her obsession with sin and guilt forces Arthur to confess, a move that Morgaine rightly interprets as putting "Arthur into the hands of his priests" (552). Gwenhwyfar sometimes believes that her inability to have a child must be the result of God's punishment for sin,[11] but she also uses that belief, out of jealousy, to have power over her husband, to punish him for loving Morgaine.

The importance of Bradley's depiction of Gwenhwyfar's character to the status of her book as a feminist rewriting has been recognized by scholars. Barbara Ann Gordon-Wise calls *Mists* "revisionist" (147) because Gwenhwyfar's "dependence, timidity and paralyzing terror of open spaces are all a result of her upbringing within a patriarchal culture" (144) rather than an innate, female weakness. Similarly, Lee Ann Tobin argues that "Bradley's most important contribution to the Arthurian tradition is her use of its primary female character to show how women lost power in Western civilization" (150). She notes, as I have noted, several instances in which Gwenhwyfar clearly is being "trained to be submissive by her family and her Christian church" (150). Tobin goes on to argue that the placement of these scenes with Gwenhwyfar makes the reader question the "naturalness" of her upbringing. Because it is depicted first, Avalon's "training of women for power

... [seems] natural. ... The patriarchal Christian tradition has been effectively decentered" (Tobin 151). Although Avalon's training may be seen as "natural" in the novel, it is not completely benevolent. Morgaine's training has been rigorous, and she leaves Avalon feeling betrayed and trapped by the pregnancy that Viviane had arranged for her; as Viviane had warned, the priestesses can be "cruel" (*Mists* 136) in using people to fulfill the will of the Goddess. Still, Morgaine from the beginning has been allowed to choose; Viviane teaches her that following the Goddess's will "is too heavy a burden to be borne unconsenting" (*Mists* 171). Furthermore, Morgaine reaches a stage in her training "where obedience may be tempered with [her] own judgment" (*Mists* 169). Gwenhwyfar's father, by contrast, assumes that his daughter, by virtue of her gender, does not have any judgement. The reader, knowing Arthur's admiration for strong women and Lancelet's preference for fragile helpless women, knows that Gwenhwyfar, in the matter of her marriage, has better judgement than her father.

Bradley's novel has been recognized as "the feminist version" (Sampson, *Herself* 305) of the Arthurian legend. The creation of a plausibly motivated and therefore complex Gwenhwyfar, despite the queen's frequent role as the main character's opponent, contributes greatly to that status.[12] Moreover, the queen's complex motivations are shown to be influenced by the assumptions about gender made by her society, and the contrast between Avalon and Arthur's court suggests that all such assumptions are ideological rather than natural or common sense.

CONCLUSION

Since the medieval versions of the legend, Guenevere has been one of the most widely recognized of the Arthurian characters. The image of a young, beautiful queen captures our imaginations in many ways, as testified to by the idolization of Princess Diana in our own time. Contemporary rewritings of the Arthurian legend can use such royal women as Igerne, Niniane, Anna, Alice, or more often Guenevere to explore the constraints that society imposes on women whose personal lives are most glaringly subjected to public scrutiny, whose personal feelings have the most political consequences. The images contemporary writers give us of these women indicate the problematic nature of the ideals and expectations our society bases on gender.

NOTES

1. In my Conclusion I will discuss the ideological implications of this individualisation of character.

2. Merlin's existence and non-warrior-like bearing threaten the orderly inheritance of the kingdom: his grandfather dismisses him as "all I'm left with" (*Cave* 21). Camlach, however, fears that Merlin will present a competing claim to the kingdom, so, once sure that Niniane will not remove herself and her son to a distant land by marriage, he tries to poison Merlin (*Cave* 40). Niniane, by having Merlin out of wedlock and then refusing to marry at all, foils her father's and brother's plans to use her to gain an alliance with another kingdom.

3. Harold J. Herman also discusses the importance of Ygraine in Stewart's novels, seeing this character as an example of the way Stewart challenges "the traditional role of women as merely sex objects and mothers" by creating "strong-willed women who seek other positions in society" (108).

4. Compare Merlin's statement to Mary Ellman's comment from 1968: "Probably no group of people, steadily scrutinized by another, can afford to be open. Such people (employees, Negroes, women) are driven to subtlety, a sanctuary from examination. . . . [A]ll but the least vulnerable feint, hide, circumlocute" (190).

5. This story appears in Book X, chapters 32 to 39, of *Le Morte D'Arthur*.

6. Muriel Whitaker, in "'The Hollow Hills': A Celtic Motif in Modern Fantasy," argues that Guinevere is "willing . . . to be abducted and taken to the island" (174–75) by Melwas, and that "the King is deceived as to her reason for being there" (175). This is Merlin's first impression of events. Arthur then repeats what the queen has told him, and Merlin "did not answer straight away. . . . When at length [he] spoke, it was with certainty. 'Yes. She told the truth . . . I should have known she was afraid, and knowing that, I might have guessed that what poor weapons she had against Melwas, she would use'" (*Enchantment* 300–1).

7. This is important because, in a series where readers are positioned to sympathize with Arthur (he is a protagonist in this case), any action that hurts him tends to cast the doer of the action into a villainous, or at least unsympathetic, role.

8. In this chapter and in Chapter 4, I primarily discuss the way these novels represent women's access to, or ability to hold, power in the societies depicted. Chapters 5 and 6 will address the issue of narrative power: whose story is told and who tells it.

9. Elaine also mentions this idea when she is embarrassed to see Morgaine dressing. According to this doctrine, even for one woman to see another woman's body is shameful, for "all sin came into this world through the body of a woman" (*Mists* 520).

10. The phrasing of this passage suggests that she would not have bowed to the high king either. In this respect, the abbess resembles the Lady of the Lake, and this subtly prepares the reader for the moment when Morgaine recognizes a kinship between Avalon and the nuns at Glastonbury.

11. For example, after Arthur agrees to confess, his wife "had a moment of shattering fear and doubt" (*Mists* 554) about whether her barrenness has been caused by a cruel God's punishment.

12. Furthermore, Bradley avoids making the major male characters stereotypes as well. Arthur, Lancelet, Mordred, and the various Merlins may not be as heroic here as in other texts, but Bradley gives personal, psychological reasons for their weaknesses or villainies. Mordred, for example, is both a victim and a villain (Spivack and Staples 117–19).

Chapter 4

Images of Magical Women

The other women most notable in the Arthurian legends, whether of royal birth or not, are memorable for their magical abilities. These sorceresses have often been demonized, for in Western culture witches have been commonly associated with evil, their magical powers seen as coming from the devil. Renewed interest in paganism and New Age spiritualism in the last fifty years has increased the profile of witches as heroes, but the long tradition of Arthurian sorceresses as opponents of Arthur's reign continues as well. In contemporary rewritings, women with supernatural powers may be given complex motivation or remain stereotypical evil witches, depending to a great extent on the narrative role they fill. Bradshaw's Morgawse, for example, opposes Gwalchmai, Arthur, and Gwynhwyfar and is the incarnation of evil. Stewart's Morgan and Morgause plot against Merlin and Arthur, but Nimue helps the two men, and the characterizations of these women vary accordingly. Sampson's characterization of Arthur's three sisters uses goddess imagery to make them more complex whereas her portrait of the villain, Nimue, is closer to that of the stereotypical witch. Bradley's sorceresses, the most numerous and important of her women characters, are the most complex, but even here characterization depends on the narrative role, as Morgause displays more stereotypical qualities when she plays the role of villain.

GILLIAN BRADSHAW

Gillian Bradshaw's series sets up an opposition between those working for Light or Good and those working for Darkness or Evil;[1] of the two main female characters, Gwynhwyfar works for Light and Morgawse for Darkness. As noted in the previous chapter, Gwynhwyfar's inner conflicts and believable motivations make her a more complex character. Morgawse, on the other hand, is the main villain of the first two novels, and so she appears as a stereotypical witch.

However, she, like Gwynhwyfar, is shown to be affected by society's assumptions about gender.

Stereotypical witches generally do evil for its own sake, or for a selfish desire for power, or capriciously, as a demonstration that they can. Bradshaw's Morgawse acts out of the desire for power and hatred for the world; no explanation is given as to why she should act this way. Although Morgawse gains power from the use of her beauty, intelligence, and magic, her sorcerous powers overshadow her other attributes and make her a horrifying, demonic figure.

Gwalchmai, the narrator of the first novel, often comments on his mother's beauty. His first description of Morgawse suggests both a model of womanhood, especially in the quality of her voice, and the Darkness she will come to represent: "Her voice was low, soft, and beautiful. She was herself beautiful: very tall, dark where Lot was fair; her eyes were darker than the sea at midnight" (*Hawk* 6). As Gwalchmai's description continues, her beauty becomes associated with danger, for "she left breathless anyone who only looked at her, and drew eyes as a whirlpool draws water" (*Hawk* 6). Her beauty gives her the ability to dominate her husband; when Lot rushes to her after returning from the wars, Gwalchmai sees "still, cold disgust in her eyes mixed with a strange pride in her power" (*Hawk* 23). She uses her beauty and "an intimate, secret smile" (*Kingdom* 224) to "bewitch" and thus control her husband, her political allies, and even her sons.

Morgawse's intelligence also allows her to influence men, especially her husband. Bradshaw presents Lot as a statesman, who "enjoyed the complicated processes by which he kept his subject kings obedient" (*Hawk* 25). He is "more cunning than a fox" (*Hawk* 25), but Morgawse surpasses him. When difficulties arise in his power games, "he would ask Morgawse, and she would tell him what she had long before thought out, and it would work" (*Hawk* 8). While Lot is away, "she controlled the realm in a way which made [Lot's] . . . grip seem light" (*Hawk* 41). Gwalchmai realizes that she holds "Lot's fate in her slim white hands" (*Hawk* 30), for Lot "is a strong man, but she is a subtle designer, and will outlast him" (*Kingdom* 124).

Morgawse uses her beauty and intelligence to rule other men besides Lot. She sleeps with Arthur in order to have a hold over him, knowing he will be horrified at the incestuous relationship (*Hawk* 300–01). Morgawse begins an affair with Maelgwn, one of Arthur's enemies, in order to find another tool to use against Arthur. Rhys observes that "Morgawse would dominate her allies' minds and subjugate them, not to a cause, but to herself, and she would start with Maelgwn" (*Kingdom* 149). She knows that by "sleeping with the king of Gwynedd, . . . [she could] dictate his counsels" (*Kingdom* 149), and she plans to use his kingdom, which lies closer to her brother's than her own islands, as a base of operations against Arthur.

The power Morgawse receives from her magic increases and intensifies her other sources of power. Thus, even when Lot overpowers her physically, she "fed upon him like a shadow upon a strong light, and drained his power slowly away" (*Hawk* 58). Rhys also senses her ability to drain men's powers. He describes her eyes as "black in such a way that they seemed to drink all the light around them, . . .

[b]lack enough to drink your life like a thirsty man gulping down a cup of water" (*Kingdom* 122). When she uses sorcery, "darkness blazed in a corona about her, and she was more beautiful than ever any mortal woman was" (*Hawk* 52). In fact, Morgawse has served Darkness so long she has become "the queen of Darkness" (*Hawk* 115) and "is scarcely human now" (*Hawk* 173). Thus, one of most important female characters in the series is hardly a woman at all. Morgawse is, instead, "a Power wrapped in human flesh, long ago consuming the mind that had invoked it" (*Hawk* 68); she is supernatural, the protagonists' opponent, and unrelentingly evil.

However, Morgawse, like Gwynhwyfar, experiences constraints in spite of her powerful position. Morgawse can command Lot's warband, but only because "they feared her greatly. Enough men have defied her only to disappear from the green earth for any of them to disobey her" (*Kingdom* 242). The warriors' loyalties, however, remain with Lot and Agravain. In part, this lack of loyalty to Morgawse results from her known use of sorcery, but her gender is also a factor: the men "hated to be ruled by a foreign woman" (*Kingdom* 242). Bradshaw thus shows that society's gender-based assumptions can affect even this supernaturally powerful woman.

MARY STEWART

Stewart's series, as demonstrated in the last chapter, expands the roles and suggests motivations for Niniane, Ygraine, Anna, Alice, and the two Gueneveres and, in doing so, emphasizes the strengths and admirable qualities of these women who support the male protagonists of the story. However, the two women, Morgause and Morgan, who fill the roles of villain remain stereotypes of power-hungry (and thus "unnatural" or evil) women. Yet contradictions in the texts regarding powerful women highlight the way representation depends on narrative roles.

Morgause is introduced when Merlin and Ector discuss the political situation in the realm, for Uther has suggested that she might be married to Lot to strengthen the younger king's allegiance. When Merlin meets her, he does not immediately think she is treacherous, but he does associate her perfume with the smell of "fruit in a sunny orchard. Strawberries, was it, or apricots" (*Hills* 209). The association of Morgause with the fruit used by Camlach (Merlin's uncle) in his attempt to poison Merlin suggests that she, like the apricot in *The Crystal Cave*, will turn out to be deadly. When she later seduces Arthur, Merlin senses death, which has a scent "like treachery, something remembered dimly from my childhood, when my uncle planned . . . to murder me" (*Hills* 391). Morgause's perfume once again is apricot-scented, and her hair is "rosy fair . . . the colour of apricots" (*Hills* 403).

Treachery, therefore, becomes Morgause's trademark as she attempts, by any means, to gain power. She conceives Mordred in order to have a hold on Arthur. She manipulates Lot into killing his own son. She poisons Merlin, expecting that it will kill him. Her dealings with Lot and Merlin can be justified by her desire to protect her own son, and by the fact that Merlin is her sworn enemy. However, the ruthlessness of her character becomes even more explicit as the series progresses.

We know that "there have been many killings [for which she is responsible] . . . and none of them clean" (*Day* 167); her use of Macha to shelter Mordred and deceive Lot only to order her killed (*Enchantment* 154) is a memorable example of one of those deaths. In *The Wicked Day*, Stewart portrays this ruthlessness even more vividly. Macha is simply a name to the reader; she only appears as a corpse. Sula's perspective, on the other hand, shapes the prologue of *The Wicked Day*; her death has more impact upon the reader, who knows both her devotion to Mordred and his affection for her. When Morgause poisons Brude and Sula and has them burned, she tells her lover that he has served her "more than faithfully" (*Day* 60); he, and the reader, reflect, "so did they" (*Day* 60). Morgause, therefore, kills both enemies and allies when it seems expedient to her.

Her ruthlessness extends into her family relationships. She takes Arthur to bed knowing he is her brother, using him in hope of gaining political power. Her relationship with her half-sister consists of envy and convenience; when they can work together to do Arthur or Merlin harm they will (*Day* 84). She has "never . . . been moved by love" (*Day* 48) so she is "an erratic parent" (*Day* 61), spending time with the children only when she is bored. She uses the principle of "divide and rule" (*Day* 62) to govern them, in order to keep them under her influence rather than to ensure their welfare. She uses the same "well-tried pattern" on her sons and her subjects: "fear and then gratitude, complicity and then devotion" (*Day* 101).

However, Stewart includes a couple of remarks in her novels to suggest possible reasons for Morgause's behaviour. In *The Hollow Hills*, although Merlin condemns Morgause's plot to trap Arthur, he recognizes why she must make such plots: "You have the Pendragon blood in you that makes you desire power, so you take it *as it mostly offers itself to women*, in a man's bed" (*Hills* 407, emphasis added). The omniscient narrator of *The Wicked Day* suggests that "without magic, and the terror she took care that it invoked, a woman could hardly have held this stark and violent kingdom" (*Day* 73–74). The novels hint that Morgause's actions result, in part, from the constraints of a patriarchal society, a society that only credits women with the power to rule if they have supernatural help.[2]

Morgan is less visible throughout the first four books of the series than her half-sister, but she too is generally selfish and ruthless. Three incidents in particular demonstrate these traits. First, Morgan attempts to replace Caliburn and depose Arthur because of "ambition. She had some idea of putting her husband on the high throne of Britain with herself as his queen" (*Enchantment* 452). She uses Accolon as a tool in this plot, likely without intending to follow through with the promised reward. Her actions show a desire for power that overwhelms any other considerations; she is not concerned with how the country might fare if Arthur were killed. Second, her relationship with Morgause reveals selfishness since she expresses concern for her half-sister only when she wants an alliance with her. She implores Arthur to allow Morgause to join her in exile in her castle, but he knows that they "had little fondness for one another, and Arthur . . . suspected that Morgan's desire to join forces with Morgause was literally that: a wish to double the baneful power of such magic as she had" (*Day* 193). Third, Stewart uses the tradition of Morgan's taking Arthur to Avalon without changing the portrait of

Morgan as selfish witch. Morgan is present at the final battle, because, even though "she had been her brother's enemy, . . . without him she was, and would be, nothing. She could be trusted now to use all her skill and vaunted magic on his behalf" (*Day* 380).

Morgan plays a larger role in *The Prince and the Pilgrim*, but her characterization follows the pattern established in the earlier novels. Alexander perceives her to be beautiful, but the descriptions of the "notable witch" (105) emphasize the artificiality of that beauty: her "brows and eyelids were carefully drawn and darkened" (116), and she surrounds herself with women who are "elderly or plain" (177) so that her beauty has no competition. The purpose of this artifice is manipulation. With beauty and drugs, Morgan seduces Alexander. His original injury weakens him "in spite of her care, or more probably because of it" (118); after they become lovers she continues to give him "delicately drugged wine" (185) to prevent him from thinking for himself. She uses emotional displays that the narrator assures us are an "art" (200) in order to get Alexander to do her will. Although Alexander is too naive to recognize Morgan's manipulative nature, the omniscient narrator emphasizes it in every description; her motives are consistently selfish and designed to destroy her brother Arthur.

Morgan thus remains a villain and a stereotypical witch. Moreover, her powers, although real, seem limited. Alexander learns the truth about her, in part because one of her women warns him, and in part because he is tired of her. Her attempts to steal the grail and its powers fail because her messengers die or, in Alexander's case, abandon her. Readers thus never see her schemes succeeding. Furthermore, the narrator assures us that Arthur has full knowledge of Morgan's conspiring against him. The king knows "all about it, and [chooses] to allow it" because Nimuë has advised him to "let her [Morgan] plot in peace, where you can watch her doing it" (183). Morgan uses magic ruthlessly, for manipulative and villainous ends, but it is ineffectual.

Morgause and Morgan, however, are not the only characters with magical powers and the determination to use them. Merlin, for example, is often ruthless; certainly several people die so that his vision of Arthur's begetting can occur. Because he narrates much of the series, however, his fears and doubts are as vivid as his ruthless actions. As well, his narration makes clear the "price to be paid for the word of power; pain and suffering are necessary accompaniments" (Watson 73). Furthermore, as Jeanie Watson notes, his "knowledge and power is of the spirit, coming from the god" (70). Merlin's actions and visions are always justified by a higher power, the god he follows, and by the fact that he is "searching after final truth" (Watson 77), rather than acting with any selfish motive. In contrast, Morgause and Morgan only desire power for themselves, for their own good. Stewart's series thus consistently emphasizes a dichotomy between the magical powers of important female characters and those of important male characters.

In the first meeting with Merlin, Morgause is straight forward about what she wants: knowledge, and through it, power. Merlin at first tells her that she is too young to be his student, although she is about the same age that he was when he met Galapas. But his reasons for refusal shift quickly from those of age to those of gender: "I doubt if any woman could go where I go and see what I see" (*Hills* 210). Likewise, he refuses to explain "the hows and wherefores of . . . power" (*Enchantment* 205) to Morgan; he also admits that he would not have begun teaching Nimuë if he had recognized her gender (*Enchantment* 351).

Merlin, therefore, distinguishes between women's and men's magical powers and suggests that the magical powers of the female characters are less legitimate than his own. After Morgause's seduction of Arthur reveals the powers she has learned, Merlin describes his own powers as given to him, whereas hers are taken "against all laws of God and men" (*Hills* 407). When Merlin is gone Morgan wonders "what power we true witches cannot grasp for ourselves?" (*Day* 84); she sees power as an asset to be fought for and snatched. Furthermore, "these dark powers" are peculiar to women; they "go from mother to daughter" (*Day* 167). Even Nimuë's powers are developed only through a trick; Merlin teaches her thinking she is a boy and even afterward believes that the boy Ninian "might have been a greater enchanter than she" (*Enchantment* 367).

Merlin does acknowledges that he inherits the Sight from his mother, but he insists that his power "is different. She saw only women's things, to do with love" (*Cave* 155). Although he is unwilling to teach Morgan his type of magic, he feels he must try to convey to her its complexity, since "as these girls see it, it is an affair of philters, and whispers in darkened rooms, spells to bind a man's heart, or bring the vision of a lover on Midsummer Eve" (*Enchantment* 205). However, other incidents in the novels contradict Merlin's statement: the women in the series who are serious about magic express little interest in using such power for aphrodisiac or erotic ends. Morgause only uses sexual magic when Merlin prevents her from learning other types. Morgan's "questions turned all on the greater power, and mainly as it had touched Arthur" (*Enchantment* 205). Nimuë had already learned such minor magic on the Island, "but still . . . was hungry" for more (*Enchantment* 358), and for greater powers (*Enchantment* 360).

Merlin is obviously wrong about women's interests in magic, and that error raises questions about the accuracy of his other declarations on the subject of women and magic. His assertion that women cannot survive the demands of true power is borne out by Niniane and Morgause. Niniane either loses or willingly gives up "what she had had of power" (*Cave* 262). Merlin suggests that "she began to fear the power, and let it be" (*Cave* 155); Stewart does not reveal any other motivation behind Merlin's mother's actions. The example of Morgause also supports Merlin's statement. Although she does not abandon the practice of magic, the omniscient narrator of *The Wicked Day* suggests that her powers are inferior to those of Merlin or even Morgan, because of her lack of discipline: "Like many women who work chiefly through their influence on men, [she] was subtle rather than clever, and she was also by temperament lazy" (*Day* 99). Morgan and Nimuë, however, survive the rigours of magic and use their powers all their lives: Morgan, identified "as sorceress or queen" (*Day* 380), arrives at Nimue's island before the final battle to help Arthur; Nimuë, after Merlin trains her, uses her powers for Arthur's kingdom until the end of the last battle.[3]

Such textual contradictions do not redeem the characters of Morgause and

Morgan; they are still villainous. However, the contradictions indicate that Merlin can be wrong, and this capacity for error highlights the way that the story, as Stewart presents it in the first three novels, comes from one person's perspective. For most of the series, we believe Merlin's assessment of events and characters, but his biases in regard to women and magic suggest that characters fill certain roles depending on who is the centre of the story, and this is reinforced by the characterization given Nimuë.

Stewart's Nimuë exhibits a transformation in terms of motivation and action. In *Le Morte D'Arthur*'s portrayal of her relationship with Merlin, Nimuë both manipulates and fears him, and her entrapment of him suggests the stereotype of a woman's using sex to get what she wants or to destroy men. Nimuë uses Merlin's attraction to her to learn his secrets: "And ever she made Merlin good cheer till she had learned of him all manner thing that she desired" (1: 117). After a while, however, "she was ever passing weary of him, and fain would have been delivered of him, for she was afeared of him because he was a devil's son, and she could not beskift him by no mean" until she learns how to trap him "under a great stone" (1:118). Stewart uses this character and episode but changes them in several ways so that Nimuë is not using sex to gain power, nor is she the stereotypical witch brewing potions. In this Stewart's novels follow the characterization of Nimuë as sympathetic to Arthur's court, which, as I mentioned in Chapter 2, also appears in Malory. Stewart must change the complexion of Nimuë's relationship with Merlin because the enchanter, as the undoubtedly human narrator of the first three books of the series, is positioned to have more reader empathy than is Malory's Merlin.

First, Nimuë does not manipulate Merlin to learn his secrets. True, he mistakes her for the boy Ninian, and she uses that mistake to gain access to him, but as Merlin points out to Arthur, "the deception was not hers in the first instance" (*Enchantment* 351). Although Nimuë admits she wanted to learn magic before Merlin spoke to her, she was not actively trying to find a way to get close to him; nor does she use her sexuality to gain power. Stewart thus avoids the stereotype of witch as evil sexual predator.

Second, throughout the novels, Stewart plays upon the possibility of Nimuë's betrayal. Merlin can see his own end, and it has to do with a young woman. Merlin realizes, however, "that a fate long dreaded can prove, in the end, merciful" (*Enchantment* 351). Nimuë's attempt to learn all of his knowledge as he lies supposedly dying seems ruthless; however, she follows Merlin's own instructions. The fact that the mage survives his cave burial also changes the complexion of her act, especially since "the joy she showed [at Merlin's return to life] was as real as the glow of the brazier" (*Enchantment* 459). Moreover, Nimuë is not responsible for Merlin's seemingly fatal illness. Arthur does not blame Nimuë, though he had been prepared, "witch or no witch, lover or no lover, . . . [to] deal with her as she deserves," if she were to hurt Merlin (*Enchantment* 352). Arthur instead summons Morgause to answer for Merlin's supposed demise since she was the one "who fed him the poison that in the end brought him to his death" (*Enchantment* 427).

Third, Nimuë is not the stereotypical witch. Stewart emphasizes this point through comparisons between Nimuë and her rivals in power, Morgause and

Morgan. Mordred, when he first enters Nimuë's house, finds that "she was not, as he half expected, brewing some concoction over the brazier" (*Day* 217). He is used to Morgause, who usually uses her "magic" to "concoct . . . unguents and lotions and perfumes, and certain subtle drugs that had the reputation of restoring beauty and the energy of youth" (*Day* 111). In contrast, Nimuë's "magic," like Merlin's, includes scientific, scholarly activity, involving "a litter of tablets and papers [and] an instrument . . . in the window embrasure, its end tilted towards the sky" (*Day* 217). Overall, Stewart portrays Nimuë as "beautiful, but with a force and edge to her" (*Day* 126). She is "a sombre lady" (*Day* 220) who reminds Mordred of "a rousing falcon" (*Day* 221). In many ways she resembles Ygraine, for both women are capable of love, devotion, and passion but are also able to act on the basis of rigorous principles.

Stewart's series, more than Bradshaw's, demonstrates that sorcery alone does not determine whether female characters remain stereotypes of evil. Narrative roles are most important in affecting characterization, and these roles in turn are affected by whose story is told and who tells the story, both issues to which I will return in subsequent chapters.

FAY SAMPSON

Fay Sampson's series *Daughter of Tintagel* explicitly recognises the issue of representations of women in fiction, particularly the representation of sorceresses. In discussing medieval Arthurian works, one of the narrators of *Herself* argues, "No man is so reviled in the romances" as Morgan is (140); later, discussing twentieth-century versions, the same narrator observes that Arthur is always good and Morgan is always evil: "any evidence that points to ambivalence . . . is rejected" (303). Besides such assertions, Sampson's series creates a social background for its female characters that emphasizes the effects of patriarchy on women's lives, whether those women are from the lower classes or the aristocracy. The usual witch-figures, Morgan, Margawse, and their older sister Elaine, here are made more complex through comparisons to goddess figures. Once again, though, narrative roles affect the complexity of characterization; like Sampson's Gwenhyvar, already discussed, Nimue remains stereotypically vain, power-hungry, and selfish.

Throughout the series, metaphors compare women to horses, cattle, or gems and indicate their status as men's possessions. Gwennol compares Uther's feast to "the midsummer horse-fair, with the men sizing up the fillies for breeding and beauty . . . [where] a duke's daughter [may] be bought and sold, the same as a slave" (*Woman* 49). Ygerne is referred to as Gorlois's "treasure" (*Woman* 21) or "his jewel" (*Woman* 48); her beauty gives him a certain rank that other men get from land or money. When Uther threatens to take her from him, Gorlois treats Ygerne and her daughters "like a prize mare and her fillies when the horse-rustlers are abroad" (*Herself* 18). As Uther takes Ygerne and her daughters back to Bossiney after killing Gorlois, Gwennol compares the festive atmosphere of the occasion to the aftermath of a cattle raid, "as though [the] women were cows herded in" (*Woman* 176). Merlyn, Uther, and Mark confine Morgan to Tintagel in order to assure themselves that there will be no "return to the old ways," which they now consider "dangerous nonsense" (*Nun* 233); they do not want Morgan to be "[a] queen to lead the chariots. A queen who would kill any man who stood in her way. A queen . . . [to] heal the wounded land" (*Nun* 233). Women's power is part of a past society that cannot be reinstated.

Yet that past power cannot be completely ignored, either; as Modred explains, "our faith lies in our mothers" (*Herself* 196) since paternity is harder to prove. Arthur's parentage and upbringing have been kept secret. His use of Caliburn legitimizes him as a war leader, but not as high king. To give him that rank Merlyn uses women for the older powers and ties they represent. Thus he has Elaine, Margawse, and Morgan perform a pagan king-making for Arthur (*Herself* 93), and he marries Arthur to Gwenhyvar, whose mother's lineage "comes of that ancient line that flows in the veins of kings and queens like the mighty Severn that is an artery from the heart of Britain" (*Herself* 196). But although the belief in the power of the mother's lineage is still strong, it has been changed and corrupted by that desire to use women as possessions and trophies. Ancestry alone cannot tempt "an ambitious man" (*Herself* 197) like Arthur; the queen must also have youth and beauty because "daughters and wives are jewels to be boasted of and displayed. Beauties to outshine other men's treasures" (*Herself* 197). If Gwenyvach's tale is true,[4] royal blood and the power that comes with it are only politically useful if joined with other, socially idolized traits, such as beauty.

Sampson's series, although mainly focussing on British royalty, also depicts the status of women in other classes. Luned is not a member of British nobility; she is the daughter of parents who own a bit of land (*Nun* 14). Yet, as a woman, she faces constraints and dangers similar to those experienced by Morgan. Because of her parents' holdings, she is expected to marry, to have her "future contracted" (*Nun* 14). She, like Gorlois's women, narrowly escapes being raped, although she asserts that she "did not go fleeing what [she] feared" (*Nun* 7) (i.e., male sexual violence) when she decides to become a nun. Rather, she chooses the Church and Bryvyth's nunnery in order to escape "the lives of the women [which consist of the] running bowels of their babies, the greasy steam of bacon and cabbage, the skirts thigh-high in mud, the nights of fleas and snores, the same stale gossip year after year" (*Nun* 14). Her connection with Morgan introduces her to sorcery, although she is the least powerful of Morgan's attendants in this respect.

Gwennol is also of a lower class. She is, however, a wise woman in a matriarchal religion, and this role gives her more status and power than others of her class have, though that power and status have limits because of her gender. On the one hand, many of the women in the duke's household fear her and what she can do (*Woman* 41). Gwennol can also claim kinship to Queen Ygerne "by the Mother's blood" (*Woman* 4), though only a select few know that fact. On the other hand, the men of the household, including Gorlois, although they know she possesses "powerful skill with charms," dismiss that skill as "no more than women's medicine" (*Woman* 10). Gorlois refuses to let Gwennol leave Bossiney in order to make the magic that might protect him (*Woman* 97), though at the end he acknowledges that she might be able to do something to keep his wife and daughters safe and tells her, "Try all you know. There's more things than morning mist that can deceive the eye" (*Woman* 123).

Sampson thus uses Luned and Gwennol, characters unique to this series, to illustrate the lives of women from different classes in the society. Of course, she also includes the usual sorceresses of the legend in her retelling. Her portrayal of Morgan, Margawse, and Elaine at times challenges stereotypes of these characters as witches by emphasizing their connection to goddess figures. Sampson's portrayal of Nimue, in contrast, maintains the stereotype of the witch as selfish and greedy for power.

Morgan, from the beginning of *Wise Woman's Telling*, is portrayed as both dangerous and vulnerable. She is the "little black witch" (*Woman* 7) who tries to make Arthur's birth more difficult by tying knots in her girdle to curse the process. She has "power in [her] . . . already" (*Woman* 6), although she has not been initiated, or whispered, into the mysteries. Her birth has supernatural aspects to it; she is born "with her hair already grown down to her waist while she was still in the womb" (*Woman* 19). Such descriptions create an image of a typical witch figure: powerful, dark, and dangerous. Yet this same Morgan is also vulnerable. She is a daughter whose parents had hoped for a son; her mother "wouldn't look at Morgan" (*Woman* 20) and leaves her to a wet nurse and Gwennol to raise. Although Morgan loves her father and makes him "mightily pleased with her" while hunting (*Woman* 12), "she could never be the son he wanted" (*Woman* 13). Her parents, therefore, teach Morgan from an early age to "make herself be loved and not to love back" (*Woman* 9). Sampson's descriptions thus evoke sympathy for this little girl emotionally abandoned by her parents.

Other aspects of Morgan's character are less sympathetic. The narrators of the first three novels in the series all suggest that she is ruthless. Luned, for example, insists that Morgan "compelled [her] to obey" (*Nun* 61), and Luned and Smith both condemn Morgan's use of them. However, Morgan as the protagonist of the series and a narrator reveals her own perspective on her use of others. She admits that "my people are more loyal than I deserve" (*Herself* 106); she knows what they have sacrificed for her. Sampson, therefore, does not make Morgan's character either wholly sympathetic or wholly villainous. Morgan is a complex character rather than simply an evil witch, partly because she is the central character of the series.[5]

Margawse's character and motives remain sketchy since she is not the focus of the story, nor a narrator; her most memorable trait is her sexuality, which Gwennol describes as "a red hunger that wouldn't be satisfied" (*Woman* 69). Margawse talks and flirts with Gorlois's soldiers and slaves; she has a "bold stare" (*Woman* 142) and likes "tossing her red hair and flashing her green eyes at every man in the dun" (*Woman* 203). Thus, Margawse uses sex as a means to power; she sleeps with her stepfather, her half-brother, her husband, and others. Portraying Margawse in this way runs the risk of vilifying her as the stereotypical witch as whore. However, Sampson suggests that sex is the weapon that society teaches Margawse to use. Ygerne uses beauty and magic to acquire the high king and greater status. Margawse herself gains favour with her stepfather and king by welcoming his advances (*Woman* 185). That same king uses her beauty as a prize to reward Lot's political solidarity. Uther's actions in arranging the marriage resemble those of a horse-trader: "He'd sell Gorlois's filly off at a fair price, to keep the north at peace" (*Woman* 212). Thus Margawse is used sexually and politically by men, and she determines to use sex for her own purpose. As early as her rendezvous with Uther, that purpose is vengeance. Morgan assures Gwennol that Margawse "doesn't love him [Uther]. . . . Margawse will avenge Father in her own way" (*Woman* 186). Later, after Margawse's seduction of Arthur, Morgan remarks that Margawse "wanted vengeance. She chose the most appropriate way" (*Herself* 69) to avenge the murder of Gorlois.

Furthermore, several characters observe and acknowledge that Margawse's seemingly casual attitude toward events masks deeper emotions. Gwennol suspects that, whereas others might show their feelings through tears, "Margawse will laugh when she has her revenge" (*Woman* 192). Morgan admits that Margawse acts out of the suffering caused by her father's murder: "Men rarely saw the bitterness with which she mourned both the murder of Gorlois and the loss of Modred. She laughed when she took her revenge. Only I knew the pain" (*Herself* 104). Smith had "always seen Margawse laughing. The whole world was a joke to her, and men the biggest laugh" (*Smith* 233), but he, too, recognizes that she can also be hurt. Sampson's portrait of Margawse, therefore, is not as complex as that of Morgan, but her actions are shown to have motivation. Furthermore, her relation to Morgan, the protagonist, shifts; she is not simply Morgan's enemy and thus not always the villain of the story.

Elaine remains a more mysterious figure. Gwennol has less to do with her because Elaine is close to Ygerne and therefore less of Gwennol's responsibility. Also "Elaine keeps her own council" (*Woman* 192) and confides in none of the series's narrators. Sampson, therefore, generally sketches Elaine's character through comparison. Elaine's face at times is as "sweet and smiling as her mother's" (*Woman* 44). Whereas Margawse is wild, Elaine is "grave and stately" (*Nun* 33). In terms of their religious beliefs, she is "a sensible maid and quick to learn" (*Woman* 98). Moreover, Smith suspects "that Elaine might be the most dangerous of the three" sisters, for she seems to see all of his secrets just by looking at him (*Smith* 163). However, as a young woman, she seems somewhat alarmed by the power she has; after helping Ygerne perform the spell of summoning, "her eyes looked scared" (*Woman* 44). She also bears "a bitter burden" (*Woman* 143): her ability to see into the future.

The extent of this burden becomes apparent in later books. *The Daughter of Tintagel* series insists that exceptional powers have exceptional costs. When Elaine appears after Morgan's wedding, she is no longer young and beautiful. Smith describes her as "a spider . . . [her features] sagging into wrinkles" (*Smith* 163), with a "shrouded sort of face" so that no one can tell what she is thinking (*Smith* 166). Smith suggests that her power has caused such changes in her body, although he would "rather not know what she'd seen or done to age her so" (*Smith* 163). He gets a glimpse of it, however. She is taken over by power as she sees what happened to Modred in the boat, and, according to Smith, even witnessing such power "can shake the strongest when it comes unasked and it's naked and screaming in the room with you" (*Smith* 233).

Smith associates Elaine with "the very first One" (*Smith* 198), some ancient goddess. Through "hundreds and hundreds of years, going back into darkness, [through] all of those women, generation before generation" (*Smith* 198), Elaine is connected to that goddess. She resembles old stone statues with "those big hips and breasts. That flat face that sees nothing or everything" (*Smith* 198). And though the description of hips and breasts suggests motherhood, Smith associates Elaine and this older goddess with death: "They wanted more blood than I knew how to give" (*Smith* 198).

All three of the sisters are associated with goddess figures, however, and Charlotte Spivack and Roberta Lynn Staples note that such associations allow authors to "redeem" traditional witch figures (40). *The Daughter of Tintagel* series uses imagery of a Triple Goddess for this purpose. Sampson links these Celtic goddesses with those from other religions and thus broadens the scope of the allusions and associations in the series:

the Muses are nine, the Fates are three, the Earth is one. Nine maidens fan the fire for the Otherworld Cauldron of Annwn. . . . Three are the Matronae, the Mothers of Europe. We must not be separated from our sister-selves. To the Greeks we are Kore, Demeter, Hecate. To the Hindus, Parvati, Derga, Kali. We are the Three-in-One. We are the Triple Goddess. Within each separate self we hold a triune being: Maiden, Mother, Crone. (*Herself* 15)

The Maiden, or Virgin Huntress, is associated with youth, virginity, the Moon. The Mother appears in images associated with fertility and sexuality. The Crone appears in images of weaving and death. Colours also indicate these aspects of the Mothers: "White for the Virgin, purity of spirit, the high ideal, the untouchable huntress. Red for the Mother, blood and life, generously given, hungrily taken. Black for the Crone, our inescapable death and no less bitterly feared though we know the white will be born afresh" (*Herself* 178). Although all of Gorlois's daughters embody each of these aspects at different times in their lives, generally descriptions and situations throughout the series link Morgan with the Maiden, or Virgin Huntress; Margawse with the Mother; and Elaine with the Crone.

Various narrators in the series associate Morgan with the Moon, and thus with the Virgin Huntress. She rides to her wedding dressed as "the May-Maiden" (*Smith* 4), and Smith always sees in her "the young moon" (*Smith* 48). When he expects her to send for him, he sees a vision of "a white face, narrow like a half-moon," which he calls his "second sight of Morgan" (*Smith* 20). Taliesin also calls Morgan "the virgin priestess of the new moon" (*Taliesin* 258). Despite her marriage and the children she bears, she remains "slender and hard" (*Smith* 186), still maiden-like. Moreover, when Merlyn gives gifts the first Christmas after Uther's and Ygerne's marriage, he gives "a little hunting-knife" to Morgan (*Woman* 208).

Margawse, associated with passion and sexuality throughout the series, represents the Mother. She is often called "Margawse the Red" (*Herself* 298). She creates "the weapon that will bring Arthur down" when she bears Modred

(*Taliesin* 76). Although all three sisters have children, Margawse's birthing of Modred is the only childbed described. Merlyn's gift to Margawse that first Christmas, "a bronze mirror . . . beautifully patterned on the back . . . with leaves and song-birds' heads" (*Woman* 207), symbolizes beauty and womanhood seeking a mate to produce children. Even surrounded by news of death, Margawse's "mother's blood rages to recreate what is taken" (*Taliesin* 257) and Taliesin associates her with the fertile earth.

Unlike her sisters, Elaine does not like to go riding or hunting. All she does is "sit over a fire, everlastingly weaving strands of coloured wool and snipping the fringes with her scissors" (*Smith* 186). Merlyn's gift to her was "a little case with fine bone needles, and a pair of scissors shaped like a swan's beak, and skeins of coloured silks" (*Woman* 207). Furthermore, Elaine tends to the bodies of the dead or dying. She "gathers up poor Anir in her arms . . . as effortlessly as if he was a baby" (*Taliesin* 114), pronounces a blessing upon the dead boy, and then proceeds to "lay . . . the boy out on his bier" (*Taliesin* 115). Similarly, when Gwenhyvar gives birth to twins who will not likely live, Bryvyth intends to baptise them, but "Elaine has already taken them in her ample arms" (*Taliesin* 254).

But Morgan takes on all three roles of Maiden, Mother, and Crone in succession. She is called "Black Morgan" (*Taliesin* 15), a colour association that links her with the Crone and death, yet white, the colour of the Maiden, is also stressed, especially in descriptions of her face, or her skin (*Smith* 20). Merlyn's gifts to her also symbolize the various roles she plays. When she is young, Merlyn gives Morgan a knife, which symbolizes the young, Maiden huntress (*Woman* 208). When she is older, he sends her a mirror, a symbol of beauty, seduction, and womanhood (*Smith* 159). Later still, he sends her "a pair of silver scissors, shaped like the beak of a heron" (*Smith* 196). She uses these scissors to cut the cloth of the poisoned cape that she sends to Arthur; once again, the scissors represent the cutting off of the thread of life, the activity of the Crone. Even more dramatic, however, is her transformation into the Morrigan, "the washer at the ford" (*Taliesin* 269) who makes men's shrouds. As Morgan washes the old shirt of Arthur's on the eve of the battle of Camlann, her physical appearance changes. Whereas she is young, with no white in her hair when Taliesin first meets her (*Taliesin* 11), she suddenly "is old . . . ugly, beyond bearing" (*Taliesin* 269), with "grizzled hair. Bones poke through withered flesh" (*Taliesin* 269). By the end of *Herself*, however, Morgan has reassumed her place as Maiden as the three sisters carry Arthur away.

The three sisters have powers but are still human, and the novels use goddess imagery to legitimize their powers. In contrast, Nimue lacks the humanizing motivation given to Morgan's sisters, and Sampson emphasizes that she is not human at all (*Smith* 118, 123). Despite this supernatural status, she is not associated with any aspect of the Triple Goddess. She is consistently Morgan's enemy and her most predominant traits are love of power and selfishness.

Nimue "relished . . . power" (*Herself* 128) in any form. Although she gives sanctuary to Arthur as he grows up, she is not dedicated to his cause, but to the status and influence that she will have as his mentor. She sees him as a possession:

"He is mine. Not yours, not Merlyn's, not the Church's" (*Smith* 254).[6] Thus when Arthur chooses to listen to the Church (*Herself* 242) after his crowning, she goes off in jealous rage. Her desire for power also means she is interested in practitioners of different religions. She keeps the blacksmith, hoping he will teach her powerful pagan magic; she keeps a priest for similar reasons. The smith compares her exploitation of him to that of a farmer or a butcher, suggesting the potentially destructive nature of her means of harvesting power: "Was I like a cow she'd come to milk daily and feed well between? Or a carcase she'd strip bare of flesh and leave just the dead skin and bones?" (*Smith* 93). Smith recognizes "her game. . . . She'd gobble up Merlyn's high magic" (*Smith* 118) by willingly trading sex for Merlyn's secrets. She boasts, "I offered him love and I got what I asked" (*Smith* 254). She thus fits the stereotype of woman as using sex to manipulate or destroy men, but what she does with that power suggests the stereotype of woman as shallow. On a whim she plays with the power she has acquired, not thinking of the long-term consequences; she uses a spell to lock Merlyn away without learning to undo it so that "Merlyn is trapped forever" (*Smith* 254, *Herself* 129).

Morgan's description of Nimue at the last battle begins on a positive note. Nimue is "brave and wonderful" (*Herself* 242), but she also possesses many stereotypical witch characteristics: she is "dangerous," "changeable," and obviously jealous; she usurps men's powers in various ways for her own ends; she "feeds" on young men (*Herself* 242). The meta-Morgan of *Herself* criticizes previous versions of the legend that cast Morgan as "the jealous woman" (107); this characteristic is here shifted to Nimue. Morgan may be re-valued, but Nimue, as the obstacle to Morgan's plans, is not.

We could claim that this negative portrayal is Morgan's. But whereas the negative portrayals of Morgan are counter-balanced by more positive ones, including her own testimony, Nimue is painted in the same way by Smith, Taliesin, and Morgan. We are given little reason to question her portrait. As a result, Nimue, to use Sampson's own word, is "vilified" (*Herself* 305), even though Sampson makes Morgan more complex, suggests possible complex motives for Margawse, and uses goddess figures to recuperate Morgan, Margawse, and Elaine.

MARION ZIMMER BRADLEY

Marion Zimmer Bradley's *The Mists of Avalon* focusses on the women of the legend and represents most of them as complex individuals, especially those usually considered evil sorceresses. Even here, however, roles affect characterization; as Morgause steps into the role of villain she becomes more stereotypical. Bradley's novel also explores the relationship between society's assumptions about gender and the way women think about themselves and act; by contrasting matriarchal and patriarchal societies the novel emphasizes that many "natural" attributes and social roles are learned.

The Mists of Avalon challenges traditional depictions of the main female sorceresses of the legend. Bradley makes these characters complex in two ways. First, she gives insight into the women's thoughts and feelings, especially when they are faced with assumptions about them based on their gender. Second, she places traditional judgements of these female characters, like labels of "witch" or "sorceress," in the mouths of other characters who are then shown to be biased in their opinions, or ignorant of the true motivations of those they condemn. The novices at Glastonbury observe that "there are ignorant priests and ignorant people, who are all too ready to cry sorcery if a woman is only a little wiser than *they* are" (874, emphasis in original), and it is such ignorant people who judge Viviane, Morgaine, and Morgause harshly.

Viviane, whose name recalls Tennyson's famous sorceress, is labelled a witch by those who have ulterior motives. Balin accuses Viviane of killing Priscilla, his mother, and calls the Lady a "foul, murdering witch" (342). Although Balin's grief is understandable, Bradley makes it clear that his accusations are false and arise out of extreme prejudice and emotion[7]. Priscilla has asked Viviane "to put an end to her suffering" (340), and Priscilla's husband, Gawan, has agreed. Gawan and Balan grieve for Priscilla; only Balin thinks that Viviane's act of mercy is "murder and evil sorcery" (342) that must be "avenged" (499). Balin is obviously mad with grief when he kills Viviane and offers to "purge this court of all their evil wizard line" (500). He is described as being "in a frenzy" (500), and Arthur questions whether the knight is "sane enough" to understand his punishment (500–01). Arthur himself speaks of Viviane as "my friend and my benefactor . . . who helped to set me on my throne" (499). No one takes Balin's side; indeed, several people, including Lancelet, wish to kill Balin to avenge Viviane (499). Gwenhwyfar is the only one who agrees that Viviane deserves death, and that agreement comes a couple of years after the event when Gwenhwyfar, too, is in the grip of jealous rage. Her anger at Morgaine's relationship to Arthur leads Gwenhwyfar to condemn Morgaine, Avalon, and Viviane, "that evil old witch whom Balin rightly killed for her heathen sorceries" (552). Although Viviane's actions do at times seem cruel and calculating, the condemnation of characters like Balin and Gwenhwyfar, since it arises out of wrongs they feel she has done to them, loses credibility as an accurate assessment of her character. Meanwhile, the "fierce love" (227) that Viviane feels for Morgaine does much to mitigate her unsympathetic traits.[8]

Morgaine herself is seen by other characters as a sorceress, but, again, it is the ignorance and lack of education of most people that make her knowledge seem magical in contrast. Some of Camelot's women think that her ability to make ale, medicines, and perfumes proves she has "magic art" (439). Morgaine knows that with proper instruction "any woman . . . could do what she did, if she was neat-handed and willing to take the time and trouble to see to it" (440). Morgaine is also most often accused of sorcery by those who think her a threat. Gwenhwyfar, after begging for a charm from Morgaine, thinks of her as "the damnable sorceress" (447) when Morgaine's warnings about the outcome start to come true. Furthermore, Gwenhwyfar's most violent accusations of Morgaine as evil occur when she realizes that Morgaine has done what she cannot: give Arthur a son. For other characters, such as Elaine, it is hard to reconcile what they have been taught about Avalon with what they know about Morgaine. Morgaine is "from that evil island of witches and sorceresses," yet Elaine thinks the priestess is "good" (520) and therefore trusts her to bring about Elaine's marriage to Lancelet.

These women do, of course, have real magic powers, but those powers themselves do not make them villains. The supernatural powers of Viviane and Morgaine result from study and belief in a religion, whose tenets and principles they follow.[9] Furthermore, their powers bring with them sacrifice and pain. At each of the two times when Morgaine uses her magic to try to kill someone, she is deathly ill herself. When she becomes connected with the Great Sow in order to kill Avalloch, "she must suffer the death throes" (672) and even much later "could not move a muscle without griping, terrifying pain" (672). The conflict between Arthur and Accolon occurs at the same time as her miscarriage; as the men wound each other, "excruciating pain stabbed through Morgaine's whole body" (739), and she is then ill for months afterward.

The character of Morgause most clearly demonstrates the effect of narrative roles on complex characterization. On the one hand, Bradley adds depth to the evil sorceress of many versions of the legend. T. H. White memorably depicts the queen of the Orkneys boiling a black cat alive in search of a bone to make her invisible, although she mainly wants "an excuse for lingering with the mirror" (215).[10] In Bradshaw's series, Morgawse is truly an agent of "Darkness" who uses spells to enchant her sons and who plots against Arthur. In *The Mists of Avalon*, in contrast, Morgause herself speaks of her reputation as sorceress and links it to her political influence. Her husband listens to her opinions regarding the running of their land, and as a result, Morgause notes, "the priests are very sour about me and say I do not keep my place as befits a woman—no doubt they think I am some kind of evil sorceress or witch because I do not sit modestly at my spinning and weaving" (212). Other reports of her sorcery are passed on as gossip regarding her ability to charm men. For example, her popularity and the number of her lovers lead people to "say she practices magic arts to spellbind men to her" (436). Morgaine, however, suggests that it is more likely "henna from Egypt" (436) than magic that makes Morgause still look young.

By the end of the novel, however, Morgause is acting as the villain; it is she, for example, who helps Mordred trap Gwenhwyfar and Lancelet. As she becomes more established in that narrative role,[11] she becomes more like a stereotypical witch. In a scene reminiscent of White's, Morgause cuts the throat of a white dog in order to acquire the Sight (816); she also uses a serving woman as a medium and eventually kills her (818). This picture of Morgause is still different from White's, however. Bradley shows the scene from Morgause's perspective, so that we know that, even though she will not stop, Morgause still has "a dispassionate sympathy" for the dog, "a moment of genuine revulsion as she cut its throat" (816), and "a certain squeamishness at the preliminaries" (817). Her character is not completely hardened.

The novel also invokes the stereotype of the witch as insatiable in her desire for young men to assure herself continuing beauty and sexual power. In various medieval versions, Morgan was so characterized and the escape of these young men provided occasions for the tales to ridicule the witch's age and ugliness. The last time Morgause appears in *Mists*, her advances to a young man are rejected.

When the chance of ruling the entire kingdom as queen mother to Mordred's king disappears, Morgause turns to Cormac to reassure herself that she still has sexual power. He refuses her because she is like his "own grandmother . . . an old woman" (859). However, this rejection is not accompanied by intentional ridicule, though the lad's suggestion of "a nice possett" instead (859) is insensitive to the older woman's passions. On the whole, though, Cormac's attitude toward Morgause is one of "respect" and "loyalty" rather than malice, and Morgause's own realization at that moment that she has lost everything and "lived too long" (860) creates sympathy for her. Therefore, although Morgause comes closest to the stereotypes of witches at the point in the story when she fills the narrative role of villain, for the most part she is a character who, if not always sympathetic, has at least some sympathetic traits, such as her real love for her sons and Morgaine,[12] mixed in with unsympathetic ones, such as her ruthlessness and ambition. She is also one of the most lonely figures in the book. Unlike other women—Morgaine, Igraine, Viviane, Gwenhwyfar, and Niniane—Morgause never belongs to a community of women for any length of time. After she marries Lot, when she is about fourteen, she is cut off from any group of "sisters" except during brief visits to other courts.[13]

By contrasting judgements made about Viviane, Morgaine, and Morgause with their own interpretations of their actions, Bradley shows women coping with a patriarchal society, for, although Avalon is matriarchal, the rest of the kingdom is not. Within this patriarchal society, women are limited to certain social roles. The gossip in the queen's sewing room makes two of these roles explicit. The women talk about the possibility of Morgaine's marriage, the marriage and pregnancy of one of the women, and the possibility of the queen's pregnancy. Marriage and motherhood thus are women's goals; the only alternative is a nunnery.

Bradley creates some female characters, such as Morgaine, who challenge these ideas, but society's reaction to them is often hostile. Arthur seems to find nothing wrong with the fact that his "sister is a woman grown and her own mistress. She need not seek . . . leave to be here or there" (374). However, men like Leodegranz feel that a man should be "lord of all," including his "womenfolk," and these men react antagonistically when that does not happen (375). Gwenhwyfar's affair with Lancelet brings out the same point; Elaine realizes that Arthur's subjects will question his ability to "rule a kingdom" if he cannot "rule his wife" (522).

Women also have mixed reactions to a woman's freedom from usual social constraints and expectations. Gwenhwyfar both admires and resents Morgaine's independence; she is amused at the men's plans to "tame" Morgaine through marriage, "and then she grew angry. Why should Morgaine please herself? No other woman was allowed to do her own will" (375). Gwenhwyfar also dislikes Morgause, because the older woman "does what she will and cares not if all men criticize her" (606). Gwenhwyfar disapproves of the way that Morgaine and Morgause hold political power and rule, or help to rule, kingdoms (602). When Arthur cites Boadicea as a precedent for British queens' ruling, she says, "bitterly, 'I hope they killed her'" (602).

The novel thus presents two types of society: the matriarchal world of Avalon, whose religion worships the Goddess; and the patriarchal, romanized, Christian world that is superseding it. Bradley's representation of these two worlds is crucial to her representation of the women of the legend, for, in either case, societal expectations and assumptions about gendered roles shape the women who grow up in them.

One of the important features of Avalon's religion is the status it gives to women. Bradley constructs a society that is matriarchal, that "count[s] their lineage . . . sensibly through the mother" (7), and worships an Earth Goddess who is Mother of all. This has several consequences for women's status and for the degree of power they can attain. First, though the Merlin is required to kneel before a king, the Lady is not, "for she was not only the priestess of the Goddess, but incorporated the Goddess within herself in a way the man-priests of male Gods could never know or understand" (200); she can, "in her own place, precede . . . even a king" (203). Their religion gives these women jurisdiction over their own actions as well. Kevin reminds Morgaine, when she returns from the fairy world, that as "a priestess, . . . [her] conscience is not in the keeping of any man alive" (418).

Furthermore, women who are priestess-raised have dominion over their own bodies. Niniane responds to Mordred's jealousy by reminding him that her body is not his property, but her own: "I account to no man on this earth for what I do with what is mine—yes, mine and not yours. I am not Roman, to let some man tell me what I may do with what the Goddess gave me" (849). Igraine also contrasts the Roman attitude toward women with the Tribal one and suggests the difference results from the way each culture determines lineage. Because the Romans trace lineage through the father, they "made a great matter of worrying over who lay with their women, and locked them up and spied on them" (7). This attitude, when taken to the extreme, results also in a callousness towards daughters and an obsession to have sons: Gorlois "was discontented" because Morgaine was not a son (7), and Avalloch "was really angry" when Maline bears another girl instead of a boy (669). Morgaine resents this Roman way of thinking, which makes "women . . . the chattels of their menfolk" (312) and thus on a par with "horses or dogs" (312), whose masters "could fondle or beat" them whenever they liked (720). When she seduces Lancelet, it is, in part, a deliberate rejection of the Roman and Christian way of conducting a relationship (323); she feels that the tribal festivals, which acknowledge human passion as separate from the desire for marriage, are "more honest" (323). When Morgaine labels herself a "whore" (625), it is because she allows herself to be used by her husband, instead of following her conscience.

Because of their attitude toward their own sexuality, the priestesses of Avalon cannot fully condemn Gwenhwyfar for her affair with Lancelet. Morgaine, although believing in the principle of woman's free choice, still blames Gwenhwyfar because the queen, unlike Morgaine, Morgause, and Isotta, "had been married to a man who was handsome, and no more than her own age" (621); however, this condemnation arises from jealousy, not reason. Niniane, knowing that Arthur has broken his vows to Avalon, still refuses to depose him "by betraying a woman who has taken the right the Goddess has given to all women" (851). Mordred points out that "Gwenhwyfar has done no more than is right—the lady shall choose who she will for a consort" (851). Mordred suggests that picking a king on the basis of her choice is ridiculous, but the problem, which he does not acknowledge, is not in the principle of the lady's picking the king, but in the identity of the woman. Gwenhwyfar is not queen in her own right. Morgaine, as part of the royal line of Avalon and Maiden to the King Stag, is the real Lady, whose mating with Arthur makes him king. Despite the damage that Gwenhwyfar's principles do to Avalon, none of the priestesses betrays her.[14]

Avalon, and the religion it represents, also allows women political power as well as spiritual and personal power. Their way of calculating kinship means that "the sister's son was the natural heir, [for] . . . rule passed through the blood of the woman" (616). Gawaine believes that the Tribes' system of "women to stay home and rule, and men to wander about and make war" (614) makes more sense than Arthur's court's way. Gawaine acknowledges that Morgause rules better than he would since she has "talent" for it, whereas he does not (614). In addition, the contrast between the women who have political interests and talents and those who do not is not flattering to the latter. Gwenhwyfar's ladies "have . . . nothing better to do than gossip . . . [because] their most Christian husbands and fathers make sure they . . . have nothing else to occupy their minds" (707) except "mindless jests and gossip" (724).

The way that Avalon allows women to develop their full potential is also demonstrated in the first encounter we are shown between Morgaine and Lancelet. Because of Morgaine's small size and her gender, Lancelet fears that the slope of the Tor would be "too long and steep for a girl" to climb, in part because of the "long skirts" that Morgaine wears (149). She beats him to the top and is "not even short of breath," whereas he is (149). Thus Avalon's training allows women to be capable, active people.

CONCLUSION

Creating complex characters and carefully portraying plausible motivations for their actions are fairly common in contemporary novels using the Arthurian legend; when applied to the female characters they suggest an engagement with feminist critiques of representations of women in literature. The characters thus created can disrupt the conventions of the legend, for detailing the psychological motivations of the female characters may put more focus on the women than expected in a legend of knightly adventures. However, other narrative conventions remain and may influence, in the case of those surrounding the narrative role of villain, the degree of complexity possible in the characterization. Thus, although the strategy I label "Images of Women" commonly appears in feminist rewritings, it often combines with strategies that create female heroes or that affect the way the story is told. Such strategies are the focus of the following chapters.

NOTES

1. This binary will be discussed more fully in Chapter 6.

2. The same type of assumptions affect Morgan as well. Alexander, the narrator of *The Prince and the Pilgrim* tells us, is not completely swayed by Morgan's account of her ill treatment by Arthur because "he was still young enough to think that she had all the kinds of power that a woman needs" (216).

3. Nimue's role as Lady of the Lake convent (*Day* 380) means that she is obviously the Lady who will keep the sword and who says: "I shall take him [Arthur] to Applegarth, where we shall see to the healing of his wounds" (*Day* 385).

4. Gwenyvach claims that she is the true daughter descended from the royal line; Gwenhyvar is illegitimate but more beautiful, so she is passed off as the "real" daughter.

5. I will discuss the effect of different narrators in this series in Chapter 6.

6. Gwenhyvar has no power or magic (*Smith* 216), and Morgan thinks it odd that Merlyn would choose her for Arthur. The choice becomes more logical if Nimue helped make it, since she does not like to share influence. Though we are not told specifically that she helps choose Gwenhyvar, we do know that she was involved with Merlyn at the time.

7. Note that in Malory this is not so clear: "He [Balin] saw the Lady of the Lake, that by her means had slain Balin's mother" (1:64). After he slays her, he tells Arthur that she "was the untruest lady living, and by enchantment and sorcery she hath been the destroyer of many good knights, and she was causer that my mother was burnt" (1:65). When Merlin explicates the events, he neither confirms nor denies Balin's accusations (1:66–67).

8. Viviane loves Morgaine as a daughter, "as she had never loved Igraine, or Morgause . . . [or] any of the men who had shared her bed" (*Mists* 227).

9. This religion resembles a Neo-paganist system of belief, for "most Neo Pagans seek to recreate what they believe was a primitive nature religion in Western Europe that flourished before Christianity. Adherents say that this ancient religion focussed on worship of the Goddess" (Fry 68). Carrol L. Fry emphasizes that "Neo Pagans ardently deny any connection to Satanism" (69); since Bradley seems to follow a Neo-paganist model (although the accuracy of her portrayal of the religion is open to debate), Morgaine's and Viviane's powers do not come from a devil figure, and that means those powers do not automatically seem villainous to the reader.

10. This occurs in *The Queen of Air and Darkness*. Page numbers refer to this work as it appears in *The Once and Future King*.

11. Most of the chapters where Morgause is the focal character occur in the last two books of the novel when her political schemes are coming to fruition. The earlier chapter that she focalizes involves Mordred's birth and shows her caring for and worrying about Morgaine.

12. For example, she cries with "the weight of anxiety" over Morgaine's difficult childbirth (*Mists* 247).

13. A fuller discussion of the significance of sisterhood appears in the next chapter.

14. Morgause does so.

Chapter 5

Women as Protagonists

Fay Sampson's Morgan, commenting on the traditional roles assigned to her in Arthurian stories, says, "For each telling, I become what you need me to be. Lover, mother, enemy" (*Herself* 302). Morgan is the helper or obstacle to the male protagonist, never the protagonist herself; that is, "Never till now" (*Herself* 302). As Raymond Thompson notes, one of the "trends in the modern treatment of Arthurian legend" (176), has been "the greater attention paid to women. Their lack of power in a male-oriented warrior society and their heroic attempts to break with convention by taking an active role in events" (177) become important themes in many rewritings. Furthermore, writers often make these themes central to the story by choosing Morgan, Guenevere, or another female character, for the role of protagonist; in addition, many of these protagonists also narrate their own stories. Maureen Fries attributes this "interest in Arthurian women" to both "the twentieth-century rebirth of feminism" and "the concomitant search for new narrators from whose viewpoints to tell the old story" ("Trends" 219). Both Fries, in her article, and Charlotte Spivack and Roberta Lynn Staples, in their book, select *The Mists of Avalon* to discuss the phenomenon of Morgan as protagonist, but many other writers, too, centre narratives on Morgan.[1] Spivack and Staples also discuss four authors who "make Guenevere the narrator of her own experiences" (83) and the protagonist of her own story, but they suggest there could be more examples given.[2] The number of Arthurian short stories and novels continually appearing that use female protagonists suggests that both male and female writers still find this trend a productive one.

Making women the protagonists of their own stories is not unique to contemporary Arthurian fiction, of course. Nevertheless, such protagonists can be important indicators of feminist discourses in these novels. Joanna Russ, discussing the literary tradition, asserts that "the one occupation of a female protagonist . . . is [to be] the protagonist of a Love Story" (9). However, some of the Arthurian rewritings that use female protagonists go beyond this tradition to create new roles for their protagonists, often by emphasizing the nation-building aspects of the story rather than the courtly love aspects. The various Gueneveres and Morgans of contemporary rewritings may be motivated by heterosexual love, but that motivation is often equalled or excelled by their concern for community and their religious or political convictions. Their actions are, therefore, as often directed toward matters of state as toward matters of the heart. And although some of these female heroes are exceptions in their societies, others belong to groups of similarly motivated, exceptional women.

This chapter examines Mary Stewart's use of Alice as one of the protagonists of *The Prince and the Pilgrim* and Gillian Bradshaw's use of Gwynhwyfar as narrator and subject of her own story in *In Winter's Shadow*. It then considers some of the disadvantages of having a lone female protagonist and moves on to discuss the creation of communities of women in texts as a feminist technique. Close relationships between women are often portrayed as mother-daughter or sisterly ties. Fay Sampson explores such relationships in her portrayal of Morgan's family in her novels. However, in this series the women compete as often as they co-operate, and although competition can illustrate the strength of these characters, it can also cast certain of them in the role of villain, the consequences of which have already been discussed. Furthermore, *Daughter of Tintagel* primarily tells Morgan's story. In Marion Zimmer Bradley's *The Mists of Avalon*, competition between women still exists, but the novel includes many female characters' perspectives and the emphasis on sisterly or mother-daughter relationships provides a crucial feminist element in the novel.

EXCEPTIONAL HEROINES

Mary Stewart's *The Prince and the Pilgrim* focalizes half of the novel through Alice. As a result, it emphasizes the ways in which Alice is an extraordinary person. She differs from the conventional women of her society: "I believe it's thought strange for a young girl . . . to go on these long journeys and mingle with rough folk on the road, and sometimes meet with danger, or at any rate the risk of it" (234–35). Alice is a perceptive woman, and her travelling endows her with greater understanding than many have in her society. She recognizes the political machinery behind the Church, the way it works as an industry and not just a faith. She is the one who explains to Alexander that "there are men who make a living from this trade [in relics]" (237). Although Alexander, like the traditional hero of many twentieth-century romances, is the more sexually experienced because of his liaison with Morgan, Alice has the broader experience of the world; she has travelled and experienced more.

The Prince and the Pilgrim, however, is basically a love story. Alice, although exceptional, is not exceptional in the type of story of which she is allowed to be protagonist. However, she is not the only one; Alexander too is the protagonist of a love story. Although his adventures begin with his seeking justice and going on a quest for the grail, he abandons these when he meets Alice. March dies without

Alexander's intervention, and with his marriage to Alice, Alexander has no need to claim the lands of Cornwall for his own. The quest that Morgan gave him is an evil one and therefore abandoned. The novel ends by acknowledging that "Alexander never did get to Camelot" (283), but the narrator then asserts that "he knew . . . that he had found it" in his love for Alice (283). If Alice as heroine is made more active only to fill a fairly traditional narrative role, Alexander as the questing hero is made more passive to take on the same role.

Gillian Bradshaw's queen, in contrast, is the protagonist of more than a love story, though her love for Arthur is a component of her story. Previously, I discussed Bradshaw's creation of a queen who was beautiful, intelligent, and hard-working. Gwalchmai's and Rhys's observations in the first two books contribute to this portrait: Gwalchmai comments on Gwynhwyfar's strength, intelligence, and warmth when he meets her at her father's holding (*Hawk* 288); Rhys describes her demeanour and duties as she manages "the household of Camlann" (*Kingdom* 107). Nevertheless, Gwynhwyfar is only a minor character in these novels; her presence as part of the social background is acknowledged, but she seldom takes part in events. *In Winter's Shadow*, in contrast, tells the end of the Arthurian story, making Gwynhwyfar the protagonist and narrator. This emphasizes the events in which she participates, but it also gives the reader Gwynhwyfar's own perspective on and the motivations behind the two events of the legend most known: her affair and the fall of the kingdom.

The affair with Bedwyr is Gwynhwyfar's one instance of selfishness. Needing comfort and "forgiveness not of the empress but of the woman" (*Shadow* 99), she turns to Bedwyr and the love he can share with her. Bedwyr allows her to be a person instead of a role, a woman instead of an empress. As a result of that understanding and their shared guilt, she "could be whole only with him [Bedwyr]" (*Shadow* 152). Her love for Arthur and her love for his vision of empire do not diminish: she insists that she "loved [Arthur] even when [she] was unfaithful" (*Shadow* 238). This portrayal of events and motivations is psychologically realistic because Gwynhwyfar's point of view allows the reader to see the pain and loneliness leading up to the affair and the guilt and grief that accompany it.

Although Bradshaw incorporates some traditional condemnations of Gwynhwyfar's behaviour, they have a different effect in this novel because the queen herself is the one most often employing them. She characterizes "the empire [as] . . . a thorn brake against the wind" (*Shadow* 280) and describes herself as "the weak point in the barrier, the place where it had given" (*Shadow* 280). Years later, she still lives with that grief, for "it is a terrible thing to have worked the ruin of all one loved best, but it is worse to survive that ruin, and grow old, forgetting" (*Shadow* 318). Gwynhwyfar articulates the traditional verdict of her actions: her adultery destroys the kingdom. Yet the events of Bradshaw's novel and the opinions of its other characters contradict that verdict. Barbara Ann Gordon-Wise points out various ways in which Bradshaw "disassociates the queen from the doom of Camelot" (134), but most importantly, quarrels and disunity in the Family occur before the affair (135). Events after the affair also remove blame from the queen. Arthur forgives her, and even blames himself for not realizing that Gwynhwyfar, like a strong warrior, "need[s] rest sometimes" (*Shadow* 238); his understanding and acceptance of her actions reinforce our empathy for the queen while his comparison of her to a warrior prevents any suggestion of the "weak woman" stereotype. Others of Arthur's supporters also forgive her because they admire her courage for returning to take Arthur's side in the stand-off with Macsen. Cei expresses the soldiers' view: "She has paid her penalty already! . . . [I]t was a bold deed, escaping from Macsen's fortress dressed as a man; the warband will pardon her anything, after that" (*Shadow* 231). In addition, the traditional penance, retirement to a convent, is postponed, so that Gwynhwyfar once again gives practical, logistical support to Arthur's war with Darkness.

Bradshaw creates a character who is an emotional, private person and who accepts the responsibilities and obligations of her political role as well. As a result, the tragedy of the story operates on several levels. Eivlin recognizes that Gwynhwyfar grieves for Arthur's loss for personal, emotional reasons. When Eivlin embraces Gwynhwyfar, they are not servant and empress but "only two women who had lost the men they loved" (*Shadow* 310). The grief of this personal loss is the greater because it ends the possibility of a reconciliation between Arthur and Gwynhwyfar and a renewal of their relationship. However, Gwynhwyfar also grieves that "there is nothing left of the empire, and nothing remaining from which we could build again, and nothing to show for our lives' effort but guilt, shame and a few lying songs" (*Shadow* 312); she mourns as an empress, for a political vision that will not be fulfilled.

Bradshaw's Gwynhwyfar, then, fulfills the requirements of a tragic hero. *In Winter's Shadow*, like a "medieval tragedy of fortune . . . describes the fall of some ruler or other noble person from success or happiness into ruin or misery" (Matthews 105). At the beginning of the novel, Gwynhwyfar is "Augusta, Empress of Britain" (*Shadow* 1), and Camlann is her "fortress, the strong heart of the visionary empire" (*Shadow* 16). The queen loses her high status through a combination of her own weaknesses (her loneliness) and external pressures (Medraut's desire to wreck Arthur's kingdom). Again, the reasons for the protagonist's change of status resemble those of medieval versions, in which "the fall [is] brought about not only by capricious Fortune, but also by the change that takes place in the hero's character" (Krishna 21). Whereas *The Alliterative Morte Arthure* and Malory's *Le Morte D'Arthur* create Arthurian tragedies whose hero is Arthur,[3] Bradshaw makes a woman the protagonist, thus questioning readers' assumptions, namely, that the acting subject of such a political tragedy is "naturally" male.

Gwynhwyfar, therefore, has real power in the society depicted by *In Winter's Shadow*, and narrative power as well. She is an exception, however. She is different from other women and is often isolated from them. Her "female cousins . . . had to learn to spin and weave and sew, to butcher and cook an animal or to heal it of various common ills, to make cheese and mead, to keep bees, keep house, manage servants, and see to the holding accounts" (*Shadow* 7); Gwynhwyfar tries, often successfully, to avoid all but the last two in this list of women's duties. Her desire to read sets her apart from many men in her society as well; her "male cousins were not much interested in reading, beyond what was obviously useful" (*Shadow* 7). Her inability to have children also distinguishes her; she is not "an ordinary woman" (*Shadow* 45). Moreover, she is the only female protagonist in the series and the only female narrator; she is the only woman to have narrative power as subject and teller of the story.

Having an exceptional person as hero is not unusual. Joseph Campbell describes the hero as "a personage of exceptional gifts" (37); Northrop Frye suggests that "attributes of divinity" may still be associated with the hero (*Anatomy* 187). Merlin, in Mary Stewart's series, exemplifies this mixed status; he is human, yet he is also a vehicle or instrument of the god and therefore at times more than human. The female protagonists of Sampson's and Bradley's works are also extraordinary in some way.

Morgan, in Sampson's series, is exceptional, even in a family whose women all have the old powers. Gwennol implies that Morgan has great abilities, "a spirit buried inside her that made the rest of the world seem half dead" (*Woman* 3). As a nine-year-old, Morgan realizes, "I had power over people. . . . The Goddess was already present in me" (*Herself* 30–31). She merely has to concentrate to make her mother, for example, do what she wants (*Herself* 31).

What makes Morgaine different from most of the women in *The Mists of Avalon* is the length of time that she spends *not* fulfilling any one of the typical female roles of wife, mother, or religious figure, and *not* working to become part of them either. She refuses to marry Cai, for though the women think his status makes him a good match for her, both she and Cai know they are not suited (304). She jokes with Balan about marriage (312), but she later recognizes "that she had no real wish to marry Lancelet or any other" (323). Although few know it, she gives up her son to Morgause, albeit somewhat unwillingly. She even, for a time, gives up her role as a priestess.

It is not just her independence that makes Morgaine different, but all the knowledge and skills that she has that allow her to be independent. Her ability to read and write is not considered magical, but it is unusual in a woman; Gwenhwyfar has more education than many of her ladies, and yet "she could do no more than write her name and read a little in her Gospel book" (440). Furthermore, Morgaine has undergone vigorous training in Avalon, so that she is capable of taking care of herself, even while travelling under adverse conditions. Unlike Gwenhwyfar, who travels seldom and then usually in a closed litter with a group of attendants (268), Morgaine makes several journeys unattended. While pregnant, she flees "over moorland and fell" to Lothian (231); later she travels both to and from Avalon and the fairy world alone. When faced with this last journey, she must travel by herself, without proper clothing, food, or transportation, and she merely reflects that "she had walked farther with less to eat" (410).[4]

Nevertheless, there is a difference between the exceptional woman created by Bradshaw and those created by Sampson and Bradley. Bradshaw's Gwynhwyfar is, most of the time, isolated from other women; once she was married to Arthur, "most of [her] work had to do with administering Camlann, and with affairs of state, and hence with men" (*Shadow* 43). Such isolation is enhanced by the fact that hers is the only female perspective in the trilogy. Sampson, in contrast, places Morgan in several groups of women, and two women, Gwennol and Luned, narrate parts of the series. In Bradley, women form communities in several places and these appear at critical plot moments. Although Morgaine is the only one who "speaks," the novel uses third-person limited narration to tell events from the perspectives of Ygraine, Viviane, Morgause, Gwenhwyfar, Nimue, and Niniane as well as Morgaine. In the rest of this chapter, I will examine the communities of women created in Sampson's series and Bradley's novel, discussing their importance to the portrayal of feminist ideas in the texts. In the following chapter, I will investigate the implications of the use of multiple narrators and perspectives for the creation of feminist stories.

COMMUNITY

Various feminist scholars have recognized the importance of community in women's writing. Charlotte Spivack comments that one thing female protagonists in feminist fiction usually strive for is "protection of the community" (8). Melinda Hughes, in "Dark Sisters and Light Sisters," an article on Marion Zimmer Bradley and Diana Paxson, suggests that "women writers of fantasy are beginning to recognize the importance of portraying the quest for positive female bonding and 'sisterhood' in their fantasy novels" (24). Barbara Ann Gordon-Wise argues that "the ultimate sisterhood" experienced by the women in *The Mists of Avalon* is significant to the revision of the Arthurian legend (147). Emily Toth claims that "the new frontier in women's writing is not the sensitive man / career woman coupling—but the love and friendship between women" (791). This love and friendship can occur between mothers and daughters or between sisters. The Arthurian legend inherited by twentieth-century writers includes such relationships already: Morgan and Morgause, for example, are daughters of Ygraine and sisters to one another, and through Arthur, sisters-in-law to Guenevere. Contemporary writers may expand these kinships to include other women associated with the legend.

However, blood ties are not the only way to define a mother-daughter or sister relationship, and fantasy writers take advantage of this. As Hughes notes, "sisterhood" in fantasy novels "encompasses not only the relationship between women related by blood or marriage but the relationship found in any woman-to-woman dyad in which each woman searches for an identity . . . through interaction with a sister or sister-surrogate" (24), or, I would add, with a mother or mother-surrogate. Sometimes these relationships involve conflict and competition as well as support and nurturing; regardless, relationships between women shape the primary characters and the action of Sampson's and Bradley's rewritings and affect the role of the protagonist. Although one woman may be the subject of the story, foregrounding communities of women in the text means that women also fill the roles of important supporting characters, so that strong women are not portrayed as exceptions. Moreover, these communities often reflect the priority of the protagonist, whose quest is not just personal; it is undertaken with the help and for the benefit of a group.

In Sampson's series Ygerne has three daughters; she has the strongest ties with Elaine, the eldest. Partly these ties are religious; Ygerne passes on her own knowledge to her daughter (*Woman* 3) and includes her when making the spell that will draw Uther to her (*Woman* 43–44). Gwennol sees this passing of secrets from "mother to daughter. Woman to her own blood" as a natural process (*Woman* 3), and one that she can never fully enjoy because she has no children of her own. Others see such ties as less positive, suspecting that evil may be transmitted mother to daughter. Thus Bryvyth warns that Morgan "comes of a treacherous mother. The darkness is in her blood" (*Nun* 96). Considering the lack of emotional connection between Ygerne and Morgan, this statement is somewhat ironic, but it indicates that blood ties cannot be ignored; they exert powerful influence on the women.

Morgan has a love-hate relationship with Ygerne. At times she envies and seeks to copy her mother. When she recognizes the power that Ygerne can command because of her beauty, she strives to be more lady-like, "copying [Ygerne's] steps . . . twisting her hair in her fingers as though she was thinking of braiding it with pearls" as Ygerne does (*Woman* 95). She mimics her mother's actions as well by "holding Margawse's mirror and smiling at her own reflection as she touched her hair. . . . She looked like a small, dark copy of her mother" (*Woman* 210). Morgan, however, also hates her mother for abandoning her father for Uther. She stands on the thin land bridge at Tintagel, trying to use a spell to keep Uther and Ygerne apart (*Woman* 167–69), and she tells Gwennol that neither she nor her sisters "love Mother" (*Woman* 186).

However, blood ties are not the only way that mother-daughter bonds are formed. Ygerne belongs to a different class than Gwennol; she is of the nobility and Gwennol is a peasant. Yet spiritually Ygerne acts "in place of the daughter [Gwennol] never had" (*Woman* 49); Gwennol "had the whispering of that one" (*Woman* 4) and initiated her into the "mysteries" (*Woman* 5) of their religion. As Ygerne's spiritual mother, Gwennol feels left out and abandoned when her "spirit-daughter whispers her own [Elaine], and the two of them go spell-speaking in secret" (*Woman* 49).

Gwennol, however, also mothers Ygerne's daughters. She, as their nurse, takes care of them. This responsibility alone does not create a mother-daughter relationship; Gwennol seems to see Margawse, for example, as just a responsibility. Gwennol feels real affection for Morgan, though. Gwennol, not Ygerne, goes to Morgan when the girl defies Uther at Tintagel. Gwennol acts because, as she says, "she [Morgan] was my little maid. I'd carried her in my heart these eight years" (*Woman* 167). Gwennol, in fact, is "closer to her [Morgan] than her own blood" (*Woman* 167), since Ygerne cannot or will not try to love her youngest daughter. Being Morgan's surrogate mother is not easy for Gwennol, however. The old nurse feels Morgan's pain and sympathizes with her vulnerability: "I couldn't cut the cord that bound us together, for all it hurt me" (*Woman* 191). Gwennol's devotion to Morgan even results in physical harm for the old woman. She suffers a stroke after betraying Tintagel to Mark to free Morgan (*Nun* 240).

The series depicts another mother-daughter bond, but it lasts only briefly. As she takes care of and struggles with Morgan, Luned feels a maternal bond with her. This bond may result, in part, from Luned's growing recognition of their similarities: "I thought we were akin in our pride, our estimation of our own worth compared with others', our contempt for weaker souls, our need of solitude" (*Nun* 82). The strongest recognition of this bond occurs on May Day, when Luned makes a garland of flowers to drape about Morgan's neck. To Luned the act symbolizes a transmission or re-enactment of a specifically mother-daughter ceremony. The words "Welcome Summer" (*Nun* 91) evoke a ritual that links Luned to her "mother and grandmother, and to all those other women far back beyond" (*Nun* 91). Luned begins at this moment to think of Morgan as her own "foster-daughter" (*Nun* 91, 105). Morgan's reaction to the flower garland, however, indicates that she thinks of their relationship differently. She sees herself as Luned's "queen" (*Nun* 91), with Luned, therefore, merely a servant, and consequently she does not help Luned with her pregnancy because Luned did not act suppliant (*Nun* 201). Although this attitude seems overly harsh and proud, Morgan makes an accusation about Luned's feelings for her that is not disproved or rebutted and that therefore alters our perception of Morgan. She askes Luned: "When have you ever loved me more than yourself?" (*Nun* 203). Luned's refusal to answer suggests that Morgan's assessment of the self-centred nature of the nun's maternal feelings is correct.

Morgan has other mother figures as well, although we see less of those ties. Morgan claims, "Elaine was all the mother of my own blood I had ever known" (*Herself* 116) and remembers being "cradled in my sister's lap" (*Herself* 116). Morgan also addresses Bryvyth as Mother. Although Bryvyth's rank as abbess would demand such a title from her followers, Morgan is not Christian. Nevertheless, Bryvyth's concern for Morgan is a motherly one, though it mostly addresses spiritual matters.

Little is shown of the relationship between Morgan and her own daughter, Morfudd.[5] Although Morfudd's testimony against Arthur convinces Morgan to vote for Gwenhyvar as high queen (*Herself* 189), Morgan reacts less out of outrage for her daughter's suffering than out of sorrow for what she, Morgan, has lost. An element of competition pervades Morgan's relationship with her daughter. Morgan votes for Gwenhyvar, not because Arthur harmed Morfudd, but because "he had forced on [her] daughter what he had never offered" to Morgan (*Herself* 189).

Sisterhood is not much in evidence at the beginning of *Wise Woman's Telling*. The two older daughters of Ygerne and Gorlois continually compete with one another. Most memorably, they fist-fight and wrestle over whether or not Margawse will go to London tòo. Margawse uses threats against her sister to get permission to go along: if she were not allowed to go she vows to "put such scratches on Elaine's face that no one will marry her, now or ever" (*Woman* 51). Later in the series, after Margawse seduces Arthur, a similar fight takes place, this time between Margawse and Morgan; "those two queens wrestled together, rolling on the ground . . . there was damage done. Margawse had the worst of it" (*Smith* 181). Nevertheless, despite differences in the way they respond to situations, and despite the competition between them, Morgan suggests that the three women still share a degree of common feeling. None of them loves Ygerne; all of them seem to be waiting for a chance to avenge their father and restore their name (*Woman* 186).

As the series progresses, the sense of these women working together yet being also in competition deepens. Every time there is a major event, the three queens get together to consult and to act. After Arthur's marriage, they meet to discuss what can be done about the Pendragon's growing power. Each of them has some weapon against Arthur; Elaine has stolen Caliburn, Margawse has borne him a son, and Morgan has stolen the scabbard, Arthur's power to heal. They are working for similar ends, yet the scene suggests they are still competing in trying to outdo each other in hurting Arthur. Thus when Morgan reveals what she has taken from him, "Elaine smiled, a bit coolly. It had taken some of the shine off her deed" (*Smith* 232). Morgan's challenge to Margawse to do as well is "pretty vicious" (*Smith* 232), considering that Arthur has supposedly killed Margawse's child.

As the end of the tale draws closer, however, the sisters put aside their differences. They draw together, either because they have a sense of impending, inevitable tragedy or because they have always fought among themselves but acted in unison against those who would threaten their family honour and their rights. Thus they act as one in the matter of Gwenhyvar; Morgan leads, but the others do not disagree with her solution. Together, they face down Nimue. Nimue comes to talk to Morgan, thinking her the most reachable of the sisters, but Elaine and Margawse act as a chorus for their younger sister. The three together answer Nimue's question about their right to have any power with three lines: "The right to heal? The right to bear? The right to embrace?" (*Taliesin* 264).

The other communities of women that appear throughout the series often show a lack of unity or cohesion. In part, this sense of fragmentation or struggle within the community results from the narrators who tell the story. Gwennol is reporting to her sisters what she has done, and what events have lead to the decision they must make; it is therefore the story of an individual, more than of a group. Luned never seems to be one with Tintagel's nuns, in part because she has already lost her position when she tells the story. In addition, her class, ambition, and abilities keep her in competition with other nuns; she admits, "I could have begged my sister nuns to teach me what they knew. . . . But I was too proud to ask" (*Nun* 35). Neither is Luned a willing or happy member of Morgan's band; she fears the powers of the wise too much. Likewise, Smith is an unwilling follower of Morgan and, because of his gender, always somewhat of an outsider among them; his version of events consequently emphasizes isolation rather than community.

Moments of women working together, therefore, are more often reported than seen, or are simply assumed. For example, Taliesin describes Morgan's ladies-in-waiting as "her tribe, not her hirelings. Loyal to her as Urien's warband to him" (*Taliesin* 10). Morgan and her sisters take Gwenhyvar to the convent and find Bryvyth still managing it with her old high principles and scorn of rank; Bryvyth's group of nuns have obviously survived their expulsion from Tintagel, and that suggests they must be a strong community. Although we see comparatively little of them, Nimue's women also seem to be a strong community. They fight together as "a small tight band of warriors" (*Taliesin* 132), and together they train Arthur and his companions (*Smith* 133). Nevertheless, the series does suggest a context for the actions of the female protagonists and narrators that is usually a community of women: for Gwennol, it is her sister worshippers; for Luned, it is first the nuns and then Morgan's followers; for Morgan, it is the alliance with her sisters.

Bradley, in contrast, emphasizes moments of community between women. Competition between the major female characters occurs, but the sisterhood among women is often reaffirmed after divisive episodes. Thus, the relationships portrayed are generally quite complex; love and friendship are gained in spite of, or perhaps because of, tensions between women arising from different beliefs. Bradley depicts the way strong women can join in hard-won communities, some of which last years.

The first community of women we see in *The Mists of Avalon* is one defined by family ties. Viviane and Taliesin arrive at Tintagel to visit Igraine. This visit reunites women who had been separated by marriage, fostering, or duty: Viviane, the Lady of the Lake; Igraine, Viviane's half-sister and wife of Gorlois, duke of Cornwall; Morgause, Igraine's sister and Viviane's foster child, who had been sent to live with Igraine a year previously; and Morgaine, Igraine's daughter. In this scene the permutations of female familial relationships are quite complex. Igraine and Morgaine are mother and daughter, and the other women are sisters, but more than blood ties connect them. Viviane, for example, is sister to Igraine and Morgause, but as their spiritual leader she also represents the Goddess, a mother figure. Furthermore, she acted as a wet nurse for Morgause; she is Morgause's foster mother. Thus a pattern is introduced here that will appear again and again throughout the novel: women bound to one another in relationships that are described through family metaphors of sister, mother, and daughter. These are not fixed relationships, but rather roles that women adopt for one another, depending on the situation. The women related to Morgaine by blood take on these various roles, but other women also play the parts of sisters, mothers, and daughters to Morgaine.[6]

Two factors commonly appear in the disintegration of these communities of women: sexual ties with men and religious beliefs. Thus the initial community of Viviane, Igraine, Morgause, and Morgaine alters when Igraine marries Uther. As Igraine's spiritual and physical connection to Uther and her allegiance to Christianity are formally acknowledged, her ties to her sisters and daughter diminish. Paradoxically, Igraine's belief in the ways of Avalon's priestesses is strongest during the events that lead up to that formalized marriage to Uther. Igraine rejects Gorlois's Christianity for "she would not have her daughter brought up to feel shame at her own womanhood" (79). She uses the Sight to learn news of her sister and to warn Uther of Gorlois's plans. In order to accomplish this, she invokes the Goddess and for a brief moment in the mirror even sees "the awesome face of the Goddess, with the rowanberries bound about her brow" (83). After Gorlois's death, however, when she is about to be crowned Uther's queen, she deliberately turns to Christianity. In some ways this is a rejection of one father for another; she turns from the Merlin, her blood father, to Father Columba, the priest (107–8). Since Merlin is associated with the Goddess worship of Avalon, this is also a turning away from a matriarchal religion to a patriarchal one; she rejects Viviane's religion for Christianity. After Igraine's wedding, Morgause marries Lot and moves away, in part because Igraine "fancied Morgause looked on Uther lustfully" (110). And Uther, rather than Morgaine, "was always at the center of [Igraine's] heart" (108) afterward.

However, shortly after Morgaine's words record this diminishment of these women's sense of community, Morgaine begins to form relationships with other women. Viviane meets Morgaine again at Morgause's wedding and swears that Morgaine "shall never go into a nunnery while there is life and breath in my body" (112); she, not Igraine, determines to protect Morgaine from the priests and their ideas of proper roles for women. Again Bradley incorporates a variation on the mother-daughter tie and a community defined by certain religious beliefs. After she has been in Avalon for several years Morgaine feels she has forgotten her own mother, her own blood ties, for "she had learned to live without need of any mother save the Goddess, and she had many sisters among the priestesses" (148).

Even when no real community is formed, temporary tableaux of sisters, mothers, and daughters mark important events in the story. Igraine's relationship with Morgaine has been distant for many years, and Morgaine resents Gwenhwyfar, but the three of them come together at Arthur and Gwenhwyfar's wedding. Gwenhwyfar calls Morgaine and Igraine "my own sister and my own mother" (285); when "the three of them stood in a brief embrace," Morgaine reflects that they "are sisters under the Goddess" (285). This triangle of Igraine-Morgaine-Gwenhwyfar recurs at Igraine's death-bed, even though Morgaine is not physically present. Gwenhwyfar acts as daughter to Igraine in her last hours and Igraine appreciates her daughter-in-law's presence, but she asks for Morgaine as well.

Therefore, these mother-daughter bonds reassert themselves at crucial points in the novel. Characters turn, almost instinctively, back to those roles, and the emotional ties they represent, in times of crisis, thus demonstrating the strength of those bonds. For example, when Morgaine gives birth to her son, the old ties among her, Morgause, and Igraine are invoked. Morgause combs and braids Morgaine's hair as she did when they were both at Tintagel (239). Morgause has had only sons, no daughters, and quiets Morgaine's restlessness and protests with the following appeal to mother-daughter roles: "You must just be my little daughter now when you need me" (239). Later, during the difficult birth, Morgaine says that Morgause is "so like [her own] mother" (245) and wishes for Igraine's presence. When Morgaine cries out for "Mother" later, it is not clear whether the appeal is meant for Morgause, Igraine, or the Goddess (248). Igraine, far away in her nunnery, senses that appeal even though she has renounced the Sight.

Likewise, Igraine, as she is dying, assumes that the mother-daughter bond should overcome any obstacle, and that Morgaine should be able to sense her mother's approaching death. Morgaine realizes later that Igraine's appeal to her may have reached even into the fairy world when she saw "Igraine's face in the forest pool" (412). As Morgaine recognizes, at the end of the novel, the similarity between the convent and Avalon, she feels close to the Goddess, and "it seemed to

Morgaine that it was Igraine's voice that whispered to her . . . and Igraine's hands that touched her head" (876). Even after a character's death, therefore, the mother-daughter bond still influences the survivors.

Another temporary community of women is formed when Morgaine miscarries. Morgaine and the women of Gwenhwyfar's court do not like each other, yet when she miscarries, the women gather around in support. One woman scoffs at Uriens's possible anger about the miscarriage: "Who chose him for God? . . . [I]t is dangerous for a woman to miscarry at your age! Shame on the old lecher for putting you so at risk!" (740). The mid-wife takes care of Morgaine; her role is similar to that which Morgaine played when Gwenhwyfar first miscarried. The mid-wife knows Morgaine used herbs to instigate the miscarriage, but she will not tell Uriens because "if he has no more sense than to let a woman of your years try to bear him a child, then what he does not know will do him no harm" (740). Morgaine calls out for Igraine (741) and the mid-wife acts as mother and comforts her.

Gwenhwyfar also creates her own community of women at court, where women's roles of sister, mother, or daughter to one another shift with circumstances. Gwenhwyfar and Morgaine are sisters-in-law, but they also have moments of sisterhood. "There was real affection between them sometimes" (307) so that Gwenhwyfar understands and does not pry when Morgaine is upset by an unwilled vision. Although Gwenhwyfar is sometimes afraid of what sinful aspects of her personality Morgaine might know because of the Sight, Gwenhwyfar admits that "Morgaine had never shown her anything but a sister's kindness" (316). Although Morgaine despises the gossipy circle of women who make up Gwenhwyfar's court, she feels a common bond with Gwenhwyfar and Elaine, who "had some learning, and occasionally . . . with them, she could almost imagine herself peacefully among the priestesses in the House of Maidens" (308), women whom Morgaine described previously as "sisters" (148). Furthermore, Morgaine characterizes her attendence on the queen as not servitude, but the result of sisterly feeling (493). This sense of sisterhood remains, though marred by sibling rivalry over the men in their lives, and it resurfaces at various points in the book. Gwenhwyfar is able to sympathize when Morgaine miscarries; they have that experience in common, though Morgaine wants to lose the baby for fear she would die in childbirth (740). Morgaine realizes "that in spite of all old enmities, there was love too" between her and Gwenhwyfar (725), and in fact, "it was not Gwenhwyfar herself that she hated, it was the priests who had so much influence over her" (723). As Gwenhwyfar enters the convent where she will live out her days, she thinks of Morgaine "with a sudden passion of love and tenderness" and prays to "Mary, Holy Mother of God" for her sister-in-law's spiritual well-being (864).

These women play other roles for each other. During Gwenhwyfar's first miscarriage, Morgaine "care[s] for her almost like a mother" (316). Again, when Morgaine agrees to prepare a charm for Gwenhwyfar to help her get pregnant, the queen follows her sister-in-law "like a child being led by her mother" (443). Gwenhwyfar herself acts "even as a mother" to the younger women of her court

(421), and therefore she "guards her maidens well, and makes good marriages for them" (311). Gwenhwyfar, however, wishes to be a real mother; she suffers great distress because she has no child, as she reveals to Morgaine when asking for a charm to help her conceive (441).[7]

The last community of women portrayed in the book is that of the nuns at Glastonbury. As she introduces this group of women, Bradley again invokes sisterly and mother-daughter bonds. The abbess treats Gwenhwyfar as a child and calls her "my daughter" (863); Gwenhwyfar realizes that she will become one of a group of sisters (863). When Morgaine goes to the convent with a slip of the Holy Thorn, so that it will not be lost as Avalon moves into the mists, she discovers that this community of sisters is much like her own. She is called "Mother" by the novices who help her plant the Thorn, and she compares them to "her own maidens in the House of Maidens" (874). Brigid, whom they see as a saint, is the Irish equivalent of the Goddess. Thus Morgaine realizes that "these women know the power of the Immortal" (875) just as she does. The novices also offer to say prayers for Viviane and invite Morgaine to pray for them, too; this suggests a kinship between these women, even though they do not have the same religious beliefs. Furthermore, as Barbara Ann Gordon-Wise comments, this community of women outlasts the male companionship of the Round Table; "the profound revision of this novel lies in the fact that . . . it is the sisterhood on the Isle of Glastonbury which endures" (147).

Throughout *The Mists of Avalon*, then, it becomes evident that such communities of women are necessary to, or recognized as important by, a wide variety of female characters. Igraine, whose love with Uther exemplifies typical idealized heterosexual passion, looks for community with other women once Uther has died. Arthur offers to secure her another husband so that she will not be lonely, but she replies, "It is hard to be lonely in a nunnery, son, with other women" (218). Morgause regrets her lack of "woman friends" with whom she could have intelligent conversations (454). Viviane does not like Gwenhwyfar and resents her power over Arthur and the kingdom, but she refuses to create false scandal about the queen or criticize her sexuality. Viviane asks, "What woman would betray a fellow woman like that?" (473). Thus, relationships and feelings of kinship between women transcend the divisions caused by different personalities or religious beliefs.

Moreover, both Christian and Goddess-based belief systems, as Bradley depicts them, recognize the importance of the mother-daughter tie. For the Christian priests, this tie is a negative one. Gorlois, repeating their teachings, explains to Igraine that "women bear the blood of their mothers, and . . . that what is within women, who are filled with sin, cannot be overcome by a woman-child" (86).[8] For the women of the Tribes, this tie is to be celebrated; Viviane "longed for a daughter" (21), as does Morgause later (239), and Igraine contrasts their concern for daughters with the Roman desire for sons (8). However, both Christian women and women who worship the Goddess find comfort, support, and nurturing in relationships with other women, whether they live in a convent, in Avalon, or at court.

Bradley makes these relationships the focus of the novel, rather than knightly deeds of arms, so that Morgaine's relationships with her "sisters" shape the narrative. As a result, the community of Avalon can be seen as the protagonist; the survival of its beliefs, its community, is the quest that shapes the story as many of the women who focalize the story—Viviane, Morgaine, Niniane, and Nimue—work toward that end. Furthermore, interaction with the most important of her surrogate sisters, Raven and Gwenhwyfar, defines Morgaine. These women are more than sisters; they are mirror images or alter egos of one another. It is these relationships, rather than relationships with men, that develop Morgaine's character.

Raven, as Viviane's servant, is present when Morgaine first arrives in Avalon. Two of Morgaine's first important assignments are performed with Raven; Morgaine works with her in the ceremony in the ring stones (165–68) and Raven serves and supports Morgaine during the making of the scabbard (197). Furthermore, when Viviane thinks of suitable successors for herself, she always contemplates these two: "Morgaine would someday grow to that stature; but not yet. Raven—Raven might have had that strength. But Raven had given her voice to the Gods" (192). When Morgaine disappears for several years into the fairy world, Viviane suggests that Raven become Lady "if Morgaine does not return" (353). Morgaine, while in the fairy world, speaks of a sexual encounter with a maiden who "looked somewhat like Raven" (405). It is Raven's voice, crying out in prophecy, that finally recalls Morgaine to her own world, and it is the thought of speaking and being with Raven that makes Morgaine long to return to Avalon (410).

Gwenhwyfar and Morgaine also are doubles for one another. Physically, they are opposites: Gwenhwyfar is "all white and gold, her skin pale as ivory . . . her hair long and pale and shining . . . like living gold" (157); Morgaine is "little and ugly like one of the fairyfolk" (158). Morgaine makes their doubling explicit when she sees herself "as the Queen's shadow" (533). She believes they have been bound together by divine "blunders": "she, Morgaine, had had Arthur and borne him a son, which Gwenhwyfar longed to do; Gwenhwyfar had had Lancelet's love for which Morgaine would willingly have given her soul" (533). Two scenes that emphasize their duality involve the working of symbols in cloth. Morgaine creates for Arthur the scabbard that protects his life in battle; Gwenhwyfar creates the Christian standard that he carries into the battle of Badon. Morgaine weaves "the magical spells and their symbols" into the scabbard (197); similarly Gwenhwyfar weaves "prayers for [Arthur] and [his] Companions into every stitch" (392) of the banner.

As the initial community of women in the novel, centred on Igraine, breaks down at the time of her marriage to Uther, so does the sisterhood of Morgaine and Gwenhwyfar during a period that is marked by two weddings. The first, Lancelet's to Elaine, has been arranged by Morgaine because Elaine requested it, but also because Morgaine fears what will happen to Arthur and his kingdom if Lancelet remains at court with the queen. Both Gwenhwyfar and Lancelet blame Morgaine, not Elaine, for this marriage.[9] Then the revelation that Morgaine has borne Arthur's son further damages Morgaine's relationship with the queen. This knowledge triggers in Gwenhwyfar a series of outbursts against Morgaine; it is one of the most sustained diatribes against Avalon and its priestesses in the entire book (550–61). Gwenhwyfar calls Morgaine a "harlot" (550), a "damned sorceress" (552), and describes her as "incestuous, heathen, witch" (559). Although Gwenhwyfar concentrates on the sinfulness of Morgaine's union with Arthur, Morgaine, and the reader with her, suspects that jealousy drives her piety. The queen resents that her virtue has not been rewarded with a child, whereas Morgaine, a heathen, has borne Arthur a son. She becomes furious when Arthur defends Morgaine's part in it all, for "even now all [he] can think of is the wrong . . . done to Morgaine" (552) and not to her, Gwenhwyfar, his queen. The root issue is that, as Morgaine realizes, "Arthur loves me best" (558–59). Knowing that, Gwenhwyfar "fears that [Morgaine] will beckon . . . and . . . seduce him to [her] bed again" (559). Indeed, Gwenhwyfar envies not just their sexual past, but all ties between them; Arthur never comes to Gwenhwyfar for comfort (552), and it is Morgaine who wipes Arthur's eyes and holds him (551). Gwenhwyfar's revenge, suggesting to Arthur that Morgaine marry Uriens, sends Morgaine far from the court. Thus the relationship between these two women, as Meredith J. Ross argues, forms "the crux of the novel" for three reasons: because "Arthur's actions arise out of his desire to hurt neither of them"; because their relationship helps define others in the novel as they arrange marriages or compete for others' loyalties; and because their conflicts mirror the religious and political struggles of the nation (426).

Although in the novel heterosexuality often strains sisterly relationships, sisterhood itself can be erotically charged. Erotic episodes occur between Morgaine and other women in the fairy world, although Morgaine is not completely comfortable with them and thinks of them "as dreams or madness" (408). Furthermore, Morgaine occasionally senses erotic possibilities in the relationships between her and Gwenhwyfar and Elaine. Morgaine, helping Gwenhwyfar get ready for a Pentecost feast, "put her arms around her, laying her cheek for a moment against Gwenhwyfar's. It seemed enough, for a moment, to touch that beauty" (486). When she prepares Elaine to entrap Lancelet, she "embraced and kissed her [Elaine]; the warm body in her arms somehow roused her, whether to desire or tenderness she could not tell" (540). In these scenes, sisterhood and motherhood have erotic dimensions that are portrayed as natural, even if usually latent.

The most explicit lesbian scenes in the book involve Morgaine and Raven. Marilyn R. Farwell calls the night that Raven welcomes Morgaine back to Avalon a "crucial scene" (92), which is "an unmistakeably charged lesbian scene" (92). This scene is important because it initiates Morgaine's return to a matriarchal community. Another important scene of "women's bonding" (Farwell 93) occurs between Morgaine and Raven the night before the Easter feast where the grail appears. Raven, frightened of the fate she sees for herself, turns to Morgaine for comfort. Morgaine holds "Raven against her, touching her, caressing her" (Mists 765). The description of this erotic moment emphasizes its religious, "sacramental" context (Mists 765). The two women are on their way to act in the name of their Goddess, and it is during the "dark moon" (Mists 765) that they as "priestesses of

Avalon together called on the life of the Goddess" (*Mists* 766). The erotic scene between the two women therefore "affirm[s] . . . life in the shadow of death" (*Mists* 765). As Farwell notes, "All of the depictions of women loving women in Avalon are made without negative comment" (101).

Although Avalon is a community of women existing relatively independently of men, even they have ties to male followers of the Goddess. Viviane and Taliesin, and for a time Morgaine and Kevin, work together toward common religious goals. And although Bradley depicts strong emotional, even sensual interludes between women such as Raven and Morgaine, there are also more traditional heterosexual romantic ties. Igraine's ability to contact Uther psychically culminates in a sensual love scene in which, in a very Harlequinesque way, the woman becomes virgin-like in her wonder at the experience possible with one's true love.[10]   Similarly, Morgaine and Arthur share a bond that is both mother-son and sister-brother; that bond, however, gains power from their heterosexual love. Days after their sexual union, she has an unwilled vision of Arthur at the important moment when he drew Uther's sword, thus proving himself Uther's son. Morgaine realizes that "there would always be a bond between them now. Would any blow which struck him always fall like this, a sword into her naked heart?" (*Mists* 202).

Such features of the story have led critics such as Susan Signe Morrison to argue that such erotic scenes subvert Bradley's attempt to revision the Arthurian story from a feminist perspective. Lee Ann Tobin asserts that "Bradley's work embodies an important feature of women's popular fiction: simultaneous conservatism and subversion" (154). The moments of subversion in popular fiction, however, should not be dismissed. Anne Cranny-Francis suggests that such novels are "not untenable for a feminist writer or reader [because they] . . . challeng[e] the reader's acceptance of conservative ideological discourses" (71). The use of a female protagonist to tell a woman's version of events or the use of communities of women to demonstrate that strong women are not alone or exceptional, to emphasize the communal goals of the protagonist, and to create "a subtext that explores female desire" (Farwell 102), all help to redefine common cultural perceptions of the role of the protagonist, and of women's roles in general.

NOTES

1. Some of the other novels that either use Morgan as a narrator or use her point of view are Fay Sampson's *Herself*, Courtway Jones's *The Witch of the North*, Welwyn Wilton Katz's *The Third Magic*, and Harry Robin's *I, Morgain*.

2. They preface the figure four with "at least" (Spivack and Staples 83); the authors they discuss are Sharan Newman, Parke Godwin, Persia Woolley, and Gillian Bradshaw. Nancy McKenzie has published *The Child Queen* and *The High Queen*, which are narrated by Guenevere, as is Jennifer Roberson's short story "Guinevere's Truth." Lynne Pledger's short story "Gwynhwyfar" uses the future queen as the main character, as does Heather Rose Jones's "The Treasures of Britain."   Although Morgan's and Guenevere's are the most popular female perspectives to use in rewriting the legend, other women also appear as protagonists.   In Diana Paxson's *The White Raven*, Branwen tells the Tristan and Isolde story; C. J. Cherryh's science fiction novel *Port Eternity* uses a robot named Elaine as a

narrator; Barbara Ferry Johnson uses a minor female character from Malory to narrate *Lionors*; Niviane, a fey, narrates Anne Eliot Crompton's *Merlin's Harp*, and another fey, Lili, is one of the narrators of Crompton's *Percival's Angel*; Gwenhyfar's daughter Argante is the protagonist of Mary J. Jones's *Avalon*. In the genre of short stories, Phyllis Ann Karr focusses on the lady who loved Gawain in "The Lady of Belec" and Amide in "Galahad's Lady"; Nimue is the protagonist in Madeleine E. Robins's "Nimue's Tale" and in Karen Haber's "The Spell Between Worlds"; two young women seeking the grail are the protagonists of Mercedes Lackey's "The Cup and the Cauldron"; the faery who will become Lady of the Lake narrates Anne E. Crompton's "Excalibur"; a woman who has been the Lady narrates Paxson's "Lady of Avalon." These are just some of the possibilities, and new versions, of course, are appearing all the time.

3. William Matthews argues that "the *Morte Arthure* poet selects from the chronicles the climatic part of a single reign and adapts that material to the design of a tragedy of fortune" (109). D. S. Brewer sees the same design in Malory's work, where the writer "postponed the fall . . . to dilate on the splendour of Arthur's achievement and on the achievements of Arthur's knights . . . [so that] the downward turn of Fortune's wheel is all the more tragic" (8).

4. This makes Uriens's concern that a trip to Bath "would be a long journey for" Morgaine (*Mists* 582) quite ironic, and underscores the way the Roman Christian ways make it possible for a woman to do less and to be seen as capable of less.

5. Smith focusses on other aspects of Morgan's life, and Taliesin arrives in Rheged after Morfudd has gone to live at court.

6. Bradley uses Neo-paganism to reinforce this sense that women play shifting roles. In the novel, as in Neo-paganism, the Goddess is "Maiden, Mother and Crone, the three stages of a woman's life" (Fry 73). The importance of this Triple Goddess to a feminist rewriting of the legend is the value it places on all stages of women's lives. Carrol L. Fry notes that "worship of the Triple Goddess . . . enables women to value themselves and their knowledge and experience even when their beauty has dimmed" (73–74). In the first section of the book Morgaine is the maiden, Igraine is the mother, Viviane is the wisewoman. Through the book, just as women represent different aspects of the Goddess, they represent sisters, mothers, or daughters to one another.

7. Unlike other women in the book who wish for daughters (Viviane, Morgause), Gwenhwyfar is desperate to have a son. She wishes to bear Arthur's heir in order to give herself more power, knowing that Arthur has promised to do anything for her, should she bear him a son. This is ironic since he offered her joint rule of the kingdom when they were first wed and she refused.

8. Even Gwenhwyfar, usually devout and obedient, has doubts and moments of rebellion against this Christian religion, whose "God cares nothing for women—all his priests are men, and again and again the Scriptures tell us that women are the temptress and evil" (*Mists* 442). She concludes from this evidence that "that is why he does not hear" her prayers for a child (*Mists* 442).

9. Lancelet feels "bound in honor to try to make her [Elaine] as happy as he could" (605). Gwenhwyfar resents Elaine because she will have Lancelet's "sons and daughters" (603), and sometimes she feels that Elaine scorns her for her barrenness (546), but the queen does not attack Elaine's character, nor does she plot revenge against her.

10. This is, furthermore, a love that literally transcends time, since they have been reincarnated (*Mists* 104).

Chapter 6

Narrative Techniques

This chapter investigates the way conflicts are structured in Arthurian rewritings, as well as "who sees" and "who speaks."[1] The first section discusses the binary oppositions that traditionally drive the plot and affect the characterization in fantasy; I examine Gillian Bradshaw's and Fay Sampson's series for the ways these authors use and problematize such plot structures.[2] In the second section I consider authority and narration, examining the way Marion Zimmer Bradley and Fay Sampson shift between characters in the telling of their stories to avoid authoritarian judgements and to raise questions about the biases in all narratives.

GOOD VERSUS EVIL

Why are there only two sides to every story? In romance, conflict between these opposing sides creates the plot. Thus Rosemary Jackson, in her study of fantasy, notes that "romance narratives, especially classic fairy tales, represented all action unfolding under the influence of good or evil powers" (56). Mark Rose, speaking about science fiction and fantasy in *Alien Encounters: Anatomy of Science Fiction*, describes it this way: "At the core of all romance forms appears to be a Manichaean vision of the universe as a struggle between good and bad magic" (9). Like Jackson and Rose, Frederic Jameson identifies an "intimate and constitutive relationship between the form [of romance as a mode] itself . . . and this deep-rooted ideology" ("Magical Narratives" 140), which he calls "the conceptual opposition between good and evil" (140). Moreover, this ethically inflected opposition distinguishes romance. Jameson notes the absence of "the ethical opposition" in tragedy and comedy, although the latter usually places in opposition "youth and age" (*Political Unconscious* 116).

Thus opposition shapes many of our culture's fictional narratives; we accept that "a story needs conflict, desire or unhappiness to generate the energy required to launch it" (Peel 35). Narratologists confirm this requirement, claiming that "the structure of the fabula is determined by confrontation" (Bal, *Narratology* 16).[3] Binary opposition is the simplest form of confrontation; binary oppositions based on ethics (good and evil) pervade our fictions. As the comments of Jackson and Rose suggest, romance forms the basis for a variety of narratives, from fairy tales to science fiction, from medieval works to twentieth-century ones. Furthermore, Frederic Jameson links twentieth-century popular fiction to romance and follows Northrop Frye in exploring this mode as "the ultimate source and paradigm of all storytelling" (*Political Unconscious* 105).[4]

However, fictional narratives are not the only ones shaped by binary oppositions. Hélène Cixous, for example, suggests that binary thinking goes beyond "[m]yths, legends, books [to] [p]hilosophical systems. Everywhere (where) ordering intervenes, . . . a law organizes what is thinkable by oppositions" (64). Consequently, as Jameson observes, "the concept of evil is at one with the category of Otherness itself: evil characterizes whatever is radically different from me" ("Magical Narratives" 140). This division between Self and Other (or ours and theirs, or the Good Guys and the Bad Guys) is therefore not a characteristic just of fictional narratives, but of other cultural narratives, of which political rhetoric is perhaps the most noticeable example.[5]

However, recognition of the implications of such binaries leads to questions about their purposes and their influence. Jameson notes Nietzsche's work on ethics and Derrida's "unmasking and demystification" of binaries as examples of our culture's "reexamination" of such structures (*Political Unconscious* 114). Furthermore, feminists have also been concerned with the ramifications of such ethically inflected binaries in our society. Susan S. Lanser notes that "oppositional thinking has, of course, been sharply disadvantageous to women, as to other dominated groups. Binary pairs of the variety P / not-P are precisely the structures that create hierarchy" (359). Cixous connects such "organization by hierarchy . . . [to] male privilege" (64); the Other is often female or represented as feminine in contrast to a masculine Self or standard. Alice Jardine, following Cixous, also argues that "the dichotomies necessary to those [philosophical] structures have never been sexually neuter; they are the classically heterosexual couples of Western philosophy" (72). In her list of examples of such "couples," Jardine includes, besides "male" and "female," "Day" and "Night" (72).

Gillian Bradshaw and Fay Sampson explicitly use the binary opposition of Light versus Darkness in their rewritings of the Arthurian legend. In Bradshaw, the opposition is most noticeable in the first two books of the series; the last novel, which includes fewer fantastic elements, depends less on such binaries. Thus, there seems to be a correspondence, in this series at least, between the extent of the supernatural and the use of binary oppositions; this supports Jameson's claim that "the belief in good and evil is precisely a magical thought mode. . . . It is difficult to imagine a conflict of magical forces which would not be marked in some way as positive or negative . . . as a struggle between good and evil" ("Magical Narratives" 141). Nevertheless, Fay Sampson does try to imagine such a conflict; her series explicitly questions any simple identification of characters and sides with good or evil.

Gillian Bradshaw

"A fantasy is a story based on and controlled by an overt violation of what is generally accepted as possibility" (Irwin 4); Gillian Bradshaw's novels include references to magical beings, places, and objects that do "violate . . . the conventional norms of possibility" (Malmgren 139). References to the supernatural occur in all three novels, but supernatural powers participate extensively only in the action of *Hawk of May* and *Kingdom of Summer*. Moreover, the conflict in these novels takes place on different levels. It has mythic aspects, in the sense that it is a struggle for supremacy between two supernatural forces; this level requires the most fantastic elements. However, it also fits Frye's description of romances, for "the conflict . . . takes place in, or at any rate primarily concerns, our world" (*Anatomy* 187); Gwalchmai's vision of "the whole island, from the Orcades in the north to the southern cliffs" (*Hawk* 209) emphasizes that the battleground is this ordinary world of "forests, fields, mountains, rivers and proud cities" (*Hawk* 209). At another level, the conflict takes place within the individual as each person chooses the values by which she or he lives; this level requires the least fantastic elements, being more concerned with depicting the psychological states of the characters. Although Light and Good against Darkness and Evil remains the central conflict of the series, the characterization of this binary and the nature of the conflict vary with the changing use of the supernatural.

The supernatural appears early in *Hawk of May*, as Morgawse begins to teach Gwalchmai about "the characteristics of that universe that exists alongside of and within our own" (38). When Gwalchmai flees Morgawse, a magical boat rescues him: "No boat should have landed so at Llyn Gwalch. The current of the stream, combined with an undertow which was often fierce, pushed any floating things onto the rocks at the side. . . . I sensed the magic woven into its fabric" (77). This boat takes Gwalchmai to a part of that other universe, which he calls "the Plain of Joy" (79) or "Isle of the Blessed" (80). After this experience, he and others suspect that he is "not quite human" (115), but now "unalterably alien" (117). Gwalchmai's Otherworldly aura increases because of his horse, his sword, and his attitude in battle. Ceincaled is one of "the steeds of the Sidhe" (126), who can run faster and farther than any other horse; Caledvwlch is the sword Gwalchmai finds in the Isle of the Blessed, which "blazed, pure, cool and brilliant" with Light when he draws it (207). Furthermore, though he was an inept warrior before, after his return from the Isle he "goes mad in battle" (257–58) so that no one can stand against him. He accomplishes great feats and notices no wounds while this madness lasts.

In *Kingdom of Summer*, the action remains in the human world; there is no visit to an Otherworld. Nonetheless, supernatural forces work in the human realm. Gwalchmai remains "a little uncanny" (11); Rhys repeats the "numerous tales, of varying probability . . . told of [Gwalchmai]. He was said to have tamed one of the horses of the Fair Ones . . . to have an enchanted sword, and to triple his strength in battle" (11). Furthermore, Gwalchmai performs two important magical feats during the novel: he defeats Morgawse in a contest of wills and opposing powers (226–30), and he uses his sword's powers to heal Eivlin of Morgawse's curse (248). Rhys describes both acts in some detail; they can only be explained as an indication of the supernatural forces present and active in the human world of the novel.

During *Hawk of May* and *Kingdom of Summer*, therefore, two sides emerge, which can be charted as follows:

Type of Being	Good	Evil
Powers—no form	Light	Darkness
Supernatural beings	Lugh Ceincaled Taliesin (?)	queen of air and Darkness demons / shadows
Natural beings	Arthur Gwalchmai Gwynhwyfar Sion / Rhys Bedwyr	Morgawse Medraut Aldwulf Cerdic

The powers, Light and Darkness, are the supernatural forces opposed on the mythic level. The clearest description of the Light occurs when Gwalchmai leaves the Isle of the Blessed: "It seemed to me that a light like a new star burned behind the sea, beyond the horizon; and in that instant, I felt that I understood . . . to what I had pledged my sword" (*Hawk* 89). Neither of these powers is given any form.

Both powers have corporeal representatives, supernatural beings who appear to various characters (Lugh) or who work actively in the world (the queen of air and Darkness).[6] Lesser supernatural beings, like Ceincaled or the demons and shadows summoned by Morgawse and Aldwulf, assist mortals in the conflict. Taliesin, a mysterious figure who "foresaw in a vision" (*Shadow* 314) the fall of the realm, and who Gwalchmai thinks "had sung in Lugh's Hall" (*Hawk* 216), can be seen either as one of the supernatural figures or as another human with special powers.

Several of the characters I have classified as natural beings possess Otherworldly powers. Gwalchmai I have already discussed. Sion and Rhys both have prophetic dreams on occasion (*Hawk* 152–54, *Kingdom* 217). Aldwulf and Medraut both practice sorcery: Aldwulf, for example, bargains with demons for Arthur's death (*Hawk* 113), and Medraut assists his mother in the duel with Gwalchmai (*Kingdom* 226).

Morgawse, of course, is the most obvious instance of a mortal with supernatural powers. In the chart, I have indicated two characters, Morgawse and the queen of air and Darkness; for most of *Hawk of May* and *Kingdom of Summer* the two are indistinguishable. Lugh says that he "know[s] of one who is called the queen of air and Darkness, who is become Morgawse" (*Hawk* 82). In a bid for power, Morgawse "had summoned it [Darkness] as a servant for her hate, had welcomed its control when she controlled it, and everyday became more it and less herself" (*Hawk* 68–69). When Gwalchmai observes that she is not mortal (*Hawk* 115), he suggests that she is now only a physical shape that Dark powers use. After Gwalchmai defeats her, "like any other woman, she grew old" (*Kingdom* 230); this suggests that the two queens (supernatural and mortal) have been separated. It is this separation that allows Morgawse's death.

Although the two sides remain fixed in terms of membership,[7] the characters paired in opposition vary. Arthur and Morgawse form a pair of opposing leaders; each has the highest rank and deepest conviction of his or her side. In the supernatural duel, however, Gwalchmai opposes Morgawse (*Kingdom* 226–30), with Rhys in some ways acting as his second, in a way analogous to Medraut's support of Morgawse.[8] Gwalchmai also forms a pair with Medraut, as the two sons trained by Morgawse. In the Saxon camp, Gwalchmai pits his knowledge and faith against that of Aldwulf. Although there is never a face-to-face confrontation, Morgawse is also placed in opposition to Gwynhwyfar. For example, Gwalchmai recalls: "I had not really spoken to a woman since Morgawse, half-afraid of all of them for my mother's sake. Gwynhwyfar taught me to think differently" (*Hawk* 287–88). Gwynhwyfar, attempting to help Arthur deal with the problem of Medraut, observes, "Morgawse had wounded him more deeply than I could heal" (*Shadow* 58). Thus, at different times in the novels, different pairs of characters with similar qualities but opposing allegiances appear. This demonstrates that although the conflict is always between two sides, Light and Darkness, it is fought in different ways by different representatives.

The chart suggests the degree to which the first two novels ascribe gender to the binary opposition of Light and Darkness. The powers themselves generally are neuter. However, Lugh refers to "the high king, the Light who shines forever" (*Hawk* 82). This reference, combined with Morgawse's presence as the main villain, whether supernatural or natural, suggests an association between Light and male, Darkness and female. However, this association is not developed further. Men who follow Darkness, like Cerdic or Aldwulf, are not feminized; women like Gwynhwyfar follow Light. Morgawse dies near the end of *Kingdom of Summer* and Lugh does not reappear, so the conflict, in *In Winter's Shadow*, becomes one between non-gendered forces of Light and Darkness. Furthermore, the changed focus of the third novel makes the binary conflict more complex.

In Winter's Shadow uses far fewer fantastic elements than the preceding novels in the series. Memories of Morgawse motivate characters like Arthur, Gwalchmai, Agravain, and Medraut, but she herself is dead, not acting in the novel. Most importantly, Gwynhwyfar now narrates, and she has never met Morgawse. As a result, Morgawse's supernatural powers become a matter of "too much poetry, too much listening to tales" (42). Gwalchmai still appears, and with him mention of his reputation for Otherworldliness: "At times . . . he looked as though he had stepped from the hollow hills" (41). As with Morgawse, though, his magical powers remain understood, remembered from the previous books, rather than displayed, partly because Gwynhwyfar never sees him in battle.

This novel's approach to the fantastic is best understood by examining

Gwynhwyfar's description of Gwalchmai's funeral. When his horse and his sword disappear after the burial, Gwynhwyfar first suggests a rational explanation: "I feared for a time that someone might have stolen it, it and the sword" (291). She then gives a reason to doubt this explanation, for "such a horse, let alone such a sword, was too fine to be mistaken for another or pass unremarked, and they were never heard of again, even in rumor" (291). She is forced to consider the possibility of a supernatural explanation, wondering whether the horse may have returned to "a day that was now entirely separate from Earth" (291). She does not insist that this is the true explanation, and her report of the horse's and sword's origins is distanced: she does not assert it, but only repeats what she has been told, that "Gwalchmai had always claimed that the sword, and the horse, had come from the Otherworld" (291). The fantastic mystery is, in the end, dismissed: "However that may be, it went, leaving only a few hoof marks around the new grave. And I did not have much time to worry about it" (291). The supernatural, as this passage shows, affects Gwynhwyfar's life very little and therefore hardly appears in her narrative at all.

The treatment of battles also exemplifies this difference between the novels in their use of the fantastic. In *Kingdom of Summer*, the climactic battle is fought with will and magic and Light clearly wins. In *In Winter's Shadow*, the battle is fought by humans with human weapons, and no one wins decisively. Gwynhwyfar's duties in scrounging supplies for the army and organizing the retrieval of the dead and wounded add detail to what could be an account of a historical battle. The disappearance of Arthur, in many Arthurian works accounted for by mystical transportation to a magical isle, is rationalized; Gwynhwyfar finally admits that "he was lost in the cavalry charge . . . I never recognized the body because the charge went over it and it was mutilated beyond recognition" (*Shadow* 312).

The mythic conflict between Light and Darkness thus recedes in importance in *In Winter's Shadow*, and even the physical human battle is reported, not experienced. This leaves internal conflicts to propel the plot. Such conflicts did occur in the earlier novels. Gwalchmai, for example, expresses doubt about the source and effect of his powers in battle: "How, in that mingling of human madness and divine passion, to distinguish between Light and Darkness?" (*Hawk* 137). Arthur admits that he is "in Darkness" (*Hawk* 299) because of his sin with Morgawse, and that this has made him misjudge Gwalchmai. *In Winter's Shadow*, however, focusses exclusively on such conflicts. Gwynhwyfar's struggle to help Arthur create and maintain the empire provides the main action, but she also gives insight into Arthur's, Bedwyr's, and Gwalchmai's personal conflicts. No supernatural object or being warns characters when they make a choice that leads to Darkness, as the sword warned Gwalchmai about Aldwulf's plans (*Hawk* 112) or the horse warned him against Morgawse (*Kingdom* 123). The reader, with Gwynhwyfar at the end of *In Winter's Shadow*, realizes that "even the best intentions of those devoted to Light can create Darkness" (243).

Moreover, characters associated with Darkness can have redeeming moments and Gwynhwyfar witnesses one of these. When she sees Medraut's reaction to news of Gwalchmai's death, she observes, "For all that Gwalchmai had said about his brother, I had never expected that under his hatred and his many masks Medraut might still love anyone. But there could be no mistaking the look with which he had greeted my news" (*Shadow* 303). For a brief moment, "the darkness could not completely enchain his will" (*Hawk* 188), just as Gwalchmai had always hoped.

Bradshaw thus suggests that "the world . . . is mixed, good and evil together, and there was no simple and clear struggle" (*Hawk* 188). Like our own reality, it is "a complicated world, where to act might be to act wrong, and not to act be even worse" (*Kingdom* 87). Bradshaw uses a binary opposition of Light and goodness versus Darkness and evil, but her characters prove that, if one is human at all, one incorporates aspects of both sides, and the right course of action is never easily distinguished.

Fay Sampson

Of all the Arthurian novels considered here, Fay Sampson's *Daughter of Tintagel* series problematizes binaries most. I make this claim because Sampson uses binaries such as Light versus Dark or Healer versus Destroyer throughout the series, but she explicitly questions their use and tries to subvert them. This questioning and the assertion that balance is necessary, rather than one or the other of the opposing positions, allow the reader to recognize the way our society incorporates binaries in many of its implicit judgements. However, Sampson's series does not itself escape the trap of binary assumptions.

The author's note at the beginning of each book in the series indicates a theme that will shape all of the events: "In physics, Dark Matter forms an unseen world that is the inverse of the matter we observe. The two were created to exist in equal proportions. Together they hold the universe in balance. But when they come into contact, the result is mutual destruction" (*Woman* vii). Sampson thus suggests that she will be using binaries, particularly one of light versus darkness, to explore the idea of balance and harmony.

Since Morgan's story is "the Dark Matter of Britain" (*Woman* vii), Morgan is associated with darkness. Other characters are associated with light. Morgan says, "When Arthur stands in the sun, then Morgan will rise from the dark" (*Nun* 178), emphasizing Arthur's link to light and her own association with darkness. Urien also plays this role; Taliesin sees Urien and Morgan as "two chieftains . . . light and darkness" (*Taliesin* 6). This association of Urien with light is appropriate, since he, of all the sons-in-law of Gorlois, is completely loyal to Arthur. These associations do not simply depend upon gender, however. Bryvyth is also associated with light, since "her vision . . . was too high, too wide, too full of sunlight" (*Herself* 41) to be aware of Tintagel's other practices of worship. And Modred is, like Morgan, called "Black" (*Taliesin* 15).

However, other binaries *are* connected to gender. Gwennol sets up a binary of destruction and procreation that associates the genders with specific sides of that binary. She "wonder[s] if that's all life is. Breeding and killing. The men to kill. The women to breed" (*Woman* 24). Men's power to wound versus women's power to heal occurs in the notion of reinstating the old society where the queen was the leader and could "heal the wounded land" (*Nun* 233). The accomplishments of Morgan and Arthur maintain this association, for her "miracles of healing have restored whole families' lives; his battles have altered the landscape of history" (*Herself* 289). Arthur's joy in battle and Morgan's role as healer reinforce gendered binary divisions.

The binaries of destruction or healing, men or women, become associated with the metaphor of the sword and scabbard. On the physical level, the properties of these items remain the same as in most versions of the legend. The sword makes Arthur invincible in war; he can defeat any opponent, or any number of opponents, as long as he holds Caliburn. The scabbard makes him invulnerable to wounds; if he is injured he will heal immediately. In the final battle at Camlann, these two magical properties play an important part; Arthur still carries the sword and therefore defeats Modred; however, he does not have the scabbard, and the wound that Modred inflicts is fatal. This incident reinforces what we already know; the two items are meant to work together, for the magic of one complements the other.

Morgan's use of sword and scabbard as metaphors to describe the way she thinks Britain should be ruled also emphasizes their complementary nature: "If he [Arthur] consents, we shall rule together, as equals. Sword and scabbard. The earth in balance" (*Nun* 134). That the sword refers to Arthur is clear from several uses of the metaphor. Morgan and Uther can never be reconciled because "the loss of Arthur lay between them like an unsheathed sword" (*Nun* 152), a threat that neither of them can forgive or forget. Arthur himself prefers to be associated with the sword. When he faces Modred at the end, he legitimizes his claim to the throne by reciting lists of warriors (and thus, the number of swords) who support him (*Herself* 233–34).[9] Arthur does not miss the scabbard when Morgan steals it, thinking it merely misplaced (*Smith* 237). He also refuses to acknowledge any need for Morgan, or for her skills. He tells her: "Healing is your job. Fighting is mine. Take the scabbard and leave the sword to me" (*Smith* 240). He thus demarcates boundaries between men's and women's work.

Smith reinforces these boundaries, but he also makes observations that undermine them. He feels that he could have remained a smith, a masculine man, if he had met Merlyn instead of Morgan: "I could have been Arthur's man now, instead of Morgan's woman. . . . It had hung on such a small thing either way, like a sword balanced on an anvil. . . . And I'd tumbled off on Morgan's side, with the women" (*Smith* 154). Morgan herself subscribes to this view of men's versus women's work. She sees the battle as being between Gorlois's daughters and the Pendragons and Merlyn. Thus, when Nimue disposes of Merlyn, Morgan asserts that no longer is "the world in balance. Sword and scabbard. It was always Merlyn and Morgan. Male and female. The left and right. And you [Nimue] have broken that" (*Smith* 255). Although Morgan suggests that this is the way it has always been, Smith's observations of the relationship between Nimue and Merlyn suggest that Nimue has been the opposing force. Smith had thought himself caught between Merlyn and Morgan, but "it was the women, Nimue and Morgan, against each other, all along" (*Smith* 132). Taliesin, too, makes assumptions about the men's being on one side and the women's being on the other, only to revise his opinion.

Standing with Morgan, Gwenhyvar, and others to greet Arthur's return from a raid, he "thought [they] were the female party welcoming back [their] fighting men" (*Taliesin* 132), but then realizes that Nimue and her women are part of the war party.

Morgan's association of men, sword, destruction versus women, scabbard, healing also is revealed to be a simplification. Arthur does try to kill the infant Modred, his son by his sister, Margawse; he therefore represents violence and destructiveness, "the male imperative," according to Morgan (*Herself* 73). But Arthur uses the sword to unite Britain against the Saxon invaders; "the killing sword may also win . . . life" (*Herself* 123), and its power is, from the British perspective at least, constructive. Likewise, Morgan pictures herself as the scabbard, or the healing, fertile, feminine principle. However, the power of healing is double-edged. Morgan refuses Merlyn's gift of a knife because it is "a man's weapon" (*Nun* 64), but she then asks, "Which . . . is worse—the power to wound, or to have the power to heal and not to use it?" (*Nun* 64). Gwennol, too, tells us that Morgan's power can be used "[t]o heal or to harm" (*Woman* 63). Moreover, Morgan asserts that "there is only a fine line between new-won life and sudden death" (*Herself* 123).

The series, then, alternates between views of Morgan as Healer and as Destroyer. From the beginning, people like Gwennol and Luned suspect that Morgan will choose the power to harm rather than to heal. Gwennol does not whisper her into the mysteries at first because of this (*Woman* 63). Luned assumes that when one of two sick cows dies, it is because Morgan poisoned it. Morgan protests that she "had only enough of the herbs . . . to heal one of them" (*Nun* 128); whether she did choose to heal or to harm remains unknown. Luned in general remains convinced that "Morgan is the Devourer. She destroys everything she touches" (*Nun* 245), including Luned. Although Smith generally thinks of Morgan as a destructive force, he recognizes that others have benefitted from her skill. Her own people, in Urien's kingdom, "are afraid of Morgan, but they love her too in a queer sort of way. She's healed many, when no one else could" (*Smith* 207). Moreover, this desire to heal people is not just a means to get power. Smith observes that Morgan "keeps far more [herbs] than Nimue. . . . But then, Nimue isn't known for a healer, is she? You don't find a rabble of poor and sick at her gate asking for help. What Nimue wants is the power from them" (*Smith* 258). Although Morgan is also obsessed with power, she uses her skills for more humanitarian reasons as well.

Consequently, binaries in the series are more complex than they first appear. Sampson seems to reinforce old dichotomies and associations, on the one hand, yet she undermines them on the other. Characters' observations and assertions, such as Smith's and Taliesin's remarks about being left with the women, are contradicted by their own experience. Women's work does seem to be herbs, healing, and seduction, yet Morgan is often likened to a man, and Nimue's women fight in wars. Sampson thus suggests that we need to get beyond "the vocabulary of the battlefield" (*Taliesin* 21) that constructs opposites and puts them in competition. Morgan's "darkness [is also a] burning, like a lantern behind a shutter, like a smothered fire, like the stars in the darkest night of storm" (*Taliesin* 21). Matters are not "Either / Or," but can be "Both / And."

Religion in the series emphasizes the need to abandon metaphors of opposition. Morgan's religion revolves around "wholeness. She [the Goddess] did not give birth to a false dichotomy of Either / Or. Her ancient wisdom embraces Both / And" (*Herself* 43). The metaphor of harvest allows for Both / And, since it incorporates "birth, fullness, and death" (*Herself* 61) in an endless cycle.[10] However, although Morgan asserts her belief in this principle, she continues to operate within binary assumptions. And although Sampson makes neither Morgan or Arthur play simply one role, Healer or Destroyer, the final scenes of the series continue to promote metaphors of opposition. Arthur, mortally wounded, can be saved by Morgan, but she will only heal him if he gives up Caliburn. After he does so, his sisters sail with him toward an Otherworld realm. Morgan assures us that "in Avalon the sword will meet its scabbard" (308) and thus all binaries will be united or dissolved.

However, there are problems with this scene and the resolution that it proposes. First, from a philosophical perspective, the resolution of binaries is displaced from the "real" world of the story to the Otherworld; this suggests that no matter how hard one tries to achieve balance, it can only happen in an Utopian afterlife. Second, from the perspective of plot, Arthur's relinquishing of the sword is reluctant and his acceptance of his sisters seems incomplete. His last words are accusations of treachery; "you have cheated me," he cries to Morgan when he realizes the ship will take him away from this world (300). Moreover, Morgan's words when Arthur gives up the sword, "he is disarmed, and I am empowered at last" (296), suggest a reversal of the extremes rather than a union.

Thus, Sampson plays with binaries and tries to undermine the idea of Either / Or, but the binaries and our traditional ways of thinking about them are not deconstructed completely.[11] As Taliesin recognizes, such metaphors of "male and female, sun and moon, day and night" are "clichés" (*Taliesin* 80). As clichés they carry with them traditional assumptions: "they speak of greater and less, of borrowed light. They make one inferior to the other" (*Taliesin* 80). He claims that they should be seen as intertwined; "light and darkness . . . are two halves of a whole, not good and bad as you have been taught to understand it" (*Taliesin* 22). What Taliesin, and I think Sampson through him, wants to convey, is a vision of "strengths rooted in separate soils, growing together to embrace and uphold each other" (*Taliesin* 80). The problem is that even these metaphors of union insist that there are two opposites to join, instead of multiple possibilities. The binary remains the basis for the way of describing the world.

Although neither Bradshaw nor Sampson dispenses with binary oppositions, they nevertheless question the simplification such binaries impose on our complex world. They accomplish this by making their use of binary metaphors (Light versus Darkness) obvious, and by having their characters realize that such simplified descriptions of the world do not work; the conflict always turns out to be more complex, and the sides not so easy to label. Sampson's series in particular extends awareness of that simplifying process to binaries that are gendered and thus questions some of the traditional associations made about, for example, men and violence, women and nurturing.

SHIFTING FOCALIZATION AND MULTIPLE NARRATORS

"Between the story and the reader is the narrator, who controls what will be told and how it will be perceived" (Martin 9), but narrators can claim different degrees of authority and make more or less obvious the biases that shape "what will be told." Furthermore, the genre of a work can influence the type of narrator and the degree of authority that she or he has. Rosemary Jackson, in *Fantasy: The Literature of Subversion*, suggests that in "marvellous narrative[s]," such as fairy tales or romances, "the narrator is impersonal and has become an authoritative, knowing voice. There is a minimum of emotional involvement in the tale—that voice is positioned with absolute confidence and certainty towards events" (33). Jackson goes on to claim that fantasy disrupts such an authoritarian voice, for in "fantastic narratives . . . the narrator is no clearer than the protagonist about what is going on, nor about interpretation" (34). Judi M. Roller, in *The Politics of the Feminist Novel*, implies that a similar narrative technique helps create feminist stories. Roller observes that, "for the female author of a feminist novel particularly, the assumption of authority poses a special problem. There is a marked inconsistency involved in adopting an authoritative posture while at the same time attacking authoritarianism" (34), and through it patriarchal hierarchies. Roller identifies two methods of storytelling employed in feminist novels: what she terms the "autobiographical point of view" (35) and "a number of speakers" (38).

In autobiography, or "pseudo-autobiography" (Roller 35), characters tell their own stories. This device avoids an "authoritarian tone" (35) because "speaking about oneself does not as easily lead to a judgmental tone as does speaking about someone else" (35). Thus, as I mentioned in the previous chapter, the condemnations of Gwenhyfar in *In Winter's Shadow*, instead of being an authoritative verdict on her actions, signal her own feelings of responsibility, a responsibility that other characters deny. This is not to say that no judgements are ever made by first-person narrators: "Of course, a first-person narrator comments on other characters, but the reader weighs such judgements with full knowledge of the narrator's perspective" (Roller 35). The narrator speaks for himself or herself as opposed to speaking automatically from a "God-like" position of authority.

However, authors can endow narrators with authority. As there are fallible narrators, so are there narrators whose versions of events we trust; their judgements of situations and other characters seem to be valid and unarguable. For example, we are invited to believe Mary Stewart's narrator, Merlin. Through his narration, he reveals his humanity, for he is at times lonely and vulnerable, but also quick-witted and daring. As a result of such traits, he is a sympathetic character whose nature inspires confidence in his sincerity. But Stewart uses Merlin's special powers to ensure belief in his judgement. Although she uses "historical detail to rationalize the supernatural" aspects of Merlin's career (Fries, "Rationalization" 261),[12] he still has visions and at times the god speaks through him. His status as vehicle for the god gives him authority among other characters in the world of the novels, but also authority as a narrator; he literally sees and knows what mere mortals cannot. As Jeanie Watson observes, he is "a voice through which the god can speak. In the course of the novels, however, Merlin, who is the word of power, becomes so closely associated with the Word that is God that he also becomes that Word and, thus, . . . [there is an] identification of Merlin with divinity" (82). As a result, his narration carries authority, whether he recounts events or makes judgements on other characters such as Morgause and Morgan.[13]

Furthermore, Merlin's authority is unchallenged in Stewart's series. His older self narrates the majority of events, and his younger self focalizes the first three novels. Thus we hear the story from him and experience the events through his character. This changes in *The Wicked Day*, which has an unidentified narrator with focalization through, primarily, Mordred. However, only about a quarter of this fourth novel involves events that Merlin has already told, and even then we are given more detail rather than contradictory judgements. Stewart's series, therefore, illustrates the importance of the second trait Roller identifies.

Using "a number of speakers" (38), Roller asserts, means that "the author can underscore a prismatic view of the world" (38). The biases that influence the judgements one narrator makes become more obvious when other narrators, with their own sets of biases, make different or similar judgements. However, an author does not have to change narrators to achieve this "prismatic . . . world" (Roller 38), but can change the agent of focalization instead. Focalization indicates "who sees" and experiences events; shifting focalization[14] between several characters, as Neil Randall suggests, allows readers to "form . . . an understanding of the character of the focalizant" while also co-ordinating events and contributing to suspense (42). Marion Zimmer Bradley uses shifting focalization in *The Mists of Avalon*; Fay Sampson uses five narrators who focalize their own stories in *Daughter of Tintagel*; both authors use these techniques to help create feminist rewritings of the Arthurian legend.

Marion Zimmer Bradley

Throughout *The Mists of Avalon*, there are italicized passages in which "Morgaine speaks"[15] and reflects on the events told by the heterodiegetic narrator of the rest of the novel.[16] These passages provide a frame for the story, for "Morgaine speaks" the Prologue. There she informs the reader: "I will tell this tale" (x); the rest of the novel, then, recounts the events of her lifetime. In the other italicized passages, her reflections on events provide valuable information about her. For example, her relations with other characters become more clear. She reveals the origin of her feelings for Arthur when she tells us how at first she "would have killed the crying thing [the baby Arthur] and thrown him over the cliffs" (109) because of jealousy; she also remembers her decision that he was hers "to look after" (110) and love. In another section, she thinks back on her wedding and stresses the importance of Uriens's "kindness" (568), though later she will despise him for not supporting her efforts to remind Arthur of his vows to Avalon

(717). The italicized passages, therefore, help reveal the complex nature of relationships between characters.

However, these passages serve other purposes as well. First, Bradley often uses them as transitions, to indicate when a period of time elapses. Thus the second such passage (108–12) moves the action from the time of Arthur's conception to a time when he is six years old, mentioning intervening events like Uther and Igraine's marriage (108), Arthur's birth (109), and Morgause's wedding of Lot (110). In the third such passage (136–37), "seven times Beltane-eve came and went" (136); Morgaine here summarizes the time spent during her training as a priestess. Two other sections (566–70, 588–91) each advance the time of the action by one year. Second, Morgaine sometimes "speaks" in order to elaborate on events. When she returns from the fairy world, an italicized passage contains musings on the nature of time, so that the reader knows that although Morgaine spent "no fewer than five and no more than thirteen" days there, in the outer world "some five years passed" (407). The reasons for Morgaine's decision to have her baby in Morgause's court appear in another section (230–31). Third, some of these passages create suspense through foreshadowing. Because the Morgaine who "speaks" is older, she knows the outcome of events and can hint at the consequences of her younger self's actions. Thus, she remarks that "Gwenhwyfar had her revenge" (544) two years after Morgaine arranged Lancelet's marriage to Elaine; the nature of that revenge is only revealed two chapters later, when Gwenhwyfar arranges Morgaine's marriage to Uriens (564). Moreover, each passage can function in more than one way; in the example of Gwenhwyfar's revenge cited, Morgaine's words move the events along by two years as well as foreshadowing coming events.

The shifting of focalization between characters has complementary effects on the action of the novel. Changing focalization overcomes the limits of any one character's knowledge. For example, in Chapter 20 of "The Mistress of Magic" (222–30), both Morgaine and Viviane focalize the action; Bradley thus communicates Viviane's political purposes, which Morgaine does not completely understand, as well as Morgaine's despair, the extent of which Viviane does not completely understand. The first chapter of "The King Stag" (453–74) is focalized through Morgause; since she has raised Gwydion (later called Mordred), her perceptions of him supply information on his character and his relationship to her. No other woman in the book has access to that information, and it explains some of his later actions.

Shifting focalization also tends to slow climactic moments, as they are focalized through different characters. The events leading up to and including Arthur and Gwenhwyfar's wedding celebrations (Chapters 3 through 6 of "The High Queen") are focalized through Igraine, Gwenhwyfar, and Morgaine. This emphasizes the significance of the event, and the different reasons for its importance to these particular women. Morgaine and Gwenhwyfar focalize the appearance of the grail (Chapters 9 and 10 in "The Prisoner in the Oak"), showing the event from the perspectives of both participant and observer, believer in the Goddess and believer in Christ.

Furthermore, shifting the focalization also creates suspense. After Morgaine "took horse, and rode eastward through the hills" (327), no one knows what happened to her: "She is not in Avalon. Nor is she in Tintagel with Igraine, nor yet at the court of Lot of Orkney" (337). Only when Morgaine once again focalizes the action (some seventy pages later) does the reader discover where she has been. Meanwhile, four chapters are focalized through Gwenhwyfar and Viviane. This supplies details about events in the kingdom of which Morgaine is unaware, and it also provides suspense. The reader, with Viviane, wonders whether Morgaine "might have been captured by one of the marauders or masterless men who throng the country—she might have lost her memory or have been raped, murdered, flung into a ditch somewhere" (337). Because of her privileged position in the narrative as protagonist, Morgaine's death seems unlikely, but her disappearance as focalizing agent arouses curiosity in the reader, just as her disappearance from the world of the novel causes speculation among other characters.

As in the case of the italicized passages, the shifts in focalization can create more than one effect, and they can work in combination with the italicized passages to create those effects. For example, Morgaine's comment on Gwenhwyfar's revenge, mentioned earlier, acts as a transition and as foreshadowing. In addition, the shifting of focalization between Gwenhwyfar and Morgaine in the chapters that follow (Chapters 7 and 8 of "The King Stag") slows the action (most of Chapter 7 concerns the revelation that Morgaine had borne Arthur's son) and provides both Gwenhwyfar's and Morgaine's reaction to that revelation. Furthermore, it works out the foreshadowed revenge: Gwenhwyfar realizes, though Arthur never does, that Morgaine agreed to marry into the house of North Wales thinking it was Accolon, not his father Uriens, who would be her husband.

The most important effect of the shifting focalization for the feminist status of *The Mists of Avalon*, however, is the way "the technique of focalization, through its internalization, forces an understanding of the character of the focalizant" (Randall 42). Throughout the novel, Morgaine, Gwenhwyfar, Igraine, Viviane, Morgause, Niniane, and Nimue focalize parts of the story. Not all of these women focalize equal amounts of the narrative: Morgaine and Gwenhwyfar are the focalizing agents in thirty-one and twenty chapters or partial chapters, respectively, followed by Igraine in eleven, Viviane in eight, Morgause in seven, and Niniane and Nimue in two each. This division of the focalizing reinforces Morgaine's status as protagonist, and Gwenhwyfar's importance as a character.

Nevertheless, the access given to a variety of women's perceptions of events affects the reader's perception of the conflicts portrayed in the novel. "In general," as Wallace Martin observes, "our sympathies are enlisted by those whose thoughts we know" (146); shifting focalization means that we get a greater understanding of what feelings, ambitions, and confusions drive all of the women to act as they do. Viviane, after being accused by Morgaine of believing herself to be the Goddess and infallible, "wonder[s] if she was, after all, what Morgaine thought her—drunk with power, believing that all things were at her command to play with as she thought good" (191). Such a moment of self-doubt communicates Viviane's difficulties in filling the dual roles of priestess and aunt to Morgaine. Similarly, Gwenhwyfar's focalizing of certain events, such as her abduction by Meleagrant, makes her character more complex; she has many unsympathetic qualities, but she also can have a "flash of grim humor" (515) in a desperate situation. Consequently, Bradley creates not just one fully developed woman in *Mists*, but several, all with strengths and weaknesses, sympathetic traits and unsympathetic ones. The communities that these women form, then, represent a coming together of equals. Furthermore, these different perspectives prevent Morgaine from being an authoritative voice. She has narrative predominance, but her perspective does not completely control the reader's perceptions; other focalizers of events interrogate her interpretations.

Fay Sampson

Fay Sampson's retelling of the legend takes five books to complete; they are, in order, *Wise Woman's Telling, White Nun's Telling, Black Smith's Telling, Taliesin's Telling*, and *Herself*. Each of the first four books tells a segment of Morgan's life. Although the story focusses on Morgan throughout, Sampson uses a different narrator for each book. The changing of narrators performs some of the same functions as the shifting focalization in *The Mists of Avalon*. Gwennol and Luned, the narrators of *Wise Woman's Telling* and *White Nun's Telling*, respectively, foreshadow future events at the ends of their narratives. Gwennol refers to the nuns' disgrace and expulsion from Tintagel, as well as Morgan's marriage and Arthur's reappearance (*Woman* 229); the first occurs late in *White Nun's Telling*; the other two do not happen until the third book of the series. Luned believes, looking at her hands, that she knows how Morgan plans to destroy Arthur (*Nun* 245); this foreshadows Luned's errand to Arthur with the poisoned cloak in *Black Smith's Telling* (268–72). Suspense can also be created by the change in narrators; as each tells her / his own story as well as Morgan's, it is sometimes a while before the new narrator relates the foreshadowed events. This is true of the nuns' expulsion and Morgan's marriage, but also true of the climactic battle of the series. *Taliesin's Telling* ends with Urien's and the remnant of Arthur's army's searching for their king, but *Herself* retells all of Morgan's life story before revealing the events at Camlann.

As different agents of focalization in *Mists* supply more information about events than any one character could, so, too, do the narrators of *Daughter of Tintagel* provide different opinions and assessments of events and characters. In particular, the various narrators present different versions of the "truth" of Morgan's character, for the narrators all have different relationships with her. Each novel, therefore, functions as a dramatic monologue; Sampson develops the character of Morgan through the narrators' observations, but she also develops the character of each narrator through the mannerisms displayed when telling the story.

What these narrators reveal about themselves in some cases creates suspicion about the trustworthiness of their stories. For example, the nun, Luned, calls Morgan "the Destroyer"; she characterizes Morgan as evil, and as manipulative. Luned blames the destruction of her dreams on Morgan's evil will, but Luned's tale reveals the excessive pride and selfishness of the nun. She claims to love Morgan, yet Morgan accuses her of loving only what could benefit her and give her more power (*Nun* 203). Luned also blames Bryvyth for placing too much trust in her, saying that the abbess "should have seen how great a danger I was in" (*Nun* 159); however, if Luned had not been so ambitious, she would have fully confessed to Bryvyth the degree of influence the old ways held at Tintagel. Similarly, Teilo Smith blames Morgan for his transformation from a smith, and representative of the god, to Woman, and servant of Morgan. He admits, at times, to over-reaching himself, but he always moves from that admission of responsibility for his actions to blaming Morgan for them: "I must have been bewitched to think I could match myself against Morgan. That's it. It was her doing. She'd put her spell on me, there in her castle. How else do you think a man of my wisdom would have done what I did, and in such a way? I was forced to it" (*Smith* 53). The "spell" that really affects Smith is his own lust for power, and his own arrogance. He is the one who interprets Morgan's words in a certain way; he chooses to use "woman's" arts of herblore to impress her instead of his own skills with metals. Furthermore, his wife's death, which he attributes to Morgan's curse, can more prosaically be explained by Smith's own carelessness. Having "brewed, and rightly spoken over" the poison, he leaves the pots unwashed "in a corner by the fire with a bit of sacking over them" (*Smith* 55). Given the strength of the potion, it is possible that Annis simply found and handled the pots in some way and therefore died. Such examples reveal that those characters, the nun and the blacksmith, who most harshly condemn Morgan as evil exhibit excessive self-pity, which makes their criticisms of Morgan suspect. They *need* her to be evil so they will not have to accept responsibility for their own actions.

The series, then, foregrounds the reader's dependence on intertextuality; as we read each novel we compare the new narrator's perspective of Morgan with those of previous narrators, trying to shape the contradictory information into a coherent picture of the character. But every time we read a new version of the Arthurian legend we must compare, contrast, and recreate our image of the characters; each new version is, in this sense, a metafiction.[17] Sampson makes this process obvious, since the reader must try to reconcile contrasting views of narrators within a single series. This also makes explicit the way characterizations develop, and the fact that these characterizations are not disinterested, but depend on the motives of the teller of the story.

Herself, the fifth book, goes back to the beginning, briefly retelling the major events from Morgan's point of view. After such a range of characters expressing such a range of views, it is tempting to see Morgan's version of her story as the one "true" story, and two features of the narrative confirm this tendency. First, the change in title style suggests that this is the true version; instead of "Morgan's Telling," whose structural similarity to the other titles would suggest that it is just another version, it is called *Herself*, which suggests that the true self will be revealed. Second, Morgan retells events from the beginning; the fact that she is the only one to have access to the entire span of her life reinforces the tendency to see hers as a corrective to the previous texts.

However, Morgan reveals some of the same character traits that made the nun's and the blacksmith's versions suspect. For example, when Morgan retells the episode of the cloak that she sends to Arthur, she claims to have worked on it for weeks without ever realizing that her sister was putting highly poisonous thorns in it (*Herself* 132–36). She denies all responsibility, but her explanation of events seems incredible. She characterizes Gwenhyvar and Nimue as evil, shallow, power-hungry women, but we know she is jealous of their closeness to Arthur. Thus, the series keeps in suspense the reader's desire to know the "true" story, by using unreliable narrators and conflicting versions, but also through explicitly commenting on the process of character development.

For there is a second narrator in *Herself*. Chapters written in normal type feature Morgan retelling the story that we have already seen in the previous books of the series. Chapters written in italicized script feature another narrator, whose name is also Morgan. She is, if you like, a meta-Morgan, an embodiment of the idea of the character separate from the supposedly flesh-and-blood character who narrates the other half of the book. Indeed, she is supposedly separate from all literary representations of her, and it is precisely those representations that she discusses. She recounts her many appearances in folktale, romance, and other forms of literature. She comments, often sarcastically, on the changes made to her character over the years. For example, on the *Vulgate Cycle*, in which Lancelot calls Morgan "the most disloyal woman in all the world," she remarks, "This, from the man who is committing adultery with his king's wife" (150). Such comments question the logic motivating the depictions, over the centuries, of Morgan as purely evil enchantress. They also insist that portrayals of characters are not neutral but are created by deliberate choices of the author for particular purposes. Therefore, it is not just these five narrators in this one series who are biased, but all tellers of tales, for "authorship is the art of selection" (*Herself* 261), and "others will always doctor the evidence they find uncomfortable" (*Herself* 24). Morgan suggests that in her story, too, "some editing . . . will clearly be necessary" (*Herself* 1) to make it acceptable. Even Fay Sampson, the meta-Morgan admits, "is using me here for her own ends" (*Herself* 306). The series' concern with Morgan's characterization and the meta-Morgan's approval of *The Mists of Avalon*, which she calls "the feminist version" (*Herself* 305), suggest that Fay Sampson's "end" is the creation of a feminist rewriting of the legend.

I am not arguing that the use of different focal characters or narrators automatically makes a text feminist; rather, these are techniques that can be used in the service of feminist ideals. Bradley focalizes events through several female characters; that, in conjunction with the communities these women form, makes her work a feminist rewriting. Likewise, Sampson uses different narrators to question explicitly the interests that shape the way stories are told; a brief comparison to Bradshaw's use of multiple narrators illustrates the importance of that questioning.

Gillian Bradshaw, like Sampson, uses a different narrator for each book: Gwalchmai for *Hawk of May*, Rhys ap Sion for *Kingdom of Summer*, and Gwynhwyfar for *In Winter's Shadow*. As mentioned earlier in this chapter, these narrators represent different degrees of access to the supernatural. Gwalchmai visits the Otherworld and has Otherworldly powers; Rhys witnesses supernatural events and participates in them, though he has no special powers himself;[18] Gwynhwyfar neither witnesses nor participates in the supernatural. The differences between these narrators, then, help the series move from fantasy toward historical fiction.[19] In addition, Bradshaw's use of these three narrators allows her to focalize the struggle between Light and Darkness through people of different classes; Gwynhwyfar is an empress and Gwalchmai is a nobleman, and Rhys is a freeborn farmer who becomes a servant. Such differences indicate that Arthur's vision of the kingdom is shared by people with different backgrounds. This adds significance and scope to the conflict; it is not simply a quarrel between rival aristocrats.

However, these narrators do not differ on fundamental issues: all side with the Light, and all wish to follow Arthur and defeat Morgawse. Furthermore, each tells a different section of the story. Unlike in Sampson's series, in Bradshaw's trilogy there is no overlap; events are narrated once from one perspective. Bradshaw, as a result, does not address the problem of who gets to tell the story. In contrast, Sampson foregrounds this issue and illustrates the important connections between who speaks and what the story says.

CONCLUSION

The use of binaries and focalizing agents or multiple narrators in these Arthurian rewritings disrupts the conventions of popular fiction in two main ways. First, the use of the binary of Light / Good and Dark / Evil in Bradshaw's and Sampson's novels reveals such binaries to be inadequate to describe the way the world works. As a result, these rewritings, especially Sampson's, make this structural principle of much popular fiction obvious and questions that principle. Second, the use of multiple focalizing agents in Bradley and multiple narrators in Sampson suggests that there is not one, "true" story possible; every character has her or his own perspective of events and sees or tells the story slightly differently. Sampson explicitly connects this narrative strategy with feminist politics by showing that stories told about Morgan make ideological choices when they represent her as old, ugly, incompetent, and evil, or when they restore her original connections with divinity, healing, and wisdom. Both Bradley's novel and Sampson's series question narrative authority, and within the worlds depicted by the rewritings similar types of authority are shown to operate in all political and social narratives.

NOTES

1.   These phrases appear in Gérard Genette's *Narrative Discourse* when he is distinguishing between his concept of focalization and the concept of narration.

2.   Bradshaw and Sampson both use the binary of Light and Darkness as a metaphor that structures their novels. Although Marion Zimmer Bradley's series involves a conflict between Roman Christian Britain and Celtic pagan Avalon, she does not construct the novel around a binary metaphor as the other two authors do, and I therefore do not discuss *The Mists of Avalon* in the section on binaries.

3. Mieke Bal refers to William Hendricks for this part of her analysis of narratological methodology. She notes that "although it has not been proven that this [confrontation] is true of all fabulas, it is probably possible in most instances to view the actors as two contrasting groups" (*Narratology* 16–17).

4. In *The Secular Scripture: A Study of the Structure of Romance*, Frye comments that "the bulk of popular literature," whether Greek romances or twentieth-century detective fiction, "consists of . . . sentimental romance" (23).

5. I am thinking here in particular of the rhetoric surrounding the Cold War, as well as Desert Storm, in which the labelling of another power as Other and therefore evil justifies the expenditure of money, arms, and human lives against it. Thus, the prevalence of such oppositional thinking depends on the social conditions of the time, as Jameson notes in connection with medieval romances (*Political Unconscious* 118). The romance mode, then, appears and reappears throughout history, proposing "an imaginary 'solution' to this real contradiction, a symbolic answer to the perplexing question of how my enemy can be thought of as being *evil* (that is, as other than myself and marked by some absolute difference), when what is responsible for his being so characterized is quite simply the *identity* of his own conduct with mine" (Jameson, *Political Unconscious* 118, emphasis in original).

6. Lugh did once act in the world, as his explanation of his origins makes clear: "Once my kind ruled over the earth . . . but that time is long past" (*Hawk* 82).

7. After Gwalchmai's defection to Light, no one else changes sides.

8. Medraut helps his mother create the spell that sends Darkness "out to blacken the dimness of the room" (*Kingdom* 227). Although Rhys does not do anything magical, he earlier prevents Gwalchmai from defiling his sword by killing Morgawse (*Kingdom* 225–26), thus saving Gwalchmai and the sword from Darkness and allowing them to participate in, and win, the duel of wills and magic.

9. Modred lists women to validate his claim.

10. Morgan recognizes that Christ embodies this cycle as well. However, she accuses institutionalized Christianity of "deny[ing] the other half of creation. The un-male, the un-virgin" (*Herself* 43).

11. Welwyn Wilton Katz's *The Third Magic* provides an interesting comparison in terms of the treatment of binaries. The parallel world, Nwm, that the novel constructs is built around a binary. Territory and elements belong either to the Circle, controlled by Sisters and First Magic, or to the Line, controlled by men and Second Magic. But there is another source of magic on Nwm, prior to First and Second Magics: "There was a time when Nwm was united under a magic that was neither First Magic nor Second, but a union of both" (105). The ultimate quest of the novel's main characters, Arddu and Morgan, is to re-establish this linked magic. Katz, like Sampson, suggests that the binary opposition is destructive, and that union and harmony are necessary.

12. Maureen Fries uses the example of Roman architecture: "Part of Merlin's knowledge . . . is . . . gleaned from his youthful forays into the abandoned Roman hypocaust" ("Rationalization" 261).

13. See my discussion of women and magic in the section on Mary Stewart in Chapter 4.

14. Gérard Genette, in *Narrative Discourse*, uses the term "variable" (189) to describe focalization that changes from one character to another; these changes can be "rapid and elusive" (189). However, I agree with Neil Randall that "*shifting* seems more accurate. *Variable focalization* seems to suggest a change not only in the character focalized through but also the type of focalization" (41, emphasis in orginal). I therefore use "shifting focalization" throughout to indicate that "we perceive an event in a story *through* the senses

of a character" (Randall 41, emphasis in original), but that the character focalizing the events changes.

15. The passages appear on these pages: ix–xi, 108–12, 230–31, 327, 407–8, 502–6, 543–44, 566–70, 588–91, 751–59, 865–68.

16. Mieke Bal describes types of narrators as follows: "the narrator as agent . . . can be distinguished only in terms of his / her presence or absence in the narrative at the level in question. The narrator who is present in the story s/he tells is 'homodiegetic'; the narrator who is absent (invisible) . . . is 'heterodiegetic'" (Bal, *On Storytelling* 79). Furthermore, if homodiegetic narrators relate "a story in which they are the main character . . . they are 'autodiegetic'" (Bal, *On Storytelling* 79). Thus, in *Mists*, narration alternates between an autodiegetic narrator (the older Morgaine who "speaks") and an invisible or heterodiegetic narrator who uses various characters to focalize the narration.

17. Anne Cranny-Francis uses this term in relation to feminist rewritings of fairy tales that "operate via an implicit comparison with the traditional tale . . . as an absent referent" (94). Each Arthurian rewriting also operates as a metafiction, and many skillfully use contrast between them and traditional versions to play with readers' expectations.

18. He does have a strong Christian faith that allows him to resist Morgawse until Eivlin rescues him: "I knew suddenly that I could die, and still keep the Faith; and this knowledge was victory" (*Kingdom* 174). Later he baptizes Eivlin (194), thus saving her from Morgawse's demon, but it takes Gwalchmai to cure her (248).

19. These are the terms used by Raymond Thompson in his study *The Return from Avalon*. Two of the types of Arthurian fiction he identifies are fantasy, in which "supernatural events play a significant role and no effort is made to explain them in rational terms" (5), and historical novels, which "endeavor to recreate the spirit of the age . . . through attention to authentic detail" (4). Thompson also observes that "the supernatural conflict fades from sight in the conclusion" (89) of Bradshaw's trilogy.

Chapter 7

Rewriting Arthurian Women in Short Fiction

Since 1980, a significant trend in rewritings of the Arthurian legend has gained momentum: the use of short stories and anthologies of short stories to explore Arthurian topics. Although occasional examples of both these trends can be found earlier,[1] only in the last twenty years has short fiction become an often-used genre for Arthuriana. This chapter examines six stories by five female authors in order to discuss the possibilities for social commentary that arise when short fiction, feminism, and the Arthurian legend intersect. These writers critique our culture by revisioning three common elements of the legend: traditional symbols of power, definitions of the heroic, and binary oppositions between good and evil.

Jane Yolen's "The Sword and the Stone" (1985), Phyllis Ann Karr's "The Truth about the Lady of the Lake" (1990), Mercedes Lackey's "The Cup and the Cauldron" (1992), Phyllis Ann Karr's "Galahad's Lady" (1996), Heather Rose Jones's "The Treasures of Britain" (1996), and Diana Paxson's "Lady of Avalon" (1996) all appeared during the recent flowering of Arthurian short fiction. As noted in the Introduction of this book, the production of short fiction shows dramatic increase. In conjunction with these increases, at least fifteen anthologies devoted to Arthurian themes have appeared since 1988.[2] Whether the increase in short fiction instigated the publication of such collections or the reverse, anthologies make the presence of Arthurian short stories more noticeable and accessible to book buyers. The stories I discuss provide examples of the ways the Arthurian legend and the short story genre can be adapted for feminist storytelling.

The six short stories form a diverse group. Three deal with characters and events found in medieval Arthurian works.[3] Two use the Arthurian world as a backdrop for new characters and events.[4] One, Karr's "The Truth about the Lady of the Lake," features protagonists taken from another imaginary universe that Karr first created in a series of fantasy novels. Despite this diversity, all of these stories allow female characters to be perceived in new ways. These stories interrogate women's roles in the legend, and none of them, significantly, limits female characters to romantic roles. Whether queens (Yolen's Guenevere, Jones's Gwenhwyfar), ladies (Karr's Frostflower, Paxson's Ildierna), or saints (Karr's Amide, Lackey's Elfrida and Leonie), these female characters do not exist simply to inspire knightly lovers to deeds of prowess; they administer kingdoms, seek out adventure, risk danger, and pursue quests. Furthermore, they do all of these things successfully and without relying on knightly rescue, that favourite device of romance. Like the novels previously discussed, these stories play with our expectations of the legend through the characterization of the women of the legend, and the protagonists, focalizing agents, and / or narrators chosen. For the purposes of this discussion, they can be usefully grouped into three broad categories based on the focus of their feminist critique: those undermining traditional symbols of power (Yolen, Karr's "The Truth about the Lady in the Lake"), those redefining the heroic (Karr's "Galahad's Lady," Jones), and those problematizing binary oppositions (Lackey, Paxson).

SYMBOLS OF POWER

Power—the ability to act and the authority to command one's environment—is often represented by objects that are endowed with meaning greater than that of their physical selves. Although they acquire meaning in specific cultural contexts, symbols of power can become naturalized; their meaning, and hence the authority they bestow and the power relations they legitimize, seem inevitable rather than constructed. Feminist theory explores the nature of such symbolic representations in order to question the unequal power relations between genders in our society. Feminist fictions engage with issues of power by depicting female characters appropriating power, or symbols of power, for themselves. Simply to reverse traditional gender roles, however, has some drawbacks, since the power relations attached to the roles may remain unquestioned. Yolen and Karr raise effective questions about power by making obvious the constructedness of symbols of power and the assumptions that underlie their construction.

In the Arthurian context, the episodes in which Arthur draws the sword from the stone and takes the sword from the hand that rises above the lake provide two symbols of power. The swords legitimize Arthur as king. The sword in the stone indicates the man who "is rightwise king born of all England" (Malory 1:16); as Muriel Whitaker notes, Arthur's birthright to the crown "had to be demonstrated publicly by success in the sword test" (*Arthur's Kingdom* 11). The sword from the lake, Excalibur, is also associated with Arthur's kingship, for its "existence in the natural world coincides almost exactly with the temporal extent of Arthur's reign" (Whitaker, *Arthur's Kingdom* 12). In addition, both swords have supernatural origins; the association between these swords and magic suggests that Arthur is king by divine sanction. Although the connection between Arthur's kingship and his possession of the sword seems natural, underlying this connection are assumptions about the nature of kingship that connect it to ability in battle and to gendered roles. Battle, in Western culture, tends to be associated with men, not women, and swords, interpreted as phallic symbols, are also identified with male power.

Yolen's "The Sword in the Stone" and Karr's "The Truth about the Lady of the Lake" rewrite the episodes in which swords legitimize Arthur as king. Yolen's version appropriates the symbol of power to Guinevere and makes Guinevere Arthur's equal. Karr's story uses protagonists from another fictional world and creates estrangement, positioning readers to view their own culture differently. Whereas Yolen keeps Arthur and Merlinnus as sympathetic figures, Karr satirizes them; both stories, however, make obvious the cultural construction of symbols of power and questions the gendered assumptions implicit in such constructions.

Yolen's "The Sword and the Stone"[5] revisions Guenevere into a queen who is appreciated for her intelligence and acknowledged as an equal by Arthur and Merlinnus. Yolen's use of Merlinnus as a focalizing agent allows the surprise ending of the story, when the "boy" Gawen is revealed to be Guenevere. Because of the disguise, the reader accumulates evidence of Guenevere's character without any of the preconceptions that are attached to her name in the Arthurian tradition.[6] Instead of immediately expecting Guenevere the famous lover and inspiration of knightly action, for example, readers discover a Guenevere who acts for herself and who appropriates knightly prerogatives and symbols. Furthermore, as the duality of the name suggests, Gawen / Guenevere combines roles associated with men and those associated with women. The short story does not reverse our expectations of the queen by categorizing her as a "warrior" instead of a "lady," but it creates a figure who moves beyond stereotypes by blending qualities from both categories.

Yolen associates some stereotypical feminine qualities with Gawen to prepare the reader for the revelation at the end of the story. Though supposedly a knight-in-training, Gawen is associated with the domestic in the way he looks after the comfort of others and applies practical solutions to problems. When Arthur complains of the discomfort of hearing petitions, for example, Gawen suggests "a cushion atop the throne" (104), a solution that Merlinnus characterizes as "quiet homeyness" (104). The effect of this stereotypical equation of women and domesticity is altered somewhat by the story's emphasis on the further equation of domesticity and good government. In this story the ruling of the kingdom is not solely a matter of battles. Although Arthur's status as a warrior is mentioned at different moments (95, 105, 113), Yolen also portrays Arthur making decisions about domestic matters. He hears petitions involving two quarrelling warlords but then settles disputes about the chief cook and his mistresses, and a lady whose cat was killed by a miller (95). Although we never see Guenevere acting in the public realm like this, such evidence of Arthur's duties suggests that Guenevere has the skills to become a good ruler; moreover, her acquisition of symbols of male power suggests that she will not remain in the private domestic sphere.

Because she is disguised as Gawen, Guenevere acquires access to the world of male action. While at court, Merlinnus gives Gawen / Guenevere knight's training; the youngster recites parts of armour, for example (108), and learns to "thrust and slash" with a sword (115). She intends to become "a knight in order to challenge Sir Gawain who had dishonoured [her] sister" (115). This is not usually the duty of a sister, but "without a brother to champion her [sister, she] had to do" (115). Guenevere's most striking appropriation of male power, however, occurs in the episode of the sword in the stone. Merlinnus has set up the test of the sword to prove Arthur's right to rule. Before Arthur publicly draws the sword, Gawen / Guenevere takes and replaces the sword with the help of practical magic—melted butter (114). Unaided, she uses her intelligence to acquire the symbol of power and thus proves her right to rule the kingdom. Although Gawen / Guenevere is never shown in battle or as a public ruler, her character troubles assumptions about gendered roles, especially since, even after agreeing to marry Arthur, she keeps her sword (115).

The sword as symbol of power and of the "natural" authority of the king is itself called into question in the story. The proof of Arthur's kingship not only is appropriated by Guenevere: it is all a game. Merlinnus arranges the test so that only Arthur, with the help of the mage's "legerdemain" (106), will be able to draw the sword. Arthur is the mage's "greatest creation" (97), and Merlinnus invents the sword test to legitimize his own plan for the nation. Yolen portrays Merlinnus and Arthur as well-intentioned characters with the good of the nation in mind, but their power is nevertheless based on the conscious construction of a symbol through illusion.

In Yolen's story, the protagonists belong in the Arthurian world; they are native to an imagined realm that is supposed to be, in some degree, related to our past. Karr's "The Truth about the Lady of the Lake,"[7] however, introduces female characters from another reality—the world created in *Frostflower and Thorn* (1980) and in *Frostflower and Windbourne* (1982)—into an Arthurian world. Frostflower, a sorceress, and Thorn, a warrior, take part in Arthur's acquisition of the sword from the middle of the lake. Karr combines non-Arthurian characters with Arthurian events to critique the construction of symbols of power.

Karr's story depends on the reader's using prior knowledge of the legend to understand it fully. Arthur's and Merlin's names are never mentioned, so the reader must recognize certain plot elements as Arthurian, such as the sword's rising from the lake in a woman's hand. Frostflower and Thorn, who, as protagonists, also focalize the action, are outsiders in this male heroic world and interpret it differently than the characters of that world. Because the reader is positioned to experience the events through these cultural and gender outsiders, one of the story's effects is estrangement; we view our own cultural traditions in a new and critical way.

Through Frostflower and Thorn, the romance, magic, and heroism of the Arthurian world are deflated. Magical and heroic elements are rationalized. The hand that rises from the lake holding the sword is Frostflower's, and her ability to hold the sword in that way is not a "marvel" (191) but simply the shallowness of the lake; she is "quietly kneeling on the bottom" (191) while holding the sword aloft. The heroic nature of the legendary characters is also diminished. Arthur and Merlin are referred to by Thorn as "Metalpants" and "Whitebeard," respectively; neither title accords them much dignity.

Furthermore, the story presents two views of the sword. The first view is given little development in the story, since it is the traditional notion of the sword as mystical symbol of kingly power; from the little Frostflower and Thorn hear of Whitebeard's version of events, this is the view that he is creating. The second view, that of Frostflower, Thorn, and the reader, is more prosaic. The women see it as an unwelcome gift, since Frostflower does not carry any weapons, and Thorn calls it a "clumsy cowkiller" (189); they enter the Arthurian world to get rid of it. Nor is it magical properties that make the sword desirable; Frostflower explains that "jewels that big always dazzle people" (191).

The story thus emphasizes the process of constructing symbolic meaning and the implications of that construction. If we accept that this story is the "truth" as the title suggests we should, then we are invited to ask how the legendary portrayal of the events evolved. Karr's story mocks our culture's heroic legends by suggesting they are constructed with ulterior motives. Whitebeard begins the process of rewriting by erasing the physical realities and choosing more symbolically suitable details. His description of an "arm clothed in white samite, mystic, wonderful" (191) willfully changes the colour of Frostflower's clothes (she wears black). Mundane and farcical events metamorphose into legend in front of the reader.

Both Yolen and Karr interrogate assumptions about women's roles and political power at work in constructions of symbols of power. Yolen's Merlinnus frames the test to indicate the *man* to rule the nation; Guenevere's ability to draw the sword demonstrates the illegitimacy of this assumption about who, in terms of gender, is an appropriate ruler. When Karr's Whitebeard constructs the story of the sword, he ignores Frostflower's face to focus on the disembodied hand (191); Karr thus suggests that the creation of the symbol of male power entails the erasure of the individual woman, Frostflower, and her story. Yolen and Karr give their female characters access to symbols of power but also make them, and the reader, aware of the problematic nature of the power relations symbolized.

REDEFINING THE HEROIC

Northrop Frye describes the hero of romance narratives as "superior in degree" to other men (*Anatomy* 33), and this notion of heroism is woven into the fabric of the Arthurian legend. Knights ride forth in a series of quests and tournaments in which they encounter other knights to prove their superiority. As Maureen Fries notes, "We are accustomed by long literary tradition to think of the word 'hero' as masculine" ("Female Heroes" 5), and the action and adventure involved in the proving of heroism also are associated with masculine pursuits. Karr's "Galahad's Lady" and Jones's "The Treasures of Britain" challenge the assumptions that underlie traditional proofs of heroism and raise the question, What denotes heroism and why?

Karr, in "Galahad's Lady," rewrites Malory's quest for the grail. Whereas Malory presents the quest as Galahad's, Bors's, Percivale's, or Lancelot's by detailing their adventures, Karr supplies the experiences of a minor Malorean character, Amide. This rewriting of the quest from a different perspective creates Amide as a female hero[8] equal to the traditional male heroes of the grail quest and in doing so reveals a contradiction in the grail tradition itself.

In Malory's version of the quest, Percivale's sister meets Galahad, takes him to the ship where Bors and Percivale wait, explains the significance of the ship and its contents, and accompanies the knights until she dies after giving a dish full of her blood to heal the Leprous Lady. These events form just one segment of the adventures of the grail knights. Although the sister remains with them longer, her role is essentially that of an interpreter, like that of various other hermits and recluses (including Percivale's aunt, the queen of the Waste Lands) who explain dreams and direct knights' movements. She is unnamed: referred to as a gentlewoman, a damosel, or Percivale's sister. This lack of name emphasizes her role as interpreter (many of whom are unnamed or named simply by role or relationship to others) rather than as a questing knight (most of whom have names).

Although Karr's title, "Galahad's Lady," parallels Malory's terms for the character, the story itself refers to her as Amide. The events of Karr's story follow Malory's very closely, but Amide focalizes the action; it is therefore her story, not Galahad's, Bors's, or Percivale's. In fact, it is her adventure, and quest, and by participating as quest hero, she takes on a role usually reserved for male knights. Karr's rewriting thus makes Amide more than a temporary companion; it also emphasizes her equality with the knights. Like the knights, she is tested by temptation; although they are both chaste, she wonders whether her love for Galahad means that "she had, perhaps, broken her virginity in will" (170). She shares with them the adventure of the white hart, which only those meant to achieve the grail can see (173). Most importantly, her ordeal in the castle of the Leprous Lady becomes the equivalent of knightly battle. The wording that describes Amide's decision makes this equivalence clear. Amide argues that the knights "adventure [their] lives daily .o win praise and honour" and asks, "Allow me to adventure mine this once" (164); heroism in this story is not solely defined by deeds in battle. Knightly battle and virgin's sacrifice are both part of "the mystery of bloodshed" (158), a mystery that leads, at the end of the story, to Amide's vision of the grail and the association of her sacrifice with Christ's.

Amide's participation in the quest and her vision of the grail make more evident the contradiction that exists in the tradition itself about this quest. Karr refers to Malory's description, in which "Nascien told them [the members of the court] sternly that no woman, neither wife nor maid, was permitted to accompany her lord on this holy Quest" (152).[9] At the end of her rewriting, which emphasizes Amide's full participation in the quest for and achievement of the grail, Karr returns to this command. She points out that in the Arthurian tradition "the only three who fully achieved [the grail] were the three who did travel for part of their journey with a woman" (176). Lancelot only partially succeeded, "but only after he, too, had journeyed with Amide, drifting in the silk-shrouded barge with her body" (177). Consequently, through both the choice of protagonist and narratorial comment, this rewriting of the grail quest questions assumptions made about women's access to spirituality, and to heroic action, in some of the traditional Arthurian materials.

Like Karr, Jones questions traditional notions of the heroic, but she, like Yolen, chooses to rewrite Arthur's queen. She portrays Gwenhwyfar as a competent and wise administrator and uses her as the protagonist in this rewriting of the chastity test. The choice of Gwenhwyfar as a protagonist subverts several expectations about the test itself, allowing readers to reconsider various attitudes and actions that we are used to viewing as heroic or courageous.

Gwenhwyfar is perhaps best known in the Arthurian tradition as Lancelot's lover. Jones, however, omits any mention of a Lancelot figure; if Caradog Strong-Arm's chalice and mantle are meant to test the queen's fidelity to Arthur, the story gives no evidence of any reason for her to fail the test. Jones's rewriting also emphasizes the practical responsibilities rather than the romantic possibilities of the queen's position. Unlike Arthur and his knights, Gwenhwyfar recognizes that Caradog's "test" is merely a ploy to create dissension and "bloodshed" (210) at court. Her ability to organize the court and prevent the test demonstrates her competence and cleverness, and her plan to prevent the testing saves, not herself, but her ladies and the court as a whole.

Because Gwenhwyfar understands the intention behind and the problems with the test when Arthur and his knights do not, Jones's story reverses our expectations of the heroic. Throughout the Arthurian tradition, knights encounter magical tests (that in *Sir Gawain and the Green Knight*, for example) and the ability to step forward and accept the danger and the challenge of such tests marks the knight as heroic.[10] In "The Treasures of Britain," the knights who boast of the virtue of their ladies see the chalice as a test of their own courage; they believe that by agreeing to take the challenge they show the heroic nature of them and the court. The women concerned, however, recognize that it is they, not the men, who are at risk; it is their virtue, not the men's courage, that is tested. Jones emphasizes the test's targeting of women through the knights' first assumptions and Gwenhwyfar's comments. When Caradog says that the chalice "cannot abide impurity and faithlessness" (209), the knights assume that it will prove their loyalty to Arthur. Caradog corrects this impression: "It will not contain the drink of a man whose lady has violated her marriage or her virginity" (209). The cloak that the ladies are to wear does not, as Gwenhwyfar hopes, reveal whether a woman's "man has broken faith with her" (210), but again exposes the woman's "faithlessness." Gwenhwyfar's sarcastic response, "Delightful" (210), helps to underscore the "one-sided" nature of a test that assumes only women can be faithless. The heroic nature of the challenge is thus undermined because Jones exposes the test as unfair, whereas that unfairness is usually hidden by being constructed as natural and inevitable.

Moreover, the public pressure surrounding the test suggests that the men are not being heroic but are simply afraid not to follow the group. Owein believes he cannot refuse "after what he said before the others" (211); Gereint won't refuse because "the other men would think [Enid] had something to hide" (212); Cynon says that he "dares not be the only one to refuse" (212) the test. The magic items that Gwenhwyfar and her ladies bring to the feast prove the lack of heroism in the knights. The cauldron, the whetstone, and the shirt will not work in the presence of cowards, and they only work when the men refuse Caradog's challenge. The refusal to subject his lover to suspicion, speculation, and quite possibly ridicule and rejection marks the truly brave, heroic man in this story.

Karr and Jones, in these rewritings of traditional stories, question cultural expectations about the nature of heroism and the way it is proved. In both stories, the ability to face battle or answer other men's challenges does not necessarily indicate heroism. These writers thus create a space for their female characters in the redefined realm of heroic action: Amide adventures her life, and Gwenhwyfar saves the court.[11] Moreover, the process of redefinition reveals the gendered nature of traditional quests and challenges, in which women are placed to inspire, reward or enable, but never to achieve, heroic action.

BINARIES

As discussed in the previous chapter, romance and romance-descended genres such as fantasy fiction depend on conflict between two opposing sides to create plot. The most common form of binary in romance genres is the division of the world into "good or evil powers" (Jackson 56). The stories by Lackey and Paxson, like the novels earlier discussed, engage with feminist discourses by problematizing binaries. They deconstruct the assumptions underlying a binary opposition and show the destructiveness of such assumptions. In stories set in Arthurian or post-Arthurian worlds, Lackey and Paxson establish binary oppositions through focalizing agents who first distinguish between "us" and "them" but who then realize the falseness of this dichotomy. Only when characters move beyond such binary thinking do they achieve wholeness and community.

In "The Cup and the Cauldron,"[12] Lackey's choice of protagonists, Elfrida, a peasant girl who studies with a village wisewoman, and Leonie, a nun in a convent, redefines the grail quest in terms of gender and class. In consequence of this redefinition, the story investigates the binary oppositions of Christian and pagan, upper-class and peasant, new and old. The ideologies of both girls are based upon these binaries, but the similarity of their experiences allows the reader to see the artificiality of these categories; the resolution of the story makes explicit the union of apparent opposites.

Both of the protagonists focalize sections of the story, and their own understanding of their situations includes evidence of binary oppositions at work in their society. Elfrida recognizes "that the enmity of the priests of the White Christ might fall upon her" (3) because she is training to be a "priestess of the Old Way" (3); pagan and Christian, old beliefs and new, co-exist in uneasy tension and potential violence. Different classes of people are also set in opposition. Elfrida is scornful of nobles, for they refused to help "their liegemen and peasants to save their crops" (12). The work of trenching the gardens to drain at Leonie's convent means that "knight's daughter and villain's son" must work together, an occurrence "Leonie had never thought to see" (6). Elfrida, as a pagan and a peasant, seems to be the opposite of Leonie, who is Christian and likely of a higher class.[13]

Nevertheless, Lackey uses description and repetition of phrases to establish the similarity of her two protagonists. At the beginning, Elfrida works in the cold, "dank" (2) rainfall, with "scratched and bleeding hands" (2), trying to find food in a land that no longer produces sustenance. Leonie also works in the rain, with feet so cold they feel "like blocks of stone" (5) and hands that hurt because "she wasn't used to this" type of labour (6). For both village and convent, "starvation and plague [is] hovering over all" (6). Each girl, known for having visions, is asked by an older mentor figure (Mag and the Mother Superior, respectively) to dream a solution. Lackey describes each girl as loosing her "hold on her body" (5, 8) to begin the vision and signals the recounting of the visionary experience with "What did you see?" (8, 9). Each girl then searches for a sacred object: Elfrida looks for the "Cauldron of the Goddess" (9); Leonie leaves "to seek the Grail" (9). The parallels continue during the quest itself as they share food with others less fortunate (11, 12), enter into strange woods, and are captured by bandits.

In consequence of these narrative and descriptive similarities, the differences between the girls in religion and class decrease in significance. Their escape from the bandits reinforces the importance of their similarities. Although each despises and fears the other because of the differences between their beliefs, each girl consciously risks herself to save the other. Elfrida frees herself but also takes Leonie with her (15); Leonie supports Elfrida when she hurts her ankle running from "The Enemy" (17). The vision at the climax of the story proves that they have learned from their experiences. Elfrida sees the grail and Leonie sees the cauldron, reversing what each expects. However, the final metamorphosis of the vision into a "Being of light, neither male nor female, and a dazzling Cup as large as a Cauldron" (18–19) occurs when the two join hands, marking their recognition, not of difference, but of community.

In Paxson's "Lady of Avalon,"[14] community between women also occurs despite barriers of race and class. Paxson uses a first-person narrator, Ildierna, a priestess of Avalon, whose capture by Saxons leads to a new life for her and the Saxon woman whose slave she becomes. The use of this narrator means that the binaries are problematized as part of the narrator's own learning experience. The reader is thus positioned to learn, with Ildierna, to recognize the arbitrary barriers that categories create and the life-affirming possibilities of moving beyond the idea of opposition. The theme of renewal is emphasized as Paxson, in breaking down binary oppositions, portrays the community between the women using language that constructs their relationship as a mother-daughter one.

As in "The Cup and the Cauldron," "Lady of Avalon" evokes binary oppositions based on race and class only to show their artificiality. Ildierna confesses to Gytha: "I could not have imagined . . . any way in which our people were the same" (68), but during her time in the Saxon household, those around her "changed from faceless barbarians to people, as various in character as [her] own folk" (62). The Midsummer ritual emphasizes the similarities between Ildierna's people and her new masters. The rite that blesses the fields has different words but is otherwise equivalent to the one over which she used to preside: "For a moment I felt as if I were looking at one of my priestesses" (63).

The connection that is gradually established between Ildierna and Gytha, the Saxon king's youngest wife, continues to show the assumptions of difference that people make and the need to recognize similarities and forge bonds based on those similarities. Gytha is Saxon and Ildierna is British; Gytha has power and status in the household as the king's favourite wife (62), whereas Ildierna is a slave; Gytha as a Saxon has different religious beliefs than Ildierna, who worships the Goddess. Nevertheless, the two women discover that such oppositions are not absolute. Gytha's mother was British and Gytha can speak that language. Ildierna, although a slave now, once had power as priestess of the Goddess, and she retains her "old habit of command" (66). Gytha refers to the Norns, female deities of Norse mythology, but her vision resembles the Goddess Ildierna worships, a "woman draped in blue with an ornament of silver set with river pearls upon her brow" (68). This vision saves Ildierna's life, just as Ildierna's vision of the Goddess leads her to Gytha and allows her to save Gytha's life.

As the two women begin to move beyond cultural assumptions that put them in opposition, Paxson describes the relationship between them as a mother-daughter one. Ildierna learns of Gytha's background when the younger woman calls her "Mama" during an illness (65), and it is only after the use of that word that their relationship develops. Mother imagery also occurs when Ildierna saves Gytha from the poisoned tea; "I will give you life" (67), Ildierna's promise to Gytha, suggests a mothering or birthing process. The deities invoked, whether the Goddess or the Norns, and the religious figures referred to, such as Caillean or Walada, are all women and all manifestations of "the Great Mother" (69). As a result of this imagery and the allusions to such religious figures, the mother-daughter relationship between Ildierna and Gytha symbolizes the possibility of community between women of different backgrounds.

Both Lackey and Paxson show binaries at work and then deconstruct them, affirming community between women in the process. The stories conclude, however, with these communities set apart, either in a divine realm (Lackey) or on an island separated by magic from the rest of the world (Paxson). Consequently, neither story depicts a real-world solution for the problems created by binary thinking; however, both suggest the pervasiveness of binaries and reinforce the importance of seeking solutions.

CONCLUSION

Choosing these stories, instead of others, to discuss the engagement with feminist discourses in Arthurian short fiction is somewhat arbitrary, but it has several advantages. The stories are all products of women writers and thus help to indicate some of the ways that, as Marion Wynne-Davies observes, twentieth-century women writers are reshaping the legend (4). In addition, the range of characters featured and episodes rehearsed in these stories illustrates that there are many possible ways for the Arthurian legend to inspire feminist storytelling. Their appearance in five different publications signals that stories engaging with feminist issues are becoming a feature of many collections. Most importantly, they cover a range of years (1985–96) that follows some innovative feminist Arthurian novels (like those of Stewart, Bradshaw, Bradley, and Sampson discussed earlier) and that coincides with the increase in publication of Arthurian short fiction. The popularity of the short story form gives a venue for authors to use feminist ideas to explore new perspectives on, and to reshape single episodes of, the Arthurian legend. Rewriting the legend, in turn, creates a space for readers and writers to contemplate issues that affect many women today, not just the queens, ladies, and saints of legend.

NOTES

1. An early example of a short story that engages with social concerns, especially feminism, in an Arthurian context is "The True Story of Guenevere" (1879) by Elizabeth Stuart Phelps.

2. Parke Godwin collected previously unpublished stories in *Invitation to Camelot* (1988); Jane Yolen did the same in *Camelot* (1995), as did Lawrence Schimel and Martin H. Greenberg in *Camelot Fantastic* (1998). Richard Gilliam, Martin H. Greenberg, and Edward E. Kramer edited *Grails: Quests, Visitations and Other Occurrences* (1992); this was then expanded and divided into two volumes, *Grails: Quests of the Dawn* (1994) and *Grails: Visitations of the Night* (1994). These editors also produced *Excalibur* (1995). Mike Ashley has edited a series of anthologies: *The Pendragon Chronicles* (1990), *The Camelot Chronicles* (1992), *The Merlin Chronicles* (1995), *The Chronicles of the Holy Grail* (1996), and *The Chronicles of the Round Table* (1997); he also edited *The Mammoth Book of Arthurian Legends* (1998). Gardner Dozois and Sheila Williams gathered short stories from *Asimov's Science Fiction Magazine* to create the collection *Isaac Asimov's Camelot* (1998). Jennifer Roberson's anthology, *Return to Avalon: A Celebration of Marion Zimmer Bradley* (1996), contains many Arthurian stories based on the world created by Bradley in *The Mists of Avalon*.

3. Yolen depicts Arthur, Merlinnus, and Guenevere in the sword in the stone episode; Karr's "Galahad's Lady" follows Malorean characters on the grail quest; Jones's Gwenhwyfar faces the test of the cup and mantle.

4. Lackey's grail quest is undertaken by two young women rather than Arthur's knights; Paxson's Lady lives in a post-Arthurian Britain of Saxon invaders.

5. This short story first appeared in *The Magazine of Fantasy and Science Fiction* in 1985. It was reprinted in a collection of Yolen's stories, *Merlin's Booke* (1986). All references are to the version appearing in *Merlin's Booke*.

6. The associations attached to the name "Gawen" are avoided because Merlinnus comments that at court there is "already a great knight by a similar name" (99), indicating to the reader that the boy is not the traditional Gawain. This comment also prepares the reader for the purpose of Guenevere's disguise.

7. This story first appeared in *Marion Zimmer Bradley's Fantasy Magazine* in 1990. It was reprinted in the collection *The Best of Marion Zimmer Bradley's Fantasy Magazine* (1994). All references are to the story as it appears in the anthology.

8. Maureen Fries, in "Female Heroes, Heroines and Counter Heroes: Images of Women in Arthurian Tradition," more fully defines this role. Like the medieval characters whom Fries discusses, Amide is a virgin hero who "escape[s] male domination and, for a time at least, actualize[s] . . . [her] title by acting the man" (11).

9. In Malory, an old knight sent by Nascien warns the court "that none in this quest lead lady nor gentlewoman with him, for it is not to do in so high a service as they labour in" (2: 249).

10. For example, in *Sir Gawain and the Green Knight*, when no knight immediately answers his challenge, the Green Knight questions the reputation for valour of a court in which all are "overwhelmed by a word from one man's voice" (314).

11. Jones's story also emphasizes the community of women at court. Although it is Gwenhwyfar's knowledge and wit that allow her to prevent the test, she is assisted by three other women—Denw, Enid, and Morfudd—whose personal histories reveal that the test is designed to prove all women faithless.

12. This story first appeared in *Grails: Quests, Visitations and Other Occurrences* (1992). That anthology was then expanded and divided into two parts. All references are to the story in the revised anthology *Grails: Quests of the Dawn* (1994).

13. She could be the "knight's daughter" (6) referred to in the description of workers at the convent; her robe is "kirtled up above the knee" and she does use a shovel. The fact that her hands are not used to physical labour suggests, though it is not conclusive evidence of, a higher class status.

14. This story appears in Roberson's anthology honouring Marion Zimmer Bradley, and it is Bradley's Avalon to which Paxson's title refers. Character names, like that of Caillean, the founding priestess of Avalon who appears in a vision, and that of Senara, the priestess who becomes the next Lady, refer to characters in Bradley's novels *The Forest House* (1993) and *Lady of Avalon* (1997); Paxson's name appears in the acknowledgements of both these novels.

Contexts and Conclusions

The creation of complex female characters who defy stereotypes, the portrayal of female characters as protagonists of stories that are not solely romantic ones, the use of such protagonists as narrators or focal characters, the construction of stories that question narrative conventions—all of these strategies in popular fiction demonstrate the genre's engagement with feminist ideas. This engagement is enacted in brief stories or lengthy series, with writers adapting their focus and their strategies according to the form involved. Such stories, novels, or series admittedly entertain; they allow us to escape to fantasy worlds. Nevertheless, those worlds—the people who inhabit them, the structures of power that influence them—are analogous to our own; the struggles of characters within the power structures of these imagined places, or the narrative structures that create them, can make us, as readers, aware of our own world in new ways. Looking up from the pages, we may see the natural "way things are" as constructed and thus question the "common sense" of our society's ideology.

The preceding chapters have analysed in detail a few texts that rewrite one traditional narrative—the Arthurian legend—but these texts are not the only rewritings to use such strategies. Parke Godwin's *Beloved Exile* (1984), for example, rewrites Guenevere's life before and after Arthur; Guenevere narrates her own story and plays a variety of political roles including queen, warrior, and slave. A more recent short fiction rewriting of the sword in the stone story, "The Sword of the North" (1998) by Rosemary Edghill, equates Guenevere with the sword; the "White Shadow" is both the giver of Cale-born and sword / ruler / warrior / goddess figure in her own right. Other examples could include Anne Eliot Crompton's novels *Merlin's Harp* (1995) and *Percival's Angel* (1999), which use fey women as protagonists.[1] These women, raised in a non-human culture, view the Arthurian world and ideals somewhat differently; although Crompton, unlike Karr in "The Truth about the Lady of the Lake," does not mock these ideals so completely, her choice of protagonists creates estrangement and questions the "naturalness" of the Arthurian, human society. Moreover, other types of popular fiction—detective, romance, speculative, fantasy—exhibit the strategies I have discussed, although it is beyond the scope of this study to itemize them here. Of course, not all rewritings or all works of popular fiction engage with feminist concerns about society's systemic subordination of women and the role of gender in society's structures of power. However, enough of them do to demonstrate that popular fiction is a vital part of society's engagement with feminist discourses.

Popular fiction's involvement in feminism is significant for two reasons. First, the number of works that include feminist discourses is growing and so is the audience for them. The works of popular fiction that engage with feminism, because of their status as "popular" fiction, likely reach a large readership. Second, these texts become part of a process whereby political ideals are disseminated, changed, challenged, refined, recreated; popular fiction enables people to make sense of ideas, to make those ideas relevant to everyday experience, and thus to normalize ideas that may initially be threatening.

Acknowledgement of the importance of the cultural work performed by popular fiction is often overshadowed by dismissals of such texts as escapist or conservative. Critical discussions of Marion Zimmer Bradley's work, for example, reveal such tendencies. Marion Wynne-Davis cites Bradley's novel as "a pathbreaking work" (184), but she sees the story as ultimately reinforcing a "mythic essentialism" (179) and social structures based on a gendered binary opposition (183). Similarly Karen Fuog analyses the character of Nimue in *The Mists of Avalon* and recognizes that "a label of feminism . . . [is not] completely inappropriate for this book, as Bradley is certainly attempting feminist themes" (73). Nevertheless, Fuog concludes that the type of power structures assumed by the novel's characters means that, "at its deepest level, *The Mists of Avalon* is subsumed by the patriarchal society in which Bradley lives" (86). Susan Signe Morrison, in her analysis of *The Mists of Avalon*, concludes that the "content and structure [of] the unfortunate sex scenes are at odds with a truly feminist revisionist project," and for this reason "the text fails" (143).

As I have acknowledged throughout this book, these texts do reproduce many conventions and the ideologies that underlie them. Although that conservatism makes them accessible to a large number of people, it also means there are some qualifications on the type of feminist ideas appearing in the texts. For example, these novels tend not to engage with feminist theories regarding race and gender. The Arthurian legend, based in British culture, usually features white, Northern European protagonists. Even the cultural conflicts portrayed involve two Northern European peoples—the Celts and the Saxons. Moreover, the emphasis on the interior lives of individuals in these novels means that they participate in a social philosophy that celebrates "the autonomy of the individual" (Watt 60); this philosophy in turn "obviously depends on a special type of economic and political organisation and on an appropriate ideology" (Watt 60), namely, capitalism. As a result, these novels rarely consider the insights of Marxist or socialist feminisms, although a few texts, like Godwin's *Beloved Exile*, give some notice to the intersection of class and gender. One possible explanation for such selectivity is that the white, middle-class bias of the feminist ideas used might indicate the publishing industry's assumptions about the likely audience for such novels. Because they must be seen to appeal to large numbers of people in order to be published, their contribution to the circulation and articulation of feminist ideas happens when the various parts of the industry feel such ideas are marketable.

Popular fiction's need to appeal leads to another criticism. Do such works engage with feminist ideas or merely reflect them? Are popular fiction texts using feminism because it has become trendy? Although feminism's trendiness may influence the types of ideas engaged with in popular fiction, it does not preclude such texts from a role in our society's continual redefinition of feminism. As discussed earlier in terms of the technique of representing female characters, fiction can never "merely reflect" our society; fictions (like any other type of narrative) are always constructed and therefore selective. The desire to use a trend still entails the shaping of the story in accordance with the author's perception of that trend; thus feminist ideas are shaped, articulated, and circulated regardless of the motive behind their use. Furthermore, each reader interprets such fictions in the light of personal positioning—the combination of lived experience and previous encounters with feminist ideas. Readers' engagements with these texts, therefore, are yet another articulation of feminism.

Such criticisms, therefore, should not lead us to dismiss as worthless the ideas these novels do present. Changes made to plot, characterization, or narrative strategies stand out; their challenges to expectations are noticed. Darrell Schweitzer's negative review of *The Mists of Avalon* indicates the kind of impact that such changes have. Bradley's focus on the female characters is one of Schweitzer's reasons for not liking (and not finishing) the novel. Because it "goes to great lengths to tell the women's side of things . . . it gets boring, because *most of the interesting parts happen offstage*" (45, emphasis added). This statement assumes that the "interesting parts" of the legend must involve Arthur and his knights, battles, and quests—by implication, men's stories. In contrast, Barbara Brown Zikmund, a professor of Church history, asserts that "telling it [the legend] through the eyes of the women" makes *The Mists of Avalon* an inspirational book, because of its "feminist critique of patterns of power, sexuality and salvation which the Christian church and contemporary society take for granted" (quoted in "Favorites" 490).[2] The conflicting reception of Bradley's novel thus demonstrates the cultural work that the text is doing.

Challenging the narratives that our society takes for granted is an important way for popular fiction and its readers to take part in feminist discourses. Furthermore, writers of popular fiction make feminist ideas relevant to many women in our society, Lee Ann Tobin argues, because they "put strong women into oppressive situations and then write them out of it as a way of showing women how to at least imagine themselves out of their own oppressive or nonfulfilling situations" (156). As Rita Felski observes about women's autobiographical fiction, such imaginative models play an important role for those women still struggling to define themselves, who might have "little other access to feminist ideas" (78). Thus, although popular novels do not represent the last word on feminism, they do allow many people a way to imagine and to make feminist ideas relevant to themselves.

It is impossible to measure the material effects on readers of such feminist discourses in popular fiction. Even surveys or sociological and psychological studies cannot completely quantify the use people make of what they read, because people read differently each time, sometimes ignoring, sometimes emphasizing, oppositional ideas. John Fiske draws on Roland Barthes's concepts of "readerly" and "writerly" texts to explain these different types of readings of popular fiction, but he adds to Barthes's terms a third, the "producerly" text. The producerly text "does not faze the reader with its sense of shocking difference both from other texts and from the everyday" (*Understanding* 104), yet it can be read actively, foregrounding the oppositional discourses in which it participates. Some texts encourage this producerly reading, for they "reproduce among the discourses that comprise [them] a struggle equivalent to that experienced socially by . . . readers" (*Understanding* 168). Even then, the reading may not create dramatic, immediately visible, material effects; a novel may change the way one reads the Arthurian legend, for example, without changing the way one reads events in one's own life.

Nevertheless, the effects of political discourses in popular fiction are cumulative: the more one engages with feminist discourses in popular texts the more likely one is to create analogies, or, in Fiske's terms, to produce relevances, between the textual situations and one's own material circumstance. Moreover, the cumulation of popular novels read intersects with a host of other societal influences. The feminist discourses in popular fiction co-exist and interact with such discourses as they are developed and articulated in legal, commercial, political, and other cultural practices, and the public profile of such discourses, as Jennifer Wicke demonstrates in her article "Celebrity Material," is increasing. Although plotting all such intersections of discourses in each individual is an impossible task, we can explore and speculate upon the potential effects of popular fiction by analysing the strategies by which such texts engage with feminist discourses.

I have written this book, therefore, because I believe in a liberal feminist vision of a more just, equitable society, and because I enjoy popular fiction and the ways in which it can push the boundaries of its own generic conventions and make old stories suddenly new. Moreover, I believe in the power of stories to shape our material existence: "[t]he myths we imagine we are living . . . shape our choices" (Piercy 72). As feminists, to understand the choices made by our society, we need to know the myths that our culture creates and recreates, and the role feminism plays in them.

NOTES

1. In *Percival's Angel*, Lili focalizes about half of the novel; the other half is focalized by her co-protagonist, Percival.

2. These comments appear in a 1987 article in *The Christian Century*, "Favorites [*sic*] Books and How They Influence."   The article printed the responses of "16 prominent individuals" who were asked "to comment on the book or books that have been of special importance to them—either personally or professionally—within the past year" (490). Zikmund responded in her capacity as a "Christian feminist" (490) and as Dean and Professor of Church History at the Pacific School of Religion in Berkeley, California.

Appendix A

Publishing Background

Bourdieu used number of employees as one indication of the type of publisher; his example of a large-scale firm had 700 employees whereas the small-scale firm had 12 ("Production" 98–99). All of these Arthurian novels are published by firms that are subsidiaries of vast corporate empires that often have multi-million-dollar revenues and dozens of offices, let alone employees. Mary Stewart's novels were published by Hodder & Stoughton Ltd., which is a subsidiary of Hodder & Stoughton Holdings Ltd., which is owned by Hodder Headline PLC (*Who Owns Whom* 3: 212). Hodder Headline PLC is also the parent company of Headline Book Publishing Ltd., which published Fay Sampson's series (*Who Owns Whom* 3: 212). Gillian Bradshaw's trilogy was first published in hardcover by Simon & Schuster, a company with 9,200 employees (including those of its subsidiaries); it is itself a subsidiary of Paramount Publishing and Information Services, itself a subsidiary of Paramount Communications Inc., which is in turn owned by Viacom Inc., a subsidiary of National Amusements, Inc. (*Directory of Corporate Affiliations 1996* 4: 788–90). Bradshaw's books were reprinted by Bantam Books, which is owned by Bantam Doubleday Dell Publishing Group, Inc., a firm with 600 employees; it is owned ultimately by Bertelsmann AG (*Directory of Corporate Affiliations 1996* 5: 191–93). Marion Zimmer Bradley's novel was published by Random House, which is owned by Random House Inc., itself a subsidiary of Advance Publications Inc., which employs in its various subsidiaries a total of 19,000 people (*Directory of Corporate Affiliations 1996* 4: 17–19).

Most of the anthologies in which the short stories appeared were likewise published by large-scale firms. After a first printing in a magazine, Yolen's story was reprinted in a collection of Yolen's short fiction, *Merlin's Booke*, which was published by Berkley Publishing Group, a subsidiary of Putnam Berkley Group, Inc., which has 350 employees (*Directory of Corporate Affiliations 1999* 5 : 1051–52). Mercedes Lackey's "The Cup and the Cauldron" first appeared in an anthology that was a limited edition publication by Unnameable Press, but it was then published by ROC; Diana Paxson's "Lady of Avalon" was printed in an anthology published by DAW; both ROC and DAW have ties to Penguin, a publishing company that lists five national subsidiaries (in the United States, Britain, Australia, Canada, and New Zealand) as well as a head office on the copyright page. Penguin Publishing Co., Ltd., like Putnam Berkley Group mentioned earlier, is ultimately owned by Pearson PLC, a corporate empire with 17,215 employees (*Directory of Corporate Affiliations 1999* 5: 1049–50). Karr's "The Truth about the Lady of the Lake" made its second appearance in an anthology published by Warner Books, a subsidiary of Time Life, which is a subsidiary of Time Warner Company. This company is described as a "Media & Entertainment Company with Operations in Magazines, Filmed Entertainment, Cable Television, Recorded Music & Music Publication & Books, Broadcasting & Sports Franchises"; it has 40,215 employees (*Directory of Corporate Affiliations 1999* 5: 1591). Karr's "Galahad's Lady" and Heather Rose Jones's "The Treasures of Britain" both appeared in *Chronicles of the Holy Grail*, an anthology put out by Robinson Publishing in England; this is the only publisher not listed in directories of contemporary corporate empires.

The details available on most of these publishers indicate the massive corporate structures behind the publication of such texts and confirm their status as "popular" fiction. It also reveals the interconnections (on the corporate level at least) between publishing and other media and forms of entertainment in contemporary society.

Appendix B

Names and Roles of Characters

MARION ZIMMER BRADLEY

The Mists of Avalon

Arthur: son of Igraine and Uther, half-brother and lover of Morgaine, later high king

Balan: son of Viviane

Elaine: the queen's cousin, wife of Lancelet

Gawaine, Agravaine, Gaheris, Gareth: sons of Morgause and Lot

Gorlois: duke of Cornwall

Gwenhwyfar: high queen, wife of Arthur

Igraine: Viviane's half-sister, wife to Gorlois, then Uther

Kevin: a bard, later Merlin

Lancelet: son of Viviane, Gwenhwyfar's lover

Lot: Morgause's husband, king of Orkney

Mordred (Gwydion): son of Morgaine and Arthur

Morgaine: daughter of Igraine and Gorlois, priestess of Avalon

Morgause: Igraine's sister

Nimue: daughter of Elaine and Lancelet, priestess of Avalon

Niniane: priestess of Avalon and Mordred's lover

Raven: priestess and prophetess of Avalon

Taliesin: Merlin when the book begins

Uther: Igraine's lover and second husband, high king of Britain

Viviane: Lady of the Lake when the book begins

GILLIAN BRADSHAW

Hawk of May, Kingdom of Summer, In Winter's Shadow

Agravain: Lot and Morgawse's eldest son
Arthur: emperor of Britain
Bedwyr: Arthur's second in command, Gwynhwyfar's lover
Elidan: Gwalchmai's lover
The Family: Arthur's sworn knights
Gwalchmai: Lot and Morgawse's second son, narrator of first book
Gwyn (Gwalchaved): son of Gwalchmai and Elidan
Gwynhwyfar: empress of Britain, narrator of the third book
Lot: king of the Orcades
Medraut: son of Morgawse and Arthur
Morgawse: queen of air and Darkness, Arthur's half-sister and Lot's wife
Rhys ap Sion: Gwalchmai's servant, narrator of second book

HEATHER ROSE JONES

"The Treasures of Britain"

Arthur: high king
Caradog Strong-Arm: visitor to the court who challenges the knights to drink from a magical cup
Cynon: young man engaged to Morfudd
Denw: countess of the Fountain who married Owein after he killed her first husband in combat
Enid: one of the queen's friends who had been raped
Gereint: Enid's husband
Gwenhwyfar: queen and protagonist of the story
Morfudd: young woman at court and lover of Cynon
Owein: Denw's husband

PHYLLIS ANN KARR

"Galahad's Lady," "The Truth about the Lady of the Lake"

Amide: protagonist of "Galahad's Lady" who finds the grail
Bors: knight questing for the grail
Frostflower: a priestess and protagonist of "The Truth about the Lady of the Lake"
Galahad: Lancelot's son and knight questing for the grail
Lancelot: queen's lover who seeks the grail
Metalpants: Arthur in "The Truth about the Lady of the Lake"
Nascien: hermit who gives directions about achieving the quest
Percivale: Amide's brother and knight questing for the grail
Thorn: a warrior woman and protagonist of "The Truth about the Lady of the

Lake"
Whitebeard: Merlin in "The Truth about the Lady of the Lake"

MERCEDES LACKEY

"The Cup and The Cauldron"

Arthur: British king mentioned (he never appears in the story)
Elfrida: peasant girl training to be a priestess of the Old Way
Leonie: a novice at a Christian convent

DIANA PAXSON

"Lady of Avalon"

Arthur: British king in a period before the time of the story
Gytha: British-Saxon woman, wife of a Saxon lord
Ildierna: British priestess of Avalon

FAY SAMPSON

Wise Woman's Telling, White Nun's Telling, Black Smith's Telling, Taliesin's Telling, Herself

Arthur: son of Uther and Ygerne
Elaine: oldest daughter of Ygerne and Gorlois
Gawain, Gareth: sons of Margawse and Lot
Gorlois: duke of Cornwall
Gwenhyvar: Arthur's queen, Modred's lover
Gwennol: nurse to Ygerne's daughters, narrator of first book
Lot: Margawse's husband, king of Lothian
Luned: nun at Tintagel, narrator of second book
Margawse: second daughter of Ygerne and Gorlois
Merlyn: powerful magician
Modred: son of Margawse and Arthur
Morfudd: daughter of Morgan and Uriens
Morgan: youngest daughter of Ygerne and Gorlois, narrator of *Herself*
Nentres: Elaine's husband, king of Garlot
Nimue: an immortal and warrior woman, Merlyn's lover
Owain: son of Morgan and Urien
Taliesin: Urien's bard, narrator of fourth book
Teilo Smith: a smith in Urien's kingdom, narrator of third book
Urien: Morgan's husband, king of Rheged
Uther: high king of Britain
Ygerne: wife of Gorlois, then of Uther

MARY STEWART

The Crystal Cave, The Hollow Hills, The Last Enchantment, The Wicked Day, The Prince and the Pilgrim

Alexander: protagonist in *The Prince and the Pilgrim*, son of Anna and Baudouin

Alice: protagonist in *The Prince and the Pilgrim*, young woman who has made several journeys to the Holy Land

Ambrosius: becomes high king of Britain, Merlin's father

Anna: Baudouin's wife and Alexander's mother, who escapes King March

Arthur: son of Uther and Ygraine, later high king

Baudouin: March's brother and Anna's husband

Bedwyr: Arthur's second in command, Guinevere's lover

Gawain, Agravain, Gaheris, and Gareth: sons of Lot and Morgause

Guenever: Arthur's first wife, dies in childbirth

Guinevere: Arthur's second wife

Lot: king of the Orkneys, Morgause's husband

March: king of Cornwall who murders Baudouin out of jealousy

Merlin (Myrrdin Emrys): bastard son of Niniane and Ambrosius, tutor and advisor to Arthur

Mordred: son of Morgawse and Arthur, oldest of Morgause's sons

Morgan: daughter of Uther and Ygraine

Morgause: bastard daughter of Uther

Nimuë: Merlin's lover and king's prophet after him

Niniane: daughter of the king of South Wales, Merlin's mother

Uther: brother of Ambrosius and high king after him

Ygraine: wife of Gorlois, duke of Cornwall, then Uther's queen

JANE YOLEN

"The Sword in the Stone"

Arthur: king chosen by Merlinnus

Gawen / Guenevere: woman who draws the sword from the stone

Merlinnus: Arthur's advisor and Gawen / Guenevere's mentor

Bibliography

The Alliterative Morte Arthure: A Critical Edition. Ed. Valerie Krishna. New York: Franklin, 1976.

Ashe, Geoffrey, ed. *The Quest for Arthur's Britain*. London: Pall Mall, 1968.

Ashley, Mike, ed. *The Camelot Chronicles*. London: Robinson, 1992.

———. *The Chronicles of the Holy Grail*. London: Robinson, 1996.

———. *The Chronicles of the Round Table*. London: Robinson, 1997.

———. *The Mammoth Book of Arthurian Legends*. London: Robinson, 1998.

———. *The Merlin Chronicles*. London: Raven Books/Robinson, 1995.

———. *The Pendragon Chronicles*. London: Robinson, 1990.

Avon Camelot Books. Advertisement. *Publisher's Weekly* 219.5 (30 Jan. 1981): 42.

Bal, Mieke. *Narratology: Introduction to the Theory of Narrative*. Trans. Christine van Boheemen. Toronto: U of Toronto P, 1985.

———. *On Storytelling: Essays in Narratology*. Ed. David Jobling. Sonoma, CA: Polebridge, 1991.

Barker, Felix, and Peter Jackson. *The History of London in Maps*. London: Barrie & Jenkins, 1990.

Bennett, Tony. "The Politics of 'the Popular' and Popular Culture." *Popular Culture and Social Relations*. Eds. Tony Bennett, Colin Mercer, and Janet Woollacott. Milton Keynes: Open UP, 1986. 6–21.

Bourdieu, Pierre. "The Field of Cultural Production, or: The Economic World Reversed." Trans. Richard Nice. *Poetics* (Amsterdam) 12.4–5 (1983): 311–56. Rpt. in *The Field of Cultural Production: Essays on Art and Literature*. Ed. Randal Johnson. New York: Columbia UP, 1993. 29–73, 273–79.

———. "The Production of Belief: Contribution to an Economy of Symbolic Goods." Trans. Richard Nice. *Media Culture and Society* 2.3 (July 1980): 261–93. Rpt. in *The Field of Cultural Production: Essays on Art and Literature*. Ed. Randal Johnson. New York: Columbia UP, 1993. 74–111, 279–88. Rpt. of "Leproduction do la croyance: Contribution à une économie des biens symboliques." *Actes de la recherche en sciences sociales* 13 (Feb. 1977): 3–43.

Bradley, Marion Zimmer. *The Forest House*. 1993. New York: ROC-Penguin, 1995.

———. *Lady of Avalon*. New York: Viking Penguin, 1997.

————. *The Mists of Avalon*. 1982. New York: DelRey-Ballantine, 1984.

————. "My Search for Morgaine Le Fay." *The Vitality of the Arthurian Legend: A Symposium*. Ed. Mette Pors. Odense: Odense UP, 1988. 105–9.

————. "Responsibilities and Temptations of Women Science Fiction Writers." *Women Worldwalkers: New Dimensions of Science Fiction and Fantasy*. Ed. Jane B. Weedman. Lubbock, TX: Texas Tech, 1985. 25–41.

Bradshaw, Gillian. *Hawk of May*. 1980. New York: Bantam, 1992.

————. *In Winter's Shadow*. 1983. New York: Bantam, 1993.

————. *Kingdom of Summer*. 1981. New York: Bantam, 1992.

Brewer, D. S. Introduction. *The Morte Darthur: Parts Seven and Eight*. Evanston, IL: Northwestern UP, 1968. 1–37.

Brown, Paul A., and John J. Parry. "The Arthurian Legends: Supplement to Northup and Parry's Annotated Bibliography." *Journal of English and German Philology* 49 (1950): 208–16.

Campbell, Joseph. *The Hero with a Thousand Faces*. Bollingen Series. Princeton: Princeton UP, 1949.

Chatman, Seymour. "Characters and Narrators: Filter, Center, Slant and Interest-Focus." *Poetics Today* 7.2 (1986): 189–204.

Cherryh, C. J. *Port Eternity*. New York: DAW-New American Library, 1982.

Chrétien de Troyes. "Lancelot (The Knight of the Cart)." *Arthurian Romances*. By Chrétien de Troyes. Trans. D. D. R. Owen. Everyman's Library. London: Dent, 1987. 185–280.

Cixous, Hélène. "Sorties: Out and Out: Attacks / Ways Out / Forays." *The Newly Born Woman*. Hélène Cixous and Catherine Clément. Trans. Betsy Wing. Minneapolis: U of Minnesota P, 1986. 63–132.

Cornillion, Susan Koppelman. Preface. *Images of Women in Fiction: Feminist Perspectives*. Ed. Cornillion. Bowling Green, OH: Bowling Green U Popular P, 1972. ix–xiii.

Cranny-Francis, Anne. *Feminist Fiction: Feminist Uses of Generic Fiction*. New York: St. Martin's, 1990.

Crompton, Anne E. "Excalibur." *Camelot*. Ed. Jane Yolen. New York: Philomel, 1995. 79–90.

————. *Merlin's Harp*. New York: Fine, 1995.

————. *Percival's Angel*. New York: ROC, 1999.

Day, David. *The Search for King Arthur*. New York: Facts on File, 1995.

Dean, Christopher. "The Metamorphosis of Merlin: An Examination of the Protagonist of *The Crystal Cave* and *The Hollow Hills*." *Comparative Studies in Merlin from the Vedas to C.G. Jung*. Ed. James Gollnick. Lewiston, NY: Edwin Mellen, 1991. 63–75.

Directory of Corporate Affiliations 1996. 5 vols. New Providence, NJ: National Register, 1996.

Directory of Corporate Affiliations 1999. 5 vols. New Providence, NJ: National Register, 1999.

Dozois, Gardner, and Sheila Williams, eds. *Isaac Asimov's Camelot*. New York: Ace, 1998.

Edghill, Rosemary. "The Sword of the North." Schimel 244–85.

Ellman, Mary. *Thinking About Women*. New York: Harcourt, 1968.

The English Studies Group, 1978–1979. "Recent Developments in English Studies at the Centre." *Culture, Media, Language: Working Papers in Cultural Studies 1972–1979*. London: Hutchinson, 1980. 235–68.

Excalibur. Dir. John Boorman. Orion Pictures, 1981.

Farwell, Marilyn R. "Heterosexual Plots and Lesbian Subtexts: Toward a Theory of Lesbian Narrative Space." *Lesbian Texts and Contexts: Radical Revisions*. Eds. Karla Jay and Joanne Glasgow. New York: New York UP, 1990. 91–103.

"Favorites Books and How They Influence." *Christian Century* (20–27 May 1987): 490–95.

Felski, Rita. *Beyond Feminist Aesthetics: Feminist Literature and Social Change.* Cambridge, MA: Harvard UP, 1989.

First Knight. Dir. Jerry Zucker. Columbia Pictures, 1995.

The Fisher King. Dir. Terry Gilliam. Columbia Tristar, 1991.

Fiske, John. *Reading the Popular.* Boston: Unwin Hyman, 1989.

———. *Understanding Popular Culture.* Boston: Unwin Hyman, 1989.

Fries, Maureen. "Female Heroes, Heroines and Counter-Heroes: Images of Women in Arthurian Tradition." Slocum 5–17.

———. "The Rationalization of the Arthurian 'Matter' in T. H. White and Mary Stewart." *Philological Quarterly* 56 (1977): 258–65.

———. "Trends in the Modern Arthurian Novel." *King Arthur Through the Ages.* 2 vol. Eds. Valerie M. Lagorio and Mildred Leake Day. New York: Garland, 1990. 2: 207–22.

Fry, Carrol L. "The Goddess Ascending: Feminist Neo-Pagan Witchcraft in Marion Zimmer Bradley's Novels." *Journal of Popular Culture* 27.1 (Summer 1993): 67–80.

Frye, Northrop. *Anatomy of Criticism: Four Essays.* Princeton, NJ: Princeton UP, 1957.

———. *The Secular Scripture: A Study of the Structure of Romance.* The Charles Eliot Norton Lectures, 1974–1975. Cambridge, MA: Harvard UP, 1976.

Fuog, Karen E. "Imprisoned in the Phallic Oak: Marion Zimmer Bradley and Merlin's Seductress." *Quondam et Futurus: A Journal of Arthurian Interpretations* 1.1 (Spring 1991): 73–88.

Genette, Gérard. *Narrative Discourse: An Essay in Method.* Trans. Jane E. Lewin. Fwd. Jonathan Culler. Ithaca, NY: Cornell UP, 1980.

Geoffrey of Monmouth. *Histories of the Kings of Britain [Historia Regum Brittaniae].* Trans. Sebastian Evans. Everyman's Library. London: Dent, 1911.

———. *Life of Merlin [Vita Merlini].* Ed. and trans. Basil Clarke. Cardiff: U of Wales P, 1973.

Gilliam, Richard, Martin H. Greenberg and Edward E. Kramer, eds. *Excalibur.* New York: Warner, 1995.

———. *Grails: Quests of the Dawn.* New York: ROC, 1994.

———. *Grails: Quests, Visitations and Other Occurrences.* Atlanta: Unnameable, 1992.

———. *Grails: Visitations of the Night.* New York: ROC, 1994.

Godwin, Parke, ed. *Invitation to Camelot.* Afterword by Raymond H. Thompson. New York: Ace, 1988.

Godwin, Parke. *Beloved Exile.* 1984. New York: Bantam, 1985.

———. "The Road to Camelot: A Conversation with Marion Zimmer Bradley." *SF & Fantasy Review* (April 1984): 6–9.

Goodman, J. R. "Malory and Caxton's Chivalric Series, 1481–85." *Studies in Malory.* Ed. James W. Spisak. Kalamazoo, MI: Medieval Institute, 1985. 257–74.

Gordon-Wise, Barbara Ann. *The Reclamation of a Queen: Guinevere in Modern Fantasy.* Contributions to the Study of Science Fiction and Fantasy 44. New York: Greenwood, 1991.

Grant, Judith. *Fundamental Feminism: Contesting the Core Concepts of Feminist Theory.* New York: Routledge, 1993.

Haber, Karen. "The Spell Between Worlds." *Return to Avalon.* Ed. Jennifer Roberson. New York: DAW, 1996. 251–74.

Hall, Stuart. "Notes on Deconstructing 'the Popular.'" *People's History and Socialist Theory.* Ed. R. Samuel. London: Routledge, 1981. 227–40.

Hammer, Jacob. Introduction. *Historia Regum Britanniae: A Variant Version Edited from*

Manuscripts. Ed. Hammer. Cambridge, MA: Medieval Academy of America, 1951. 3–21.

Hartwell, David G. "Editing the Science-Fiction Novel." *Editors on Editing*. Ed. Gerald Gross. New York: Harper, 1985. 222–31.

Herman, Harold J. "The Women in Mary Stewart's Merlin Trilogy." *Interpretations* 15.2 (Spring 1984): 101–14.

Holbrook, Sue Ellen. "Nymue, The Chief Lady of the Lake, in Malory's Le Morte Darthur." *Speculum* 53.4 (1978): 761–77. Rpt. in *Arthurian Women: A Casebook*. Ed. Thelma Fenster. New York: Garland, 1996. 171–90.

Howe, Florence. "Feminism and Literature." *Soundings: An Interdisciplinary Journal* Winter 1972: 369–89. Rpt. in *Images of Women in Fiction: Feminist Perspectives*. Ed. Susan Koppelman Cornillion. Bowling Green, OH: Bowling Green U Popular P, 1972. 253–77.

Howey, Ann F., and Stephen R. Reimer. "The Arthurian Legends in Contemporary English Literature, 1981–1996." *Bulletin of Bibliography* 54.1 (March 1997): 33–65.

Hudson, Harriet E. "Toward a Theory of Popular Literature: The Case of the Middle English Romances." *Journal of Popular Culture* 23.3 (Winter 1989): 31–50.

Hughes, Melinda. "Dark Sisters and Light Sisters: Sister Doubles and the Search for Sisterhood in *The Mists of Avalon* and *The White Raven*." *Mythlore* 19.1 (Winter 1993): 24–28.

Humm, Peter, Paul Stigant, and Peter Widdowson. Introduction. *Popular Fictions: Essays in Literature and History*. Eds. Humm, Stigant, and Widdowson. London: Methuen, 1986. 1–15.

Irwin, W. R. *The Game of the Impossible*. Chicago: U of Illinois P, 1976.

Jackson, Rosemary. *Fantasy: The Literature of Subversion*. London: Methuen, 1981.

Jaggar, Alison M. *Feminist Politics and Human Nature*. Totowa, NJ: Rowman, 1983.

Jameson, Frederic. "Magical Narratives: Romance as Genre." *New Literary History* 7.1 (Autumn 1975): 135–63.

———. *The Political Unconscious: Narrative as a Socially Symbolic Act*. Ithaca, NY: Cornell UP, 1981.

Jardine, Alice A. *Gynesis: Configurations of Women and Modernity*. Ithaca, NY: Cornell UP, 1985.

Johnson, Barbara Ferry. *Lionors*. New York: Avon, 1975.

Johnson, Randal. Introduction. *The Field of Cultural Production: Essays on Art and Literature*. By Pierre Bourdieu. New York: Columbia UP, 1993. 1–25, 267–72.

Jones, Courtway. *The Witch of the North*. 1992. New York: Pocket, 1994.

Jones, Heather Rose. "The Treasures of Britain." *The Chronicles of the Holy Grail*. Ed. Mike Ashley. London: Raven Books, 1996. 208–17.

Jones, Mary J. *Avalon*. Tallahassee: Naiad, 1991.

Karr, Phyllis Ann. *Frostflower and Thorn*. New York: Berkeley, 1980.

———. *Frostflower and Windbourne*. New York: Berkeley, 1982.

———. "Galahad's Lady." *The Chronicles of the Holy Grail*. Ed. Mike Ashley. London: Raven Books, 1996. 151–77.

———. "The Lady of Belec." *The Pendragon Chronicles*. Ed. Mike Ashley. New York: Bedrick, 1990. 344–53.

———. "The Truth about the Lady of the Lake." *The Best of Marion Zimmer Bradley's Fantasy Magazine*. Ed. Marion Zimmer Bradley. New York: Warner Books, 1994. 189–92.

Katz, Welwyn Wilton. *The Third Magic*. 1988. Vancouver: Douglas, 1990.

Krishna, Valerie. Introduction. *The Alliterative Morte Arthure: A Critical Edition*. Ed.

Krishna. New York: Franklin, 1976. 1–34.

Lackey, Mercedes. "The Cup and the Cauldron." *Grails: Quests of the Dawn*. Eds. Richard Gilliam, Martin H. Greenberg, and Edward E. Kramer. New York: ROC, 1994. 2–19.

Lacy, Norris J. "Popular Culture." *The New Arthurian Encyclopedia*. Ed. Lacy. New York: Garland, 1991. 363–64.

LaFramboise, Donna. *The Princess at the Window: A New Gender Morality*. Toronto: Penguin, 1996.

Lanser, Susan S. "Toward a Feminist Narratology." *Style* 20.3 (Fall 1986): 341–63.

Lawlor, John. Introduction. *Le Morte d'Arthur*. Ed. Janet Cowen. 2 vol. Harmondsworth: Penguin, 1969. 1: vii–xxxi.

Layamon. *Brut. Wace and Layamon: Arthurian Chronicles*. Trans. Eugene Mason. Intro. by Gwyn Jones. London: Dent, 1978. 117–264.

Leckie, R. William, Jr. *The Passage of Dominion: Geoffrey of Monmouth and the Periodization of Insular History in the Twelfth Century*. Toronto: U of Toronto P, 1981.

Lemon, Lee T., and Marion J. Reis. Introduction to "Art as Technique." *Russian Formalist Criticism: Four Essays*. Trans. Lee T. Lemon and Marion J. Reis. Lincoln, NE: U of Nebraska P, 1965. 3–5.

Littleton, C. Scott, and Linda A. Malcor. *From Scythia to Camelot: A Radical Reassessment of King Arthur, the Knights of the Round Table, and the Holy Grail*. New York: Garland, 1994.

Lowenthal, David. *The Past Is a Foreign Country*. Cambridge, MA: Cambridge UP, 1985.

The Mabinogion from the Welsh of the Llyfr Coch o Hergest (The Red Book of Hergest). Trans. Lady Charlotte Guest. 1877. Cardiff: Jones Cardiff, 1977.

MacDougall, Hugh A. *Racial Myth in English History: Trojans, Teutons, and Anglo-Saxons*. Montreal: Harvester House; Hanover, NH: UP of New England, 1982.

MacKinnon, Catharine A. *Toward a Feminist Theory of the State*. Cambridge, MA: Harvard UP, 1989.

Malmgren, Carl D. *Worlds Apart: Narratology of Science Fiction*. Bloomington: Indiana UP, 1991.

Malory, Sir Thomas. *Le Morte D'Arthur*. Ed. Janet Cowen. 2 vols. Harmondsworth: Penguin, 1969.

Martin, Wallace. *Recent Theories of Narrative*. Ithaca: Cornell UP, 1986.

Matthews, William. *The Tragedy of Arthur: A Study of the Alliterative* Morte Arthure. Berkeley: U of California P, 1960.

McCaffrey, Anne. *Dragonsinger*. New York: Atheneum, 1977.

McKenzie, Nancy. *The Child Queen*. New York: Ballantine, 1994.

———. *The High Queen*. New York: Ballantine, 1995.

Merriman, James Douglas. *The Flower of Kings: A Study of the Arthurian Legend in England Between 1485 and 1835*. Lawrence, KS: UP of Kansas, 1973.

The Mighty. Dir. Peter Chelsom. Miramax, 1998.

Millett, Kate. *Sexual Politics*. Garden City, NY: Doubleday, 1970.

Moers, Ellen. *Literary Women*. 1976. Garden City, NY: Anchor-Doubleday, 1977.

Moi, Toril. *Sexual/Textual Politics: Feminist Literary Theory*. 1985. New York: Routledge, 1990.

Monty Python and the Holy Grail. Dir. Terry Gilliam and Terry Jones. National Film Trustee Company Limited, 1974.

Morrison, Susan Signe. "Morgan Le Fay's Champion: Marion Zimmer Bradley's 'The Mists of Avalon' as Challenge to Sir Thomas Malory's 'Le Morte D'Arthur.'" *Mittelalter-Rezeption IV: Medien, Politik, Ideologie, Ökonomie*. Gesammelte Vorträge des 4.

Internationalen Symposions zur Mittelalter-Rezeption. Eds. Irene von Burg, Jürgen Kühnel, Ulrich Müller, Alexander Schwartz. Göppingen: Kümmerle, 1991. 133–54.

Nelles, William. "Getting Focalization into Focus." *Poetics Today* 11.2 (Summer 1990): 365–82.

Nennius. *British History and Welsh Annals*. Ed. and trans. John Morris. London: Phillimore; Totowa, NJ: Rowman, 1980.

Newman, Sharan. *Guinevere*. New York: St. Martin's, 1981.

Northup, Clark S., and John J. Parry. "The Arthurian Legends: Modern Retellings of the Old Stories." *Journal of English and German Philology* 43.2 (1944): 173–221.

Painter, George D. *William Caxton: A Quincentenary Biography of England's First Printer*. London: Chatto, 1976.

Paton, Lucy Allen. Introduction. *Histories of the Kings of Britain*. By Geoffrey of Monmouth. Everyman's Library. London: Dent, 1911. vii–xxiv.

Paxson, Diana. "Lady of Avalon." *Return to Avalon: A Celebration of Marion Zimmer Bradley*. Ed. Jennifer Roberson. New York: DAW Books, 1996. 58–79.

———. *The White Raven*. New York: Morrow, 1988.

Peel, Ellen. "Utopian Feminism, Skeptical Feminism, and Narrative Energy." *Feminism, Utopia and Narrative*. Eds. Libby Falk Jones and Sarah Webster Goodwin. Knoxville: U of Tennessee P, 1990. 34–49.

Phelps, Elizabeth Stuart. "The True Story of Guenever." *Sealed Orders*. New York: Houghton, Osgood, 1879. 65–80.

Phillips, Graham, and Martin Keatman. *King Arthur: The True Story*. London: Century, 1992.

Piercy, Marge. *To Be of Use*. Illus. Lucia Vernarelli. Garden City, NY: Doubleday, 1973.

Pledger, Lynne. "Gwenhwyfar." *Camelot*. Ed. Jane Yolen. New York: Philomel, 1995. 63–76.

Plummer, John F. "The Quest for Significance in *La Queste Del Saint Graal* and Malory's *Tale of the Sankgreal*." *Continuations: Essays on Medieval French Literature and Language*. Eds. Norris J. Lacy and Gloria Torrini-Roblin. Birmingham, AL: Summa, 1989. 107–19.

Pochoda, Elizabeth. *Arthurian Propaganda: Le Morte Darthur as an Historical Ideal of Life*. Chapel Hill: U of North Carolina P, 1971.

Pratt, Mary Louise. "The Ideology of Speech-Act Theory." *Centrum* ns 1.1 (Spring 1981): 5–18.

———. *Toward a Speech-Act Theory of Literary Discourse*. Bloomington: Indiana UP, 1977.

Rabinowitz, Peter J. *Before Reading: Narrative Conventions and the Politics of Interpretation*. Ithaca, NY: Cornell UP, 1987.

Radford, Jean. Introduction. *The Progress of Romance: The Politics of Popular Fiction*. Ed. Radford. London: Routledge, 1986. 1–20.

Radway, Janice. *Reading the Romance: Women, Patriarchy, and Popular Literature*. 2nd ed. Chapel Hill: U of North Carolina P, 1991.

Randall, Neil. "Shifting Focalization and the Strategy of Delay: The Narrative Weaving of The Fionavar Tapestry." *Canadian Literature* 129 (Summer 1991): 40–53.

Reimer, Stephen R. "The Arthurian Legends in Contemporary English Literature, 1945–1981." *Bulletin of Bibliography* 38 (1981): 128–38, 149.

Roberson, Jennifer, ed. *Return to Avalon: A Celebration of Marion Zimmer Bradley*. New York: DAW, 1996.

Roberson, Jennifer. "Guinevere's Truth." Roberson 395–98.

Robertson, Nan. "Behind the Best Sellers: Mary Stewart." *New York Times Book Review* 2

Sept. 1979: 18.

Robin, Harry. *I, Morgain*. Boston: Branden, 1995.

Robins, Madeleine E. "Nimue's Tale." *Invitation to Camelot*. Ed. Parke Godwin. New York: Ace, 1988. 145–64.

Roller, Judi M. *The Politics of the Feminist Novel*. Contributions in Women's Studies 63. Westport, CT: Greenwood, 1986.

Rose, Mark. *Alien Encounters: Anatomy of Science Fiction*. Cambridge, MA: Harvard UP, 1981.

Ross, Meredith J. "The Sublime to the Ridiculous: The Restructuring of Arthurian Materials in Selected Modern Novels." Diss. University of Wisconsin-Madison, 1985.

Russ, Joanna. "What Can a Heroine Do? or Why Women Can't Write." *Images of Women: Feminist Perspectives*. Ed. Susan Koppelman Cornillon. Bowling Green, OH: Bowling Green U Popular P, 1972. 3–20.

Sampson, Fay. *Black Smith's Telling*. London: Headline, 1990.

———. *Daughter of Tintagel*. London: Headline, 1992.

———. *Herself*. London: Headline, 1992.

———. *Taliesin's Telling*. London: Headline, 1991.

———. *White Nun's Telling*. London: Headline, 1989.

———. *Wise Woman's Telling*. London: Headline, 1989.

Schimel, Lawrence and Martin H. Greenberg, ed. *Camelot Fantastic*. New York: DAW, 1998.

Schweitzer, Darrell. "The Vivisector." *Science Fiction Review* 47 (Summer 1983): 43–46.

Shklovsky, Victor. "Art as Technique." *Russian Formalist Criticism: Four Essays*. Trans. Lee T. Lemon and Marion J. Reis. Lincoln, NE: U of Nebraska P, 1965. 5–24.

Showalter, Elaine. *A Literature of Their Own: British Women Novelists from Brontë to Lessing*. Princeton, NJ: Princeton UP, 1977.

Sir Gawain and the Green Knight. Trans. Brian Stone. 2nd ed. Harmondsworth: Penguin, 1974.

Slocum, Sally K., ed. *Popular Arthurian Traditions*. Bowling Green, OH: Bowling Green State UP, 1992.

Spivack, Charlotte. *Merlin's Daughters: Contemporary Women Writers of Fantasy*. Contributions to the Study of Science Fiction and Fantasy 23. New York: Greenwood, 1987.

Spivack, Charlotte, and Roberta Lynn Staples. *The Company of Camelot: Arthurian Characters in Romance and Fantasy*. Contributions to the Study of Science Fiction and Fantasy 61. Westport, CT: Greenwood, 1994.

Steinbeck, John. *The Acts of King Arthur and His Noble Knights*. Ed. Chase Horton. New York: Farrar, 1976.

Stewart, Mary. *The Crystal Cave*. 1970. London: Hodder, 1971.

———. *The Hollow Hills*. 1973. London: Coronet, 1974.

———. *The Last Enchantment*. 1979. New York: Fawcett, 1980.

———. *The Prince and the Pilgrim*. London: Hodder, 1995.

———. *The Wicked Day*. 1983. London: Coronet, 1984.

"The Sword of Kahless." *Star Trek: Deep Space Nine*. Dir. Levar Burton. ABC. KXLY, Spokane. 20 Nov. 1995. CITV, Edmonton. 24 Nov. 1995.

Tennyson, Alfred. *Idylls of the King*. Idylls of the King and a Selection of Poems. New York: New American Library, 1961. 13–255.

Thompson, Raymond H. *The Return from Avalon: A Study of the Arthurian Legend in Modern Fiction*. Contributions to the Study of Science Fiction and Fantasy 14. Westport, CT: Greenwood, 1985.

Tobin, Lee Ann. "Why Change the Arthur Story? Marion Zimmer Bradley's *The Mists of Avalon*." *Extrapolation* 34.2 (Summer 1993): 147–57.

Toth, Emily. "Female Wits." *The Massachusetts Review* 22.4 (Winter 1981): 783–93.

Tuttle, Lisa. *Encyclopedia of Feminism*. New York: Facts on File, 1986.

Vinaver, Eugène. Introduction. *Works*. By Thomas Malory. Ed. Vinaver. 2nd ed. Oxford: Oxford UP, 1971. v–x.

Watson, Jeanie. "Mary Stewart's Merlin: Word of Power." *Arthurian Interpretations* 1.2 (Spring 1987): 70–83.

Watt, Ian. *The Rise of the Novel: Studies in Defoe, Richardson and Fielding*. Berkeley: U of California P, 1965.

Whitaker, Muriel. *Arthur's Kingdom of Adventure: The World of Malory's Morte Darthur*. Cambridge: Brewer, 1984.

———. "'The Hollow Hills': A Celtic Motif in Modern Fantasy." *Mosaic* 13. 3–4 (Spring/Summer 1980, Double Issue): 165–78.

———. *The Legends of King Arthur in Art*. Arthurian Studies 22. Cambridge: Brewer, 1990.

White, T. H. *The Once and Future King*. 1958. Glasgow: Fontana, 1987.

Who Owns Whom 1997. 6 vols. High Wycombe, England: Dun, 1996.

Wicke, Jennifer. "Celebrity Material: Materialist Feminism and the Culture of Celebrity." *South Atlantic Quarterly* 93 (Fall 1994): 751–78.

Woolley, Persia. *Child of the Northern Spring*. New York: Simon & Schuster, 1987.

Wynne-Davies, Marion. *Women and Arthurian Literature: Seizing the Sword*. London: MacMillan; New York: St. Martin's, 1996.

Yolen, Jane, ed. *Camelot*. New York: Philomel, 1995.

Yolen, Jane. "The Sword and the Stone." *Merlin's Booke*. New York: Ace Fantasy, 1986. 94–115.

Index

About the Author

ANN F. HOWEY is a sessional lecturer in English at the University of Alberta. Her interests include contemporary uses of Arthurian legend and popular fiction. She has published articles in *Extrapolation* and *Arthuriana* and is currently coauthoring a book-length bibliography of modern Arthurian texts.